THE SAGA OF
BILLY THE KID

Skyhorse Publishing books may be purchased in bulk at special
discounts for sales promotion, corporate gifts, fund-raising, or
educational purposes. Special editions can also be created to
specifications. For details, contact the Special Sales Department,
Skyhorse Publishing, 307 West 36th Street, 11th Floor, New York,
NY 10018 or info@skyhorsepublishing.com.

Skyhorse® and Skyhorse Publishing® are registered trademarks of
Skyhorse Publishing, Inc.®, a Delaware corporation.

Visit our website at www.skyhorsepublishing.com.

10 9 8 7 6 5 4 3 2 1

Library of Congress Cataloging-in-Publication Data is available
on file.

Cover design by Rain Saukas
Cover photo credit AP Images

Print ISBN: 978-1-62914-393-4
Ebook ISBN: 978-1-63220-112-6

Printed in the United States of America

THE SAGA OF BILLY THE KID

The Thrilling Life of
America's Original Outlaw

Walter Noble Burns

Skyhorse Publishing

TO
MY WIFE

CONTENTS

The Saga of Billy the Kid

CHAPTER I

THE KING OF THE VALLEY

JOHN CHISUM knew cows. That approximated the sum of all his knowledge. So, in the fullness of years, he became a cattle king. No petty overlord of a few scattered corrals, but by the divine right of brains and vision and cow sense, an unquestioned monarch holding dominion over vast herds and illimitable ranges. He owned more cattle at the peak of his career than any other man in the United States, if not in all the world, and a hundred thousand head bearing his famous brand of the Long Rail and Jingle-Bob pastured over nearly half of New Mexico, from the escarpments of the Llano Estacado westward to the Rio Grande and from the Seven Rivers and the Jornado del Muerto northward to the Canadian River.

Chisum came to New Mexico in 1867 as a settler, but a settler on a royal scale. Bearing him and his fortunes was no prairie schooner ballooned over with hooped white canvas, with household goods and bedding packed high and pots and pans jangling at every jolt. He came with ten thousand cattle and an entourage of bronzed and weather-beaten riders of the Texas pampas, a caravan of wagons, a *remuda* of cow ponies, and all the dust and thunder and pomp and panoply of a royal frontier progress.   He filed no claim on a quarter-section of government land whereon to build a cabin and plough and toil for a scant living, but homesteaded a kingdom extending beyond the four horizons in a new range world.

From Concho County, Texas, he set out on his hegira into the farther West.   His trail led through the lands of mesquite and pear south of the Llano Estacado to the Horsehead Crossing of the Pecos.   Then his great herd headed northward up the Pecos Valley—an interminable column of cows, its head dipping over one horizon, its tail over the other, drifting onward lazily, sinuously, like a living river, ten miles a day over the short-grass billows of a treeless wilderness.

Texas cattle of the ancient longhorn breed were these of the Chisum outfit; the only kind the Southwest knew in those early times; descendants of importations brought over from Andalusia to Mexico in the days of the Spanish conquest; lean, lithe, as alert and quick as deer, half-wild from rustling their own living untended on the open range winter and summer; with long horns, white, blue, polished and gleaming, curving like scimitars, as sharp as bayonets and often six feet from tip to tip.   No such cattle are to be found now from the Rio Grande to the Canadian border.   They are gone like the buffalo, bred out of existence, only a drop of their riotous blood remaining in the fat, sleek Shorthorn, black Angus, and white-faced Hereford grades that now graze their old ranges.

Directing the course, guarding the herd against stampede or Indian raid, cowboys rode at point, swing, and drag, during the long trail days, and crooned their cow lullabies around the bedding grounds during night vigils under the stars; six-shooters at their belts, rifles swung to their pommels; themselves a half-wild breed, born to the saddle on the Texas plains, as skilful horsemen as the world ever knew, as adept in gun play as in horsemanship, rough fellows in a row; courage and loyalty as much a part of their heritage as hardship and danger.

The long journey came to an end at a point thirty-five miles north of the present little city of Roswell. There where the Pecos makes a deep curve and the valley opens out into flat meadows flanked by table-top hills, Chisum established a ranch in a grove of cottonwoods on the river's margin, later to become famous throughout the Southwest as Bosque Grande, and settled down to fight his way to prosperity and kingship.

Chisum was born in Tennessee in 1824. His family has been identified with the South from the time his first English forbear set foot on Virginia soil in the early colonial period. Claiborne and Lucy Chisum were his father and mother. No need ever to ask from what part of the country a man named Claiborne hails; the name is as Southern as grits, sorghum, or corn pone. When John Chisum was born, Tennessee itself was a frontier state. The wilderness country lying just across the Mississippi River had become United States territory only twenty-one years before by Jefferson's purchase of Louisiana from Napoleon.

Born a frontiersman, the pioneer spirit was strong in Claiborne Chisum and in 1837, with his family and all his household goods and gods stowed in a covered wagon, he trekked westward across the wild, almost untraversed lands beyond the Mississippi and settled near what is now the town of Paris just south of Red River, the northern boundary of Texas.

Texas was then a republic and remained a republic until 1845, when it joined the Union. Its war for independence had been won only the year before. Santa Ana and his Mexican army, crushed at San Jacinto, had withdrawn across the Rio Grande for ever, and the new and exultant nation was still ringing with the decisive victory of brave old Sam Houston and with the heroism of Crockett, Travis, Bowie, and the other martyrs to Texas liberty, who had fallen at the Alamo.

Here, on the frontier, John Chisum grew to manhood. If one thing distinguished him in his early years above another it was sound business sense, the ability to estimate clearly the possibilities of the future in the opportunities of to-day, the quality known as vision. While other young men were following their noses, he was following a definite policy of success. While they were dancing, he was marching steadily forward. While they were shooting at a mark for fun, he was shooting at the future in deadly earnest.

Settlers were beginning to pour in. There was plenty of land for all to be had for a song. There would be plenty of land for years. But there would come a time in the future when land would be valuable. So young Chisum acquired land. He laid out the site of Paris on his land. He helped build the first house in this city of the future. He watched the town grow, and as it grew, he grew in wealth. He became a contractor and builder. He built the first courthouse in Paris. In this work, the genius of the man found first expression. He was, by all that was in him, a builder—a town builder first, a state builder later on in New Mexico, and eventually, in his relation to the Southwest and the nation, an empire builder.

He embarked in the cattle business in 1854.   For three years he made annual drives to Shreveport on Red River in Louisiana from which his cattle were shipped by steamboat to market in Mississippi River towns—Memphis, Vicksburg, Natchez, New Orleans.   For better range he moved to Denton County in 1857 and then to Concho County in 1863.   He remained on the Concho River until he pulled up stakes and set out for New Mexico in 1867.

It was not wholly the spirit of the innate pioneer that prompted John Chisum to move farther and farther west. The lure of markets led him on.   There were no markets to the north.   From the Concho straight north to the fur posts of the Hudson's Bay Company in Canada lay one wide sweep of wild country without towns or settlers, peopled by Indians, pastured only by buffalo and antelope. Beyond the eastern borders of Texas there were markets at Shreveport, Little Rock, and Baxter Springs.   There were markets to the south among the Texas gulf ports. But the profits in these Eastern and Southern markets were small and the trail was long and difficult.   Strangely enough, Chisum's best markets lay to the west.

In the southwestern corner of the United States, Spanish settlements had been flourishing for more than two hundred and fifty years.   Oñate founded Santa Fé in 1608; the town was contemporary with Jamestown; it was a sturdy village when the Pilgrims landed at Plymouth Rock. When Chisum turned his eyes toward New Mexico, it was the metropolis of the Southwest, grown rich on the trade of the Santa Fé trail.   The population of the land that had once been suzerain to His Catholic Majesty of Spain had been vastly increased by a heavy influx of American settlers.   Santa Fé, Taos, Las Vegas, El Paso, Albuquerque held out promise of rich markets to the Texas cattleman. Tucson, Prescott, Douglas, in Arizona; Denver, Pueblo, and Trinidad in Colorado, were in the golden distance. Especially alluring were the prospects for fat government contracts to supply beef to Indian reservations and army posts. Fort Sumner was in the Pecos Valley; Fort Stanton and the reservation of the Mescalero Apaches were just beyond its western edge. So, like Coronado in search of the Seven Cities of Cibola and the golden myth of Quivira, Chisum on his cow pony followed his dream westward. The old cavalier sought a mirage, the modern cattleman a market. Coronado's quest was pure adventure, Chisum's pure business.

The Texas cattle situation was unique. The war of the Rebellion had stripped the state of men. Thousands who marched away to fight under the stars and bars of the Confederacy left their bones on distant battlefields. During the four years of war, business had been almost at a standstill; many plantations went to weeds, many ranches remained untenanted. Slaves had been freed, Confederate money rendered worthless. The Lost Cause had spelled lost fortunes, almost lost hope. Texas industry started again from scratch when Lee surrendered.

Millions of cattle on the open ranges were almost valueless. They could be bought for a dollar a head, but there were no buyers because there was no money. War-time calves had remained unbranded. Nobody knew to whom these mavericks belonged. It was no theft to take them. The man who clapped a brand on them owned them. But acquiring cattle for nothing was not looked upon with general enthusiasm. It was a speculation in futures. Why own a thousand steers that you could not sell? Branding mavericks did not become an extensive industry until prices showed signs of rising. Comparatively, only a few wise men got theirs while the getting was good and laid the foundations of fortune with a rope and branding iron. Markets would have meant the difference between poverty and riches. But there were no markets.

A new day was about to dawn. The first faint glimmer of change was beginning to show on the dark horizon. The year 1867 was big with fate in the history of the West. The day of the covered wagon and the old immigrant trails was drawing to a close. The day of the railroad was at hand. With the completion of the Union Pacific, a through transportation line joined the two oceans. The Kansas-Pacific was pushing rapidly westward. New York and San Francisco suddenly became neighbours. The rich markets of the East were at last open to the prairies.

Markets! The magic of markets transformed the whole cattle situation of Texas overnight. Prosperity swept over the ranges in an avalanche. Tragedy changed into bonanza. From cattle poor, the state became cattle rich. The dollar cow of yesterday was the twenty-dollar cow of to-day. The first herd swept north to Abilene. Soon the longhorns by hundreds of thousands were pouring toward the railroads across Red River, the Indian Nations, the Staked Plains, No Man's Land, over trails a thousand and two thousand miles long from every part of Texas— the Gulf Coast, the Rio Grande, the Nueces, the Frio, the Colorado, the Brazos.

Followed for nearly twenty years the bonanza era of the cattle trails. Abilene, Newton, Wichita, Caldwell, Ellsworth, Hays City, Ogalallah, Dodge City, lived in succession their crowded hour as trail-end capitals. The cattle drives lifted them as on a tidal wave to fame, fortune, and hectic life, and, ceasing, left them stranded in the drab

obscurity of prairie villages. But in the brief years of
their romance, they were the most colourful, the most picturesque, the most lawless, the toughest towns of the old
frontier; saloons, gambling houses, dance halls booming;
six-shooters blazing in the streets; cowboys shooting out
the lights; a man every morning for breakfast; whisky,
faro, women, revel and riot night and day; and out somewhere on the stark prairie the inevitable Boot Hill cemetery crowded with the graves of those who had paid the
fiddler and gone into the great dark with their boots on.

John Chisum failed to sense the imminent great change
that was to turn the Texas cattle ranges into gold mines.
Few men did. The new prosperity stormed up out of a
blue sky almost without sign or portent to herald its approach. But, after all, there was sound wisdom in his
westward trek. The coming of the railroads that had
boomed the price of cattle in Texas boomed it likewise in
New Mexico. A steer at Las Vegas was worth as much
as a steer at Abilene. Fifteen hundred miles lay between
the Concho ranges and the Kansas markets, and it took
two months to make the drive. Markets in New Mexico
were near at hand and the railroad shipping points in
Kansas were no farther from the Pecos than from the
Concho.

When John Chisum settled in New Mexico, the Pecos
Valley was wild country. The Mescalero Apaches, in
their mountain fastnesses to the west, looked upon his
invading herds as fair prey for constant plundering raids.
Mexican marauders came frequently on whirlwind forays
across the Rio Grande and stampeded back with his cattle
and horses. White rustlers were busy and, in the long
run, his herds suffered more serious losses from their depredations than from those of Mexicans and Indians. His

first big government contract called for the delivery of ten thousand beeves at Fort Sumner, where nearly ten thousand Indians were held as government wards. While this number of cattle were fattening on the Bosque Grande ranges, more than half of them were stolen, and he had to bring in another herd from Texas to fulfil his contract. He obtained another order for eleven hundred steers from Fort Stanton. He bought these cattle at eighteen dollars a head in gold at Trickham, Texas, and was to receive thirty-five dollars a head for them at the army post. Here was prospect of fat profits. But on the drive through the Guadalupe Mountains, Apaches attacked him and stampeded off with the entire herd. Chisum arrived at Fort Stanton with six steers. He had better luck when Mexican freebooters rounded up twelve hundred of his horses and headed back for the Rio Grande with their booty. Chisum and four of his men followed their trail, and overtaking them at the Horsehead Crossing of the Pecos, killed three of the robbers and recovered the herd. So wagged the world on that spacious and lawless frontier.

But Chisum at last had found his markets. He rose to his new opportunities in a big way. His business developed to gigantic proportions as the years went by. He made his market radius as wide as the map of the Southwest and took in Colorado and Kansas for good measure. Within two years, at the height of his prosperity, he drove five thousand cattle to Tucson, six thousand to the San Carlos Apache reservation in Arizona, four thousand to the Gila River, and six thousand to Dodge City. Never a season passed that he did not have three or four herds on the move to different markets at the same time. Despite his wholesale operations, and despite wholesale thefts, his cattle increased in numbers annually. Fifteen thousand calves were born under his brand in 1876 and fresh importations from Texas were constantly coming in.

Chisum abandoned Bosque Grande as his headquarters in 1873, and moving down the Pecos forty miles, established South Spring Ranch, which remained his home to the end of his life. Where the South Spring River gushes from the earth in a never-failing giant spring of crystal water, he built a home fit for a cattle king and made it one of the show places of the Southwest. Cottonwood trees brought from Las Vegas by mule pack-train he planted about his dwelling and in two winding rows that formed a noble avenue a quarter of a mile long leading from road to residence. He sowed eight hundred acres to alfalfa. He brought fruit trees from Arkansas and set out a vast acreage in orchards of apple, pear, peach, and plum. He imported roses from Texas to make a hedge about the house, and scarlet tanagers and bob-white quail from Tennessee—birds unknown to New Mexico—and set them at liberty in the oasis of beauty he had created.

Here, with royal hand, Chisum dispensed frontier hospitality. His great, rambling, one-story adobe house, with verandas at front and rear, stood on the highway between Texas and New Mexico, and the stranger was as free as the invited guest to bed and board for as long as he wanted to stay, and no money or questions asked. Every day at breakfast, dinner, and supper, the table in the dining hall was set for twenty-six guests, twelve on each side and one at each end, and hardly a meal was served in ten years at which every chair was not occupied.

From Texas came Pitzer, James, and Jeff Chisum, his brothers, to help him in his business. Came, too, to reign over his household for years as chatelaine, Miss Sallie Chisum, his niece, daughter of James Chisum, as pretty a girl as ever set fluttering the hearts of the rough-riding cavaliers of the Pecos country.

Miss Sallie Chisum, later Mrs. Roberts, was living in Roswell in 1924, a sweet-faced, kindly old lady of a thousand memories of frontier days.

"When I came from Texas to the Pecos in 1875," said Mrs. Roberts, "I travelled with a small wagon train. The Mescaleros were off their reservation, murdering settlers and plundering ranches. 'Keep your scalp on straight' was the laughing warning of my friends as I left home. As we drew near the Horsehead Crossing of the Pecos near sundown one afternoon, a band of Apaches appeared on a hilltop. For a long time they sat there on their ponies perfectly motionless, watching us, standing out in sharp relief against the colours of the western sky like a group of sculpture.

"There were old Indian fighters in our outfit and they hurriedly corralled the wagons, outspanned the teams, and drove them inside the enclosure. There was no sleep that night. The women huddled in the wagons; the men lay on the ground between the wheels, their rifles ready, keeping guard. A coyote tuned up somewhere out in the darkness and gave us a thrill; we thought for a moment it was an Indian yell. But no attack came.

"Next morning a dozen horsemen came thundering toward us out of a cloud of dust. 'Indians!' someone shouted. Our men cocked their guns. I thought my last hour had come and gave myself up for lost. But the supposed Redskins turned out to be a bunch of cowboys that Uncle John Chisum had sent to meet us and escort us safely to South Spring Ranch. Was I happy? I felt like kissing every one of those bronzed young fellows as they rode up laughing and took us under their protection.

"We saw no more of the Indians, but my first night at South Spring they stole upon the ranch and drove off every horse and mule on the place. They did the thing like magic; their medicine must have been good. As silent as ghosts they came and went. Not a dog barked; not a soul in the ranch house awoke from peaceful dreams. We knew nothing of the raid until we saw the empty corrals in the morning and moccasin tracks everywhere. By that time the Indians with the stolen stock were miles on their way to the hills. That was my welcome to New Mexico.

"My Uncle John Chisum was one of the best men that ever lived, big-hearted and generous. Didn't talk much. Said he didn't have time. But his silence was genial; most of the time there was a kindly smile on his face. Not that he couldn't talk. If there was ever occasion to speak his mind, he was clearly and forcibly articulate. He could say more in three words than most people can in three hundred.

"He was a plain, everyday, bacon-and-frijoles sort of man. No frills. He lived simply; what was good enough for the other fellow was good enough for him. He had good clothes for what he called 'state occasions,' but he and I differed on what circumstances constituted a 'state occasion,' and he rarely wore them. A broad-brimmed soft gray hat set squarely on his head, a blue flannel shirt, sometimes a vest, and trousers stuffed in his boots were his usual costume. Sartorially, there was little to choose between him and an ordinary cow-hand. He was particular about his footwear, and his high-heeled boots were of the softest, finest leather money could buy.

"Though he never had a fight in his life, he was a brave man. Almost everyone carried a six-shooter in those days; a gun was regarded like a shirt or a hat, as an ordinary detail of costume; the average man would have felt undressed without one. But throughout a life passed on the frontier among men bred in a hair-trigger tradition, a weapon was never part of Uncle John Chisum's personal accoutrements. He rode alone and unarmed all over the Southwest, and it took real courage to do that in that lawless time.

"Uncle John Chisum was not more widely known than his famous brand of the Long Rail and Jingle-Bob. No other brand in history ever decorated so many cows at one time. It once identified one hundred thousand cattle as his own. It is gone from the ranges now; only a few old-timers know what it was. To those who never saw it, it is a riddle. The Long Rail is easy to guess. It was just a long bar on the side of a cow, running almost from stem to stern. But what was the Jingle-Bob? Sounding like a nonsense name, it was one of the wisest brands ever invented. Many people to-day, including a few cattlemen, think of it as a bit of knifework on the dewlap. But it was the result of a deep slit in both ears so that one part of the ear flapped downward and the other part stood up in its natural way. Not every cowboy could cut the ears correctly. A botch job either left both parts of the bifurcated ear standing erect or both hanging down. It took no little skill to cut the ear so that one part hung down and the other stood upright. Uncle John assigned the work only to a few trusted cow-hands who were adept in Jingle-Bob craftsmanship.

"It was easy to identify Chisum cattle singly or in small bunches by the Long Rail. You could read that brand a mile. But it was in the work of identifying cattle in a big herd that the Jingle-Bob demonstrated its right to be classed among the fine arts. After a stampede, for instance. Night stampedes were common on the trail. Any unusual sound might cause them—a peal of thunder, the report of a gun, the howl of a wolf, the galloping of a horse. Once panic had seized the senseless, half-wild brutes, they went blundering and thundering away in the darkness. It was sometimes possible, but not often, for the cowboys to turn them and get them milling in a circle and so bring them to a halt. But they usually ran until they tired themselves out, and many a stampede has carried a terror-stricken herd twenty or thirty miles from its bedding ground.

"Often a herd on the rampage ran into another herd and stampeded it, and next day, when both herds had quieted down, it was a big job, sometimes lasting several days, to separate the cattle. Cowboys could not see the body brands on cows lost among several thousand others. They had to ride into the herd and thread their way laboriously among the animals to pick out their own brands. But no matter where a Jingle-Bob steer happened to be, whether at the centre of the herd or away across a thousand backs at the far end, there was no mistaking him. He had but to show his head to be instantly identified.

"I may say that once you had seen the Jingle-Bob you never forgot it. It had a strangely transfiguring effect on bovine beauty. A lean, long-legged steer of the old range breed, with his absurdly long horns, his half-scared, half-truculent, and wholly stupid physiognomy, was a weird beast at best; but the Jingle-Bob, which seemed to crown his gargoyle head with four ears, two pricked up and two flopping down, added the last ridiculous touch and made him, in fact, look like the devil.

"I have only happy memories of South Spring Ranch.

My Uncle John never married—too busy for that, too—and I was mistress of the house. I was busy every day from morning till night managing the household and directing the servants. During the spring and fall round-ups, when the cowboys were in off the ranges, I was kept on the jump. The house was full of people all the time; the ranch was a little world in itself; I couldn't have been lonesome if I had tried.

"Every man worth knowing in the Southwest, and many not worth knowing, were guests, one time or another, under Uncle John's hospitable roof. I met them all—governors, legislators, business men, army officers, gamblers, robbers, murderers—and treated them all alike. What they were made no difference in their welcome. Sometimes a man would ride up in a hurry, eat a meal in a hurry, and depart in a hurry. A sheriff's posse trailing in a little later would give a clue to his haste. The length of a guest's visit sometimes depended on how many jumps he was ahead of the sheriff.

"Billy the Kid used to come often and sometimes stayed for a week or two. With his reputation as a bad man and killer, I remember how frightened I was the first time he came. I was sitting in the living room when word was brought that this famous desperado had arrived. I fell into a panic. I pictured him in all the evil ugliness of a bloodthirsty ogre. I half-expected he would slit my throat if he didn't like my looks.

"My heart was in my mouth as I heard his step on the porch and knew that Uncle John was bringing him in. In a daze I heard Uncle John saying with a wave of his hand, 'Sallie, this is my friend, Billy the Kid.' A good-looking, clear-eyed boy stood there with his hat in his hand, smiling at me. I stretched out my hand automatically to him, and he grasped it in a hand as small as my own.

"'Howdy, Miss Chisum, I'm pleased to meet you,' he said with a deferential bow in the phrase that was *de rigueur* on the frontier.

"'You're Billy the Kid?' I gasped.

"'That's what they call me,' he drawled in a soft voice.

"I sank down on the sofa and laughed until the tears came. He must have thought I was crazy but he laughed, too.

"'Well,' I said when I was able to speak, 'of course I owe you an explanation and an apology. But, you see, I —I didn't expect to find you looking like you do.'

"'Yes,' he answered good-naturedly, 'I understand.'

"And we both fell laughing again.

"Billy the Kid and I became great friends. Bad he surely was, but surely not all bad. He had many admirable qualities. When he was an enemy, he was an enemy, but when he was a friend, he was a friend. He was brimming over with light-hearted gaiety and good humour. As far as dress was concerned, he always looked as if he had just stepped out of a band-box. In broad-brimmed white hat, dark coat and vest, gray trousers worn over his boots, a gray flannel shirt and black four-in-hand tie, and sometimes—would you believe it?—a flower in his lapel, he was a dashing figure and quite the dandy. I suppose it sounds absurd to speak of such a character as a gentleman, but from beginning to end of our long friendship, in all his personal relations with me, he was the pink of politeness and as courteous a little gentleman as I ever met.

"Many a gallop across country Billy the Kid and I took together, and many a pleasant evening we sat talking for hours on the front gallery. There was a brook full of fish that ran under the house across a corner of the kitchen and I often sat on the back porch in a rocking chair, with Billy to bait my hook for me, and caught a string of perch for dinner.

"When Uncle John set out his cottonwoods he and his brothers, Pitzer and James, planted three young trees close to one another and, bending their stems inward, bound them together. In time the three trees grew into one, and it stands to-day, a towering giant, supported at the bottom on wide triple arches formed of the three original trunks. The first time I showed Billy the 'Tree of the Three Brothers' and told him it typified the love the three men bore for one another, as Uncle John said it should when the saplings were planted, I remember how touched Billy was at such an example of brotherly affection. He was only a boy, you know, and deep down in his hard little heart there must have been a little sentiment left; and thinking, perhaps, of the love and tenderness his own life had missed, he looked so wistful and woebegone I felt called on to cheer him up. 'You needn't cry,' I said to my sentimental desperado.

"Sheriff Pat Garrett was another frequent visitor at the ranch. A tremendously tall man, but not ungainly or awkward; moving, in fact, with a certain swinging grace which suggested power and sureness. Despite his crooked mouth and crooked smile which made his whole face seem crooked, he was a remarkably handsome man. A calm, poised spirit seemed to look at you out of his steady gray eyes. There was mighty little poetry in Garrett—he was about as lyric as one of his own six-shooters—but the face of the old border fighter suggested in some vague way that of Edgar Allan Poe. He looked melancholy and tragic but he could be genial and sociable, and when his cockles were warmed by a stiff, old-fashioned toddy, he was the life of the company that used to sit on the porch of an evening. He was a picturesque story-teller; his life as buffalo hunter, sheriff, fighter, and trailer of bad men had given him an interesting background, and most of his stories were drawn out of his own experience.

"He had a Southern man's ease and camaraderie, and it was easy to be his friend. But he had many enemies who cordially hated him; which was easy to understand because whatever he set out to do, he did 'in spite of hell and high water,' as he used to say, and if a man or two got hurt or killed, it didn't make any difference to him.

"After he was elected sheriff of Lincoln County and broke his close friendship with Billy the Kid to become his relentless enemy, I heard men offer to bet that if the two men ever met, Billy would kill him. Everybody thought Billy the more dangerous man and the quicker and surer shot. He undoubtedly was. But as it turned out, the bitter feud between these two—the outlaw and the sheriff —was not determined by the relative fighting ability of the men but by luck, or as some would call it, fate. Garrett killed the Kid, not because Garrett was the superior fighting man, but because it was the Kid's time to die. Years after, when it came Garrett's turn, the veteran of many battles was killed by a man who, as a fighter, might be classed as an amateur. Garrett and the Kid were resourceful, desperate fighters. But when their hour struck, they were as helpless as babes to save or defend themselves.

"I knew both these men intimately, and each made history in his own way. There was good mixed with the bad in Billy the Kid and bad mixed with the good in Pat Garrett. Both were distinctly human, both remarkable personalities. No matter what they did in the world or what the world thought of them, they were my friends. Both were real men. Both were worth knowing."

John Chisum died at Eureka Springs, Missouri, in 1884, and lies buried at Paris, Texas, his boyhood home, and the town he founded is his monument. History has dealt with him meagrely. You find his name mentioned here and there in printed chronicles with a surprising paucity of biographical detail. He remains a dim figure illuminated only by an episode now and then, like a mountain peak struck by an occasional shaft of sunlight shining through mists. There is still extant a daguerreotype portrait of the old cattle king who rode to fortune and power in his shirt sleeves on a cow pony. It shows a good, homely, honest face with alert, shrewd eyes and a suggestion of force and drive in the square chin and the set of the generous mouth. It is hardly an impressive picture. But it would be an unjust estimate that did not rank John Chisum as one of the great trail blazers and pioneers of the Southwest. He was a constructive force from first to last—a builder. Not an architect of civilization, perhaps, but a labourer laying in the sweat of his brow the foundation stones on which arose civilization and law and order.

The years have transformed the lower Pecos Valley. Northward within sight of South Spring Ranch, Roswell stands to-day, metropolis of eastern New Mexico, with ten thousand people, asphalted streets, imposing business blocks, beautiful homes embowered in trees. The once-arid plains now blossom like the rose. Artesian water from an exhaustless subterranean reservoir gushes from a thousand wells to irrigate farms and gardens. Along the trail which Chisum's herds followed to market now runs a railroad.

South Spring Ranch passed into the possession of H. J. Hagerman, former Governor of New Mexico, who built the railroad, and is still owned by his family. Leading from the smooth macadam highway to the stately brick mansion of the Hagermans is a broad royal avenue above which giant cottonwoods with boles five feet in diameter interweave their branches. These are the saplings John Chisum brought by mule train from Las Vegas. Where Chisum's longhorn cattle once cropped buffalo grass, herds of pure-blooded Herefords graze in alfalfa pastures. The great orchards that Chisum planted, now gnarled and ancient, still burgeon in season and hang heavy with apple, peach, and pear. Chisum's hedge of roses hands down the fragrant tradition of early times. Scarlet descendants of the birds Chisum brought from Tennessee, the tanagers swing from tree to bush like darts of living flame, and bob-whites set memories of the old cattle king to music as their liquid yodel rings over all the valley.

Off in a sequestered nook under towering cottonwoods near the stables stands the crumbling fragment of an old adobe wall. It is all that is left of John Chisum's former home, once the seat of comfort and good cheer and royal hospitality, meeting place of the whole Southwest. This ruined old wall is tragedy. The past beats against it like a shadowy surge. It stands in monumental vigil over the dead years. Back of it are ghosts. The wind in the cottonwoods above it is like a threnody. It is like a poignant song burdened with the sadness of memories. Gone are the days.

CHAPTER II

FROM South Spring Ranch you can see in clear weather across bare, rolling plains one hundred miles west as the crow flies the purple peak of El Capitan standing up against the horizon. Almost in the shadow of that mountain, a new power was rising to challenge Chisum's supremacy—a power bold, sinister, and predaceous. It was inevitable that eventually the King of the Valley and the Lord of the Mountains should clash. They were competitors in business; their dominions adjoined; self-interest begot jealousy and hatred. So war clouds began to gather; at first no bigger than a man's hand, darkening and bellying out portentously as the years went by and breaking at last in the thunder-drive of the Lincoln County war, bloodiest vendetta in the history of the Southwest.

About the time that Chisum settled in the Pecos Valley, Major L. G. Murphy, who had come to New Mexico with the California Column in Civil War days, was mustered out of the United States Army at Fort Stanton, an old military post dating back to 1854 and nine miles from Lincoln. For several years in partnership with Colonel Emil Fritz, mustered out at the same time, he ran a sutler's store at the fort. He sold out his interest in this establishment at the suggestion of Major Glendenning, the commandant, who expressed disapprobation of his business methods.

But Murphy had come to know the business possibilities of the well-populated mountain region isolated on every side by semi-arid plains from all other settlements in New Mexico, and he moved over to Lincoln and opened another store with John Riley and James Dolan as partners. He developed in time other business interests—a cattle ranch, a flour mill, a hotel, a saloon—and entered politics. He became in a few years the wealthiest man in the mountains and a political power to be reckoned with in Lincoln County.

Murphy had been educated for the priesthood, but at the last moment had entered the army instead of the Church. He had a certain scholarship which gave him prestige on a rude frontier. His character was a blend of priestly subtlety and soldierly boldness. With a flair for intrigue and conspiracy that might have won him distinction at the court of some mediæval monarch, this frontier Machiavelli was a master diplomat and was never more suave and urbane than when plotting the ruin of an enemy. But whatever his impulses or his plans, they were masked behind a cold and inscrutable face. Sagacious, crafty, clandestine, he kept in the background of his machinations and left to others the carrying out of his designs. By his opponents he was called treacherous, unscrupulous, and heartless, but whether or not he was as black as he was painted, there is no need to doubt that he was as dangerous a man as ever hid a sinister purpose behind a smile.

His partners were his puppets. He was the brains, they were the tools. Riley was a sly, malignant, subterranean little busybody with a gift for tunnelling, prying, ferreting out secrets. Dolan was a fire-eater and swashbuckler. For frictionless efficiency in team work, the triumvirate was above reproach. Murphy was the generalissimo, Riley the spy and scout, Dolan the fighter.

Fate weaves strange patterns. When Murphy was at the high tide of his prosperity in 1875, Alexander A. McSween and his bride, Mrs. Susan Hummer McSween, set out overland for New Mexico from their home in Atchison, Kansas. McSween was a native of Charlottetown, Prince Edward Island, and had been educated for the Presbyterian ministry. With a pulpit open to him, he decided to take up the legal profession, moved to Kansas, graduated in law at Washington University, then a well-known school in St. Louis, hung out his shingle first at Eureka, Kansas, and later practised in Atchison. Mrs. McSween was born in Gettysburg, Pennsylvania, where her colonial ancestors settled in 1731, and traced her ancestry back to the Spanglers of Frederick Barbarossa's court, and of soldierly fame during the Crusades.

The McSweens were married in Atchison. McSween's health not being robust, they decided to migrate to New Mexico, where in perennial sunshine and dry, pure air, McSween expected to regain his strength and establish himself in practice. Their tentative destination was Santa Fé; but they intended to look about them after their arrival and settle in whatever growing town seemed to offer the most promising opportunities for an ambitious young lawyer.

Their westward journey was a honeymoon trip, and as they travelled in leisurely fashion along the Santa Fé trail, this ancient highway of romance and adventure seemed to these young honeymoon gypsies a pathway of dreams leading surely to happiness and fortune. So it might have been but for their chance meeting with Señor Miguel

Otero at Punta de Agua, once a famous landmark on the old freight trail, a short journey from Las Vegas.

Of a distinguished family, Otero was a member of the territorial legislature and knew almost everybody in New Mexico. He was bound on an eastern trip, and his camp at Punta de Agua was near that of the McSweens. While he smoked a cigarette after his camp-fire supper, a coyote began a serenade in the hills.

"That fellow," called Otero to the McSweens, "sounds like he is a dozen."

Well, so he did. The McSweens laughed. And Otero strolled over to their camp fire for a casual visit. As he stepped into the circle of light, the McSweens saw a dapper young Spaniard beaming friendliness. "I am Señor Otero," he said. He might better have said, "I am Destiny." If the coyote in the hills had kept silence that night, one of the chapters of New Mexico's history that was written in blood might never have been written at all.

So, Señor McSween was a young lawyer looking for a good town in which to settle and build up a fine practice. Very well, Señor Otero knew just the place. Lincoln. The McSweens did not know there was such a place on the map. But Señor Otero should not be surprised to see it become a great centre some day. It was in the midst of a wonderful country. Growing. Becoming important.

But doubtless Señor McSween and his charming wife had heard of Señor Murphy. No? Never heard of Señor Murphy? Passing strange. Señor Otero gasped in astonishment to find two persons in the world who had never heard of Señor Murphy. A great man, rich, powerful, destined to wonderful things. If Señor McSween should desire to go to Lincoln, Señor Otero would be glad to give him a letter of introduction to his dear friend, Señor

Murphy. Well, that might not be a bad idea, after all. So the letter was written by the light of the camp fire. Next morning the McSweens set out for Lincoln.

The little incident seems absurdly trifling. No rhyme or reason to it; it came out of thin air; just happened. Yet it is a sphinx's riddle as inexplicable as life or gravity or the swing of the stars. Why did it occur? Why should it have occurred? What gods were asleep at the switch? Was the coyote some demon of darkness? Was Otero Mephistopheles in masquerade? Did some witch riding her broomstick against the moon hurl down a curse? A letter of casual courtesy, written by a stranger, met by accident, to a man they had never heard of in a town of whose existence they had never dreamed, changed the whole course of life for the McSweens, turned them aside from the happiness which apparently was their just due, and involved them in a strange tangle of tragedies which apparently they did not deserve. Fate crooked a beckoning finger from the Capitans, and without hesitation, blindly, blithely, they obeyed the summons.

The arrival of the McSweens in Lincoln was an event. Well-bred, well-dressed, well-educated, the couple introduced a new note into the village life. McSween's scholarly attainments gave the gossips something to roll over their tongues, and when the pretty Mrs. McSween had unpacked her trunks and appeared on the street, tricked out in gowns that were the last word in Kansas City and St. Louis fashions, she caused a flutter among the wives and daughters of the town who had never feasted their eyes on apparel of such chic and elegance. Murphy received the couple with great cordiality. McSween in a short time was comfortably settled in a newly built home, a spacious adobe of one story after the manner of the country, and began the practice of his profession under singularly auspicious circumstances with Murphy's firm as his most lucrative client.   The favour of such an important personage as Murphy gave the young lawyer immediate prestige; the frontier took with considerable enthusiasm to litigation, if not to law, and McSween's practice grew with amazing rapidity.

To add the completing detail to her pleasant and hospitable home, Mrs. McSween, an accomplished musician, ordered a piano shipped out from St. Louis, and her announcement of the coming of the instrument was the most exciting piece of news Lincoln had had since the Harold boys shot up the town.   The remote mountain village had only vague knowledge of pianos, based chiefly on pictures in infrequent newspapers and on the hearsay evidence of such of its citizens as had made the grand tour to Santa Fé. It knew fiddles, guitars, banjos, accordions, mouth-harps, and tin whistles, but not pianos.   There never had been a piano in Lincoln and there probably was not, at that time, a piano in all the wide stretch of country between Las Vegas and the Staked Plains.

The fifteen-hundred-mile journey from St. Louis of Lincoln's pioneer piano was not without interesting adventures.   There was not a mile of railroad in New Mexico. The Santa Fe had reached only as far west as Trinidad in southern Colorado and was not to get south of the Raton Mountains until 1878.   From St. Louis to Trinidad the piano travelled by rail.   From Trinidad to Lincoln it was borne in state on a wagon drawn by four horses.   No sooner had it made the toilsome passage over Raton Pass and headed southeastward for the Capitans than its progress became a matter of public moment.   The news of its coming ran before it; the little Mexican towns along the way turned out as for a circus and watched it pass in awed silence. It was one of Lincoln's big, historic moments when the four-horse team with its precious cargo came swinging into town through lanes of people in a sort of Roman triumph and backed up at the McSween door.

Lincoln took its pioneer piano to its heart. The instrument was a civic achievement that shed a certain metropolitan lustre on the community. The village swelled out its chest and boasted of its superiority over neighbouring villages. Las Cruces, Seven Rivers, Fort Sumner were good towns, in a manner of speaking, but—Lincoln shrugged a complacent shoulder—they had no piano. And to give colour to Lincoln's proprietary interest in the piano, the whole town shared in enjoyment of its melodies. When Mrs. McSween let her fingers wander among its keys, the music could be heard in almost every house in the village, from Murphy's store at one end to Juan Patron's at the other. Mexican urchins in the street danced to it; labourers in the hay vegas along the Bonito swung their scythes to its rhythm; it set the entire village humming, singing, whistling. Lincoln came to date its lesser affairs from the red-letter day in the calendar that marked the piano's arrival. If a housewife remarked with a severe wag of her head that her dominick rooster was hatched two days after the McSween piano landed in Lincoln, that settled all arguments about that chicken's age.

For the frontier, McSween was a quaintly impossible character. A man of cultured intellect and an able lawyer, he was a visionary dwelling among ideals and dreams. He was instinctively and sincerely religious. Among the gambling, swearing, fighting men of the border, he was an island of Christian virtue entirely surrounded by tumultuous wickedness.

His religion was not a carefully kept suit of clothes to be put on for church services on the Sabbath and left to hang in the closet the rest of the week; he lived it every hour of the day. It was not a spiritual abstraction but as real to him as sunshine. "Do unto others as you would have them do unto you" was not merely a verse in the Bible, but the golden rule of his daily conduct. The Sermon on the Mount was not only gospel, but law as binding on him as if printed in one of the calf-bound statute books on his library shelves.

His ideal was the Christ ideal, and he did his honest best to live up to it. He had a childlike faith in the basic goodness of humanity. As there was no evil in him, he did not suspect evil in others. With pure motives himself, he was incapable of understanding the lengths to which passion and hatred could go. "Murder" was a dictionary word to him, but deep down in his heart he had no real conception of its meaning. So, in a sort of beautiful innocence, he moved through his tragic personal drama like Sir Galahad with serene eyes fixed on the Holy Grail.

What he lacked in physical bravery, he atoned for in moral courage. What he believed to be right he stood for unflinchingly, and neither danger, violence, nor threat of death could swerve him a hair's breadth to right or left. It was unfortunate that he had not entered the ministry in his youth. He would have made an ideal pastor of some little church in a quiet countryside, and a sheltered parsonage, with family and friends about him, would have been his logical spiritual background. He was meant for a cozy chair and a book in some cheerful fireside ingle. The way in which his career was distorted by grimly sardonic circumstances seems less a psychological problem than an ironical enigma of destiny. He became a pawn in a mad, whirlwind game. Born for a cerebral life and the peaceful happiness of home, with no adventure in his soul, he was forced into the position of leader of a fighting faction in a bloody vendetta on a swashbuckling and lawless frontier.

Mrs. McSween was an entirely different kind of character. She was a good Christian but not of the meek and lowly type; militant rather; touched with the spirit of the old Covenanters of Presbyterianism's fighting, moss-trooper days. When her husband had attained eminence as a lawyer in Lincoln, he often had to ride on long journeys to distant towns to try a case in court. Always on these trips the good man carried his Bible in his saddle-bags and no matter how hard the day's ride or wearying the day's work, he was never too tired to read a chapter and then kneel down and say his prayers before he went to bed. This met with his wife's whole-hearted approval.

"But," she urged, "if you take your Bible in one pocket of your saddlebags, carry a six-shooter in the other. And if any man attempts to smite you on the right cheek, don't lose time turning the left to him, but get out your gun and be sure to shoot first."

"Why should I carry a gun?" replied the mild McSween. "I cannot conceive of any circumstances which would lead me to take the life of a fellow man."

If McSween was an idealist and dreamer, his wife was intensely practical. She saw life clearly through the medium of sharp eyes and a shrewd brain. There was in her the quality of Ithuriel's spear at whose touch sham and fraud and deceit stood revealed in their naked truth. She had no illusions regarding the men about her. She had lived in Lincoln but a little while before she saw through Murphy's veneer of friendship and knew him for the dangerous man he was. Her personality was distinctly feminine, but it was also distinctly fearless. In the later times of feud, which tested the courage of men and women, she was no background figure sitting in silence in her home and shedding futile tears, but played her part in the thick of things and fought her own and her husband's enemies by every means at her command, and bore herself with the dauntlessness of a Bayard *sans peur, sans reproche*. Of the many brave women who suffered and bore their crosses with stout hearts and uncomplaining fortitude through the long tragedy of the Lincoln County war, she was the outstanding heroine.

Lincoln was a busy little town in those days. It was the county seat of Lincoln County, which embraced a fifth of New Mexico and was as large as Pennsylvania and included what to-day are the counties of Lincoln, Chavez, Eddy, Otero, and a part of Doña Ana. It was the principal business centre of a country two hundred miles square, of high hills, agricultural cañons, valleys, and plateaus, isolated, in a way, from the outer world by the sentinel ranges of the Capitan, Jicarillo, White, Sacramento, Guadalupe, Organ, and San Andreas mountains. The region was drained eastward into the Pecos by the Bonito, Ruidosa, Hondo, Feliz, Peñasco, and the Seven Rivers, limpid streams fed by mountain snows, brawling over bars and riffles, spreading into quiet pools, and as beautiful and as musical as their names. To Lincoln, picturesquely situated where Bonito Cañon opens out into broad vegas and farmlands, people from all this region came to trade.

The lion's share of the business went to Murphy's store, housed in a large two-story adobe building, known through the country as "the Big Store," and in fact the most important establishment of its kind in all eastern New Mexico. Murphy's teams were constantly on the trail hauling in merchandise and supplies from Las Vegas, Santa Fé, and from the railhead at Trinidad, and Lincoln in that prosperous era was filled with people who came from miles around to shop and trade. Murphy's hotel across the road from the Big Store could hardly accommodate the crowds, and money was jingling day and night across the bar of Murphy's saloon which, on a thirsty frontier, was like the shadow of a rock in a weary land.

Life in Lincoln had stepped to a lively tune since the town was founded back in the 'fifties. War parties of Apaches sometimes swarmed down upon the village. The round stone tower with embrasures and loop-holes from which the first settlers fought the Indians remains as a reminder of those grim days. Cattle thieves, outlaws, fugitives from justice found the little hamlet, snugly tucked among its mountains, a safe hiding place and rendezvous. Gamblers drifted in. Saloons opened. The town grew into a tradition of lawlessness. It was hard-boiled from the first.

The Harold boys helped along its sinister fame. There were five of them: Ben, Bill, Jack, Tom, and Bob; Texas-born, a roistering, stiff-necked, bull-headed crew. They rode in one evening from over Ruidosa way and shot up the village for fun. The villagers argued with them over the quality of the jest, and when the smoke cleared Constable Martinez, former Sheriff Gillam, Dave Warner, and Bill Harold were dead—Bill Harold, you might say, a martyr to his sense of humour. Offended at the town's lack of appreciation of their pleasantry, the remaining Harold boys declared war on Lincoln. They came again one night with some fighting Texas friends at their back, not for fun this time, but for revenge.   There was a dance going on in an adobe house that still stands under the shadow of San Juan Church.   The fiddles were playing a waltz when the Harolds stalked in and assisted with a six-shooter obbligato which left one woman and four men lifeless on the dancing floor, one of them the father of Juan Patron.   Soon afterward, the Harold boys turned their backs on their foolish but tragic little war and went home to Texas.   They still speak in Lincoln of this two-act, blood-and-thunder melodrama that grew out of a joke as the Harold war.

Many men died with their boots on in Lincoln; some went out fighting; others mysteriously disappeared; and they were buried here and there about the town.   Lincoln somehow never achieved a cemetery until recent years. The secretly murdered men were secretly buried; the graves of others were marked at first with little wooden crosses bearing names.   These crosses crumbled away in time; they were never replaced because nobody cared; the names of the dead passed out of the memories of the living, and their graves were forgotten.   You will hear in Lincoln that a certain man in his days of power had in his hire picked killers who acted as his Destroying Angels or Danites and quietly removed any of his foes he marked for destruction.   The tale is generally discredited as an invention of enemies and no evidence whatever remains to substantiate it; but in its most definite version it estimates the number of these disappearances at "about twenty-five": Mexicans mostly who, it is said, were rolled in blankets, dumped into shallow holes, and covered with earth.

From time to time the bones of the nameless dead sleeping in their forgotten graves are turned up by some Mexican ploughing or spading in a garden. Such discoveries are so numerous they pass almost without comment. "José Castro ploughed up a skull in his corn patch to-day." "Juan Silva dug up a thigh bone while hoeing his onions." Humph! That is all. And graves seem to be everywhere, their sites vaguely known.

"There is some man buried over there in the corner of my front yard," says Mrs. Lena Morgan, mine hostess of Bonito Inn. "Who? Oh, I haven't the slightest idea. I don't know the exact spot. Somewhere near that clump of rose bushes. But that's nothing. There are three or four more graves out in the orchard."

It taxes the imagination to-day to picture Lincoln as the alive, bustling mart it was fifty years ago. The village went to sleep at the close of the Lincoln County war and has never awakened again. It is still at its nap in its pleasant cañon, dreaming, perhaps, of the crimson past. If a railroad never comes to link it with the far-away world, it may slumber on for a thousand years.

You will find Lincoln now just as it was when Murphy and McSween and Billy the Kid knew it. The village is an anachronism; a sort of mummy town looking as if it had been as carefully embalmed as some old Pharaoh, to preserve for modern eyes a meticulously vivid picture of the frontier past of a half century ago.

A winding country road serves as its single street, once a mile of tragedies. Its three hundred people, mostly Mexicans, live in quaint adobe houses. There are no sidewalks, no electric lights, no piped water. Old-fashioned kerosene lamps and candles burn in the homes at night. Frugal housewives set tubs to catch foaming streams guttering from the roofs when it rains. Murphy's old store is weather-stained and dilapidated, its outer plastering crum-

bled off in patches revealing the adobe bricks.   It is called
the courthouse; a great hall on its second floor is used for
judicial purposes on court days; its ground-floor rooms
are living quarters for several families, whose numerous
progeny whoop at their play about scenes of murder
and in the cobwebby, haunted emptiness of the upper
chambers.

All day long, picturesque Mexicans lounge in sun and
shade on the long front porch of Penfield's store, which
was once the McSween store, built as a rival of Murphy's,
and smoke endless cigarettes of yellow paper and gossip
endlessly in Spanish.   If you look closely at the solid
wooden window shutters of the old building, you will find
a thick sheet of steel between outer and inner layers of
timber, meant to turn bullets in the days of feud when the
store was, after a fashion, a fortress.   Only now and then
are any signs of life in the empty, silent street.   Perhaps a
woman in a sunbonnet with a basket on her arm on her
way to market.   Or a load of alfalfa piled high on a
creaking, rattletrap wagon drawn by scarecrow ponies
ready for the boneyard.   Or a Mexican in a steeple hat
bringing in firewood from the hills on a burro.   The air is
so still you can hear the gurgle of the asequia at the back
of the roadside gardens and the drowsy song the Bonito
sings among its willows in the bottoms.   The tall, gray
cañon walls are stippled with piñon and oak brush.   Up
the cañon, Capitan Mountain shows a purple giant
shoulder through a gap in the hills.

You can hardly believe that this peaceful village was
once the stage setting of a bloody vendetta.   Only a few
old-timers are left who know, in anything like accurate
detail, the stories of the old, wild days.   If you should
ever happen to go to Lincoln, hunt up Miguel Luna or

Florencio Chavez.   They have lived there since they were boys and know every spot in town that has a history. Their quaint talk will make the forgotten past live again for you.

Right out there in the road where that hen is dusting herself in a rut, they will tell you, Sheriff Brady was killed. Yonder in front of the little Church of San Juan, George Hindman fell dead with a bullet through his heart.   Almost directly across the road is the spot where Lawyer Chapman was murdered.   In the backyard of the little vine-swung home of Julio Sales is where five men met death on the night the McSween residence went up in flames.   From that upper window near the corner of the courthouse Billy the Kid shot Ollinger; at the foot of a stairway inside the dingy old building you will find the hole in the wall made by the Kid's bullet after it had passed through Deputy Bell's heart.   Down the street on the lintel of the door in the Montaña House, half-hidden beneath white paint now, are the letters "K–I–D" which the Kid carved there in an idle moment with his pocket-knife.   The only physical evidences of the Kid's life work left in Lincoln are the bullet hole and the three letters cut in the doorpost.   The Kid was not a constructive genius.

"You see where that roan horse is standing under that cottonwood down by the river," says Miguel Luna. "Well, right there is where they found Bill Harold lying dead the morning after the fight.   Some fellow had cut his finger off to steal his ring."

CHAPTER III

JOHN CHISUM charged Murphy with stealing his cattle. There was no mincing of words in these charges. Chisum flung them broadcast to the four winds. And Murphy in his mountains laughed defiance. Where was the proof? And if there were proof, where was the law to punish him?

Murphy had his cattle ranch at first some thirty miles west of Lincoln on the Carrizoza plains. That was inconvenient to the Pecos Valley—and Chisum's herds. He moved it to the Seven Rivers country flanking the Pecos Valley; and his herd of three thousand gained fame as the miracle herd. When it was mentioned, mountain people who were friends of Murphy laughed behind their palms; valley people who were friends of Chisum glared savagely. Strangely enough, according to the story, the number of cattle in the herd never varied. Murphy sold cattle by the thousand annually but, like the widow's cruse of oil, his herd remained the same.

There was neither difficulty nor danger in stealing Chisum's cattle. Rustlers did not wait for the light of the moon. They made their raids in broad daylight. The cattle roamed unguarded over boundless, fenceless plains. There was no one to see the thieves. They had but to round up a bunch, run it into the hills, and the thing was done.

Jesse Evans, George Davis, his brother—Evans was a

frontier nom-de-guerre—Frank Baker, and Billy Morton, were, it was said, leaders of the thieves and kept their pockets lined with gold by stealing Chisum's cattle. Many others of the same kidney were said to do as well. Hardly a day passed that somewhere between Bosque Redondo and the Guadalupes freebooters did not levy toll on Chisum's herds in greater or lesser measure. Chisum's rage was futile. Once back in their mountains, the rustlers were safe among friends. The sheriff of Lincoln County was James A. Brady of Lincoln town. As sheriff he represented what semblance of law there was. But he owed his office to Murphy's political favour and Murphy's wish was to Brady a command.

Chisum at times swore out warrants for the thieves. When Sheriff Brady could find no way to avoid it, he arrested the culprits and lodged them in the Lincoln jail. Having done this much, he was legally absolved from neglect of duty. But the Lincoln jail was as great a joke as Murphy's miracle herd. It was a little two-by-four adobe hut situated just back of Murphy's store. It would have been possible for a man confined in it to whittle his way out through the brittle adobe bricks with a good pocketknife. But few prisoners cared to take such trouble. They usually preferred to kick down the door.

Such escapes, becoming common, laid the sheriff open to a charge of negligence, and he finally installed a good door which was immune to pedal assaults. Then, upon the incarceration of cattle thieves on Chisum warrants, it became fashionable for their friends to ride into town at night with great show of daredeviltry and the shooting off of guns, go through the form of forcing an obliging Murphy jailer to deliver the keys, and rescue the prisoners in style.

There came at last an impasse. Chisum brought about
the arrest of thieves who failed to kick or whittle their
way out of jail and whom their friends carelessly neglected
to rescue. The situation seemed approaching a crisis.
Murphy grew perturbed and summoned McSween, his
lawyer.

"You will defend these men in court," he said.

"I will not defend them," replied McSween.

Murphy's eyes hardened. This was rebellion.

"I retain you under pay as my attorney," he observed
coldly. "Men on my payroll obey my orders."

"These men are thieves," retorted McSween. "I know
it; you know it. As a lawyer, I refuse to defend men who
have neither legal nor moral defense."

From that moment McSween's services as Murphy's
lawyer ended.

Chisum retained McSween at once. For Chisum,
McSween prosecuted the thieves Murphy had ordered him
to defend. They were convicted and sent to prison. It
was established by evidence at their trial that Murphy was
their patron and sponsor, and not only bought their stolen
cattle, but did a regular business in buying stolen cattle
from thieves who lived by plundering Chisum's herds.

Later on, after the first blood had been spilled in the
feud and McSween had been secretly marked as the next
victim of Murphy's vengeance, John Riley, still ostensibly
friendly for reasons of his own, dropped in at the McSween
home on what he explained was merely a social call.
There was no six-shooter at his belt; as far as appearances
went, his mission was peaceable. But his social call was
at eleven o'clock at night, when he might reasonably have
expected to catch McSween and his wife alone.

But instead he found McSween sitting in his parlour

with a company of pleasant friends. The pleasant friends were suspicious of Murphy's subterranean associate, who, nevertheless, masked with cordial garrulity whatever surprise he may have felt. They unanimously covered Riley with their six-shooters in a sociable sort of way and, as he stood with his hands in the air, relieved him of a large revolver which had been concealed, not in the customary hip pocket, but in the inner pocket of his coat, from which, if one cares to make deductions, he could have whipped it out unexpectedly by a commonplace gesture not likely to arouse suspicion.

As the gun was lifted from his pocket, a notebook fell on the floor. The which Sam Corbett retrieved. After Riley had been shown the door, protesting against his inhospitable reception and proclaiming his innocence of any sinister design, McSween and his friends examined the book with interest. It contained a long list of names—twenty-five or thirty, it was said—of notorious cattle rustlers; and set down against each name was the number of cattle Murphy had bought for five dollars a head with the amount of each purchase neatly totalled in the manner of good, businesslike bookkeeping.

The illuminating entries in Riley's pocket ledger gave a tangible clue to Murphy's success in obtaining government contracts. Murphy's bids were invariably the lowest. How he was able to quote prices that represented the rock-bottom minimum on beef and supplies for army posts and Indian reservations was, for a long time, a riddle to his defeated competitors. Now the cat was out of the bag. Here was the answer in plain black and white. But cattle bought at five dollars a head were only one item in Murphy's business strategy. A United States government investigation threw additional light on his methods.

The Mescalero Apaches occupying a reservation forty miles south of Lincoln complained that the "flour" with which Murphy had supplied them was bran. On top of this, Murphy's enemies charged that on his contract he had been paid for supplies for two thousand Indians when there were only nine hundred on the reservation. The Department of Indian Affairs sent Mr. Angell from Washington to investigate. Murphy, suave, ingratiating, met the government representative at Lincoln, showered him with polite attentions, and accompanied him to the agency post. Mr. Angell examined the "flour" first. It was bran; no doubt about it. Murphy appeared astonished. Secret machinations of his enemies doubtless were responsible for the substitution. He would guard his shipments more carefully in the future. Nothing like this would happen again. All right.

Mr. Angell prepared next to count the Indians. Murphy volunteered assistance. The Indians were rounded up from every corner of the big reservation and assembled at the house of the agent. Seated on the front porch with Murphy at his side, Mr. Angell counted the Indians as they walked by in single file. The tally reached nine hundred. Still they filed by. When the procession ended, the count showed two thousand. Murphy beamed in triumph. His honesty apparently had been vindicated.

It was not until several weeks later that Mr. Angell learned that he had been tricked. In filing past him, the Indians, under coaching of Murphy emissaries, had disappeared from sight behind a hill and, doubling back, had marched past him again in a continuous circle. He hurried back to the reservation, rounded up the Indians a second time, and impounded them under guard in a great corral built for the purpose. Then he let them out one by one. There was no chance for a mistake this time, and the count showed nine hundred. Mr. Angell's official report of his investigation became a part of the government archives at Washington.

Soon after McSween had broken with Murphy, J. H. Tunstall, an Englishman of wealth and social position in England, arrived in Lincoln. He was pronouncedly British in appearance, speech, and dress, and the town folks regarded him with amused curiosity as he strolled about insouciantly in checkered cap and knickerbockers with bulldog pipe between his teeth. But he won the villagers with his jovial good humour, bluff camaraderie, and openheartedness. Frontier life fascinated him. The drypoint landscape with its white sunlight and black shadows laid its spell upon him. He drank the pure air like a tippler. The extraordinary cowboys, the extraordinary Mexicans, the extraordinary mountains delighted him. So he decided to make the extraordinary country his home. He bought a ranch on the Rio Feliz, thirty miles south of Lincoln, stocked it with horses and cattle, and settled down.

Tunstall and McSween were drawn together by common sympathies and ideas and were soon close friends. When Tunstall proposed that they enter into a business partnership and open a general merchandise store in Lincoln, which he consented to finance in major part, McSween agreed with enthusiasm, though his wife counselled against it, foreseeing perilous possibilities. But the two men carried out the plan, built the store, a great squat adobe building, and laid in an extensive stock of goods, the whole representing a rather heavy investment. From the day the new firm threw open its doors, business flourished, and the McSween-Tunstall store was soon making heavy inroads upon Murphy's trade and developing into a formidable rival of the Murphy establishment. Then, in partnership with John Chisum and Tunstall, McSween opened a bank in one end of his store, of which Chisum was president, Tunstall vice-president, and himself secretary, treasurer, and general manager. With bank and store on a prosperous basis, McSween felt that at last he was on the high road to fortune.

But Sir Galahad was riding serenely for a fall. Since his acts had been open and aboveboard, contravened no moral or legal code, and had the imprimatur of his own conscience, he was blind to their sinister effect upon Murphy. He had sent Murphy's hirelings to prison. He had exposed his dishonesty. He had set himself up as a rival merchant. He had allied himself with Chisum. As a lawyer, he continued zealously to guard Chisum's interests under Murphy's very nose. He had organized a powerful financial combination which was bound to react unfavourably, if not disastrously, on Murphy's business. But in his unsophistication and childlike faith in the inherent goodness of men, he did not realize, and was not capable of realizing, that his course had inspired Murphy with bitterness and deadly hatred and must eventually drive that overlord of the mountains to plans of retaliation and revenge. He remained unconscious of the rising danger. Wolves were dogging his footsteps unseen in the underbrush, but he pursued his heedless way whistling a careless tune.

Came now the matter of the Fritz will to add the final twist to an intricately tangled situation. Colonel Emil Fritz had been Murphy's partner in the sutier's store at Fort Stanton. He had later bought a ranch a few miles below Lincoln on the Bonito, where he lived prosperously for a number of years. In advanced age and feeble health, Colonel Fritz went back to his boyhood home in Germany, where he died, leaving a will and an insurance policy for $10,000, both of which he had entrusted for safe keeping to his old friend Murphy. Aside from his ranch and stock in Bonito Cañon, the insurance policy which had been bequeathed to his sister, Mrs. Fred Scholland, constituted the principal asset of Colonel Fritz's estate.

Upon his death, Charles Fritz, his brother, set about to wind up Colonel Fritz's affairs. But when he sought to obtain the will and insurance policy, Murphy refused to surrender either and justified his refusal on the grounds that Colonel Fritz had died owing him a large sum of money. No proof of such a debt was ever produced but Murphy declared the will contained a provision that he be reimbursed from the insurance. Murphy, it is said, kept the will in a tin can concealed in a secret crypt in the walls of his store in Lincoln, as there were few safes in the country at that time, either for private or public funds. Whether there was such a provision in the will or not never was publicly known, as the will never was probated and Murphy was charged with having destroyed it. As for the insurance policy, the thrifty Murphy had hypothecated it with Spiegelberg Brothers, merchants of Santa Fé, for merchandise billed at $900.

McSween, employed by Charles Fritz and Mrs. Scholland as their lawyers, undertook the collection of the insurance. He paid the $900 out of his own pocket to the Spiegelbergs to square Murphy's account and, gaining possession of the policy, cashed it in full on a trip to the East and deposited the $10,000 in his own name in a bank in St. Louis. Murphy, it is said, still owed a considerable sum of money to McSween for legal services in the past.

McSween's fee for collecting the insurance was set by agreement with Mrs. Scholland and Charles Fritz at $3,000 and he was to be reimbursed for the money it had been necessary to pay the Spiegelbergs in addition to the expenses of his Eastern trip. However, when he returned to Lincoln, Murphy demanded the entire amount of the insurance policy to liquidate the debt he alleged Colonel Fritz had owed him. Murphy's claim was the match which touched off the powder magazine of a dangerous situation.

Whatever became of the $10,000 insurance money, the people of Lincoln County never learned. Neither Murphy nor the Fritz heirs nor McSween, it is said, ever received a dollar of it. When the McSween home in Lincoln was burned by the Murphy faction in the ven-detta, McSween, it is declared, threw the certificates of deposit out of a window to save them from the flames, and they were found by a Murphy henchman named Hart who, in some way, managed to get them cashed. Hart, according to the story, went to Seven Rivers, where he boasted of his sudden fortune. He spent money with riotous freedom in the saloons and was found dead one day in the Pecos River, his throat cut and his pockets turned inside out.

Murphy's affairs had reached a crisis. He had been defeated all along the line. Everything had gone wrong. His enemies were gaining the upper hand. He must act decisively if he was to save himself from eclipse and ruin. The time for diplomacy had passed. Only desperate measures would answer his desperate problems. Like a wolf driven from his secret covert into the open with the pack close at his heels, he turned at bay.

CHAPTER IV

FIRST BLOOD

THERE was great bustle and stir in Lincoln town on the morning of February 13, 1878. Horsemen clattering in along the cañon roads. The hitching-rack at the Big Store lined with saddled ponies. Hard-eyed men standing in sinister groups in the street, leaning on rifles. Murphy's bar doing a rushing business, the Mexican behind the counter hardly able to set out bottles and glasses fast enough. "Step up, boys, this is on me." "*Buena salud!*" "Fill 'em up again." Important con-ferences between Murphy and Sheriff Brady in grave undertones. Dolan swaggering. The subterranean Riley padding about with bland smiles.

Then at a word twenty men swung into the saddle, six-shooters at belt, rifles across pommels, and rode off, horses caracoling and curvetting; Billy Morton in com-mand, newly made a deputy sheriff by Sheriff Brady; in the posse Frank Baker, Billy Matthews, Tom Hill, John Robinson, several Mexicans; no records existing as to who the others were; all said to have been on Murphy's payroll. Morton and Brady were veteran cowboys and had been friends of Billy the Kid, from now on to be his enemies and he theirs. Tom Hill was a rough, loud-mouthed bully said to have killed a man or two. Jesse Evans, also a friend of Billy the Kid, with genuine bold-ness of spirit and skilful with weapons, was said by some

45

to have been in the company but denied it later, saving his life doubtless by his denial.

Past the McSween home, Mrs. McSween silently watching from her front door, the posse jogged; past the McSween-Tunstall store, the little Church of San Juan, the Montaña House, the Ellis House, the store and saloon of Juan Patron, black-shawled Mexican women staring from their dooryards, dusky urchins hugging their mothers' skirts and peering with frightened eyes. So out of town southward down Bonito Cañon to disappear behind a shoulder of the hills.

Murphy had sworn out an attachment against the McSween-Tunstall store with purpose to collect the old debt he alleged against Fritz; a procedure within his right and of unquestionable legality, since McSween had collected the money on the Fritz insurance and had deposited it in the bank in his own name. But he also had sworn out an attachment for the same purpose against Tunstall's ranch and livestock on the Rio Feliz, with full knowledge that Tunstall owned the Rio Feliz property in his sole right and McSween had no part or parcel in it. This action was without colour of legality and, it would seem, judged by the upshot of the affair, was taken only to get Tunstall out of the way as a rival stockman and, as McSween's partner in the store, as a rival merchant.

The attachment against the store was never served; but Murphy had placed his attachment against Tunstall in the hands of Sheriff Brady, his handy man, who had forthwith sworn in a posse and sent it off to the Rio Feliz. Such duty as this ordinarily is a formality delegated to a single deputy, and in this instance there was no reason to assume that Tunstall would not accept service peaceably and leave it to a court to decide the issue. But here, at

Murphy's behest, was a warlike expedition setting off to serve a simple process. Plainly enough this posse of twenty men armed to the teeth was bound on no peaceful mission.

Meanwhile, on the Feliz ranch, Tunstall went about his duties with no inkling of danger. No vagrant rumour had brought him tidings of attachment or approaching posse. With business to be arranged in Lincoln, and the winter's day being warm and sunny, he set off on horseback for town accompanied by two of his men. Dick Brewer, his foreman, was one of these. The other was a quiet, gray-eyed, slender youth, only a few months in this part of the country, his name not yet bruited to any wide extent, known as Billy the Kid.

While riding across the divide between the Feliz and the Ruidosa on their way to Lincoln, the three men ran upon a flock of wild turkeys which scurried off among the chaparral thickets in the hills. With visions of a fat tom roasted to a turn and served with dressing and savoury sauce for their dinner that evening at the McSween home, Brewer and Billy the Kid set off into the hills after the turkeys. Tunstall rode on alone, his horse at a walk, expecting the other two to join him farther along the trail.

Suddenly from behind him sounded the drumming of horses' hoofs. Turning in his saddle he saw the Lincoln posse galloping full-tilt toward him. He faced his horse about and waited for them, with a quizzical smile. As they drew near, he recognized familiar faces. He had hobnobbed with these boys in Lincoln in the days just after his arrival. He believed, it seems, they were still his friends merely bent upon some madcap prank.

"By jove, boys," he exclaimed jovially as they came dashing up all about him, "what's up? Eh?"

His answer was a shot which tumbled him dead from his saddle.   Some say Billy Morton fired the shot; some say, on what seems better evidence, Tom Hill.   At least, after Tunstall had fallen to the ground, Hill leaped from his horse and, sticking a rifle to the back of his head, blew out his brains.   Half-drunk with whisky and mad with the taste of blood, the savages turned the murder of the defenseless man into an orgy.   Pantilon Gallegos, a Bonito Cañon Mexican, hammered in his head with a jagged rock.   The Britisher had thought it all a joke.   Well, they would make it a good joke while they were about it.   They killed Tunstall's horse, stretched Tunstall's body beside the dead animal, face to the sky, arms folded across his breast, feet together.   Under the man's head they placed his hat and under the horse's head his coat carefully folded by way of pillows.   So murdered man and dead horse suggested they had crawled into bed and gone to sleep together.   This was their devil's mockery, their joke, ghastly, meaningless.   Then they rode back to Lincoln, roaring drunken songs along the way.

The posse, taking a short cut across the hills from Lincoln, had ridden first to Tunstall's ranch and, finding it deserted, had overtaken Tunstall five miles from home. Lucky for Billy the Kid and Brewer that they had gone hunting wild turkeys, else they would have shared Tunstall's fate.   From a distant hillside they witnessed the murder.   It was over so quickly that no forlorn-hope effort at aid on their part would have availed.   Nothing was left to do but save themselves.   Unseen, they slipped over the crest of the hills.

Back once more in Lincoln, Morton and his men reported to Murphy and Sheriff Brady.   Ashamed of their deed, they took refuge in mendacities.   They had found

Tunstall's ranch turned into a fortress, they said, with breastworks of logs and bags of sand. He had taken flight and when, after hard pursuit, they had run him down, he had opened fire upon them. His resistance had compelled them to kill him. A plausible tale, perhaps, but given the lie later by certain of the posse men themselves, who repented of their cowardly deed. But Tunstall was dead. That was the important fact to Murphy. He set out free liquor at his bar that night, and the dawn found his liegemen still at their celebrations.

Mexicans were sent out at night by McSween to fetch in the corpse. They found Tunstall as his murderers had left him, composed as for sleep, head pillowed on his hat, the moon shining in his wide-open eyes. They laid him across a burro's back and set out on their homeward journey across the mountains by unfrequented paths. Close to the ground hung the dead man's feet on one side of the little beast and head and hands on the other. Nettles and briars beside the trail cruelly lacerated his hands and face and tore his trousers' legs to shreds. Hints of morning were showing above the eastern hilltops when the tragic journey ended at the door of McSween's store in Lincoln.

They buried Tunstall that day back of the McSween store on a bench of ground overlooking the Bonito River. Billy the Kid was in the little group that stood beside the grave as the body was returned to earth. Tunstall had been his friend as well as his employer. But there were no tears in his eyes nor any sign of grief. This boy had his own way of paying tribute to a lost friend, and tears were no part of his ritual. From the brink of this grave which was for him the brink of a new career that was to be filled with graves, he turned away and, strolling to the front porch of the McSween store, lounged against a post and rolled himself a cigarette.

News of Tunstall's murder spread through the mountains, and the clans gathered as at the summons of a fiery cross. From every direction armed men came riding into Lincoln. Fifty men soon rallied round McSween; as many aligned themselves with Murphy. Viewed impartially, it is now clear that Murphy's cause was basically wrong and McSween's basically right; that Murphy was an unscrupulous dictator, McSween the champion of a principle; that Murphy stood for lawlessness, McSween for law. However, the question of right or wrong was but lightly considered. Men ranged themselves on one side or the other according to old allegiances and personal interests. Few remained neutral. It was Murphy or McSween: take your choice or take the consequences.

Not a few on both sides were actuated by purely mercenary motives. Little standing armies were organized by both leaders, made up of fighting men hired at handsome wages. These fighters were the roughest fellows of the country, hard riders, hard drinkers, bravos ready for any adventure or desperate enterprise. There was little to choose between the rank and file of the two factions; not all the good men were on McSween's side nor all the bad ones on Murphy's.

When he became the leader of a faction organized for war, McSween stuck to his religious principles, remained through the tumult of the times a scrupulous Christian. Circumstances forced him into leadership for which he was not equipped. The swift current of events swept him into bloody vendetta. To survive he must fight. His life was in the balance. But his personal attitude from first to last was defensive. He neither planned violence nor countenanced it. The blows struck against his enemies were the work of his fighting men acting on their own initiative.

Dick Brewer, veteran of the border, was appointed leader of the McSween fighting forces, and Billy the Kid, not by appointment but by native qualities, became Brewer's chief lieutenant. Plans of campaign were discussed by McSween, Brewer, and Billy the Kid in the parlour of McSween's home.

"I'm going to shoot down like a dog every man I can find who had part in Tunstall's murder," said the Kid.

Brewer listened in grim silence. This was strong language from an unknown, beardless boy.

"Don't do that," advised McSween mildly. "Let's forget revenge. We must fight only in defense of our lives and property."

"Tunstall was my friend," declared the Kid, and that seemed to him to cover the situation.

Tunstall and Billy the Kid had been worlds apart in everything. Tunstall had had a background of breeding and culture; the Kid's background was the frontier. They differed as night from day in character, thought, outlook on life. White for Tunstall was black for the Kid. But strangely enough, a strong friendship had developed between them. Their friendship was their only common ground. Friendship was one of the few things the Kid held sacred; an injury to a friend was an injury to him, and he held by the ancient law of an eye for an eye and a tooth for a tooth.

With the murder of the Englishman, the Kid threw himself into the feud to avenge his friend's death. There seems no reason to attribute any other motive to him.

Others fought for hire. Billy the Kid's inspiration was the loyalty of friendship. But this sentiment of knightly devotion, with which he must be credited, was united with a spirit of primitive savagery which held the blood of his friend's enemies the best libation he could pour to the memory of his friend.

CHAPTER V

BILLY THE KID'S legend in New Mexico seems
destined to a mellow and genial immortality
like that which gilds the misdeeds and exaggerates
the virtues of such ancient rogues as Robin Hood, Claude
Duval, Dick Turpin, and Fra Diavolo. From the tales
you hear of him everywhere, you might be tempted to
fancy him the best-loved hero in the state's history.
His crimes are forgotten or condoned, while his loyalty,
his gay courage, his superman adventures are treasured
in affectionate memory. Men speak of him with admiration; women extol his gallantry and lament his fate. A
rude balladry in Spanish and English has grown up about
him, and in every *placeta* in New Mexico, Mexican girls
sing to their guitars songs of Billy the Kid. A halo
has been clapped upon his scapegrace brow. The boy
who never grew old has become a sort of symbol of frontier
knight-errantry, a figure of eternal youth riding for ever
through a purple glamour of romance.

Gray-beard skald at boar's-head feast when the foaming
goblets of mead went round the board in the gaunt hall
of vikings never sang to his wild harp saga more thrilling
than the story of Billy the Kid. A boy is its hero: a boy
when the tale begins, a boy when it ends; a boy born to
battle and vendetta, to hatred and murder, to tragic victory and tragic defeat, and who took it all with a smile.

Fate set a stage. Out of nowhere into the drama

stepped this unknown boy. Opposite him played Death. It was a drama of Death and the Boy. Death dogged his trail relentlessly. It was for ever clutching at him with skeleton hands. It lay in ambush for him. It edged him to the gallows' stairs. By bullets, conflagration, stratagems, every lethal trick, it sought to compass his destruction. But the boy was not to be trapped. He escaped by apparent miracles; he was saved as if by necromancy. He laughed at Death. Death was a joke. He waved Death a jaunty good-bye and was off to new adventures. But again the inexorable circle closed. Now life seemed sweet. It beckoned to love and happiness. A golden vista opened before him. He set his foot upon the sunlit road. Perhaps for a moment the boy dreamed this drama was destined to a happy ending. But no. Fate prompted from the wings. The moment of climax was at hand. The boy had had his hour. It was Death's turn. And so the curtain.

Billy the Kid was the Southwest's most famous desperado and its last great outlaw. He died when he was twenty-one years old and was credited with having killed twenty-one men—a man for every year of his life. Few careers in pioneer annals have been more colourful; certain of his exploits rank among the classic adventures of the West. He lived at a transitional period of New Mexican history. His life closed the past; his death opened the present. His destructive and seemingly futile career served a constructive purpose: it drove home the lesson that New Mexico's prosperity could be built only upon a basis of stability and peace. After him came the great change for which he involuntarily had cleared the way. Law and order came in on the flash and smoke of the six-shooter that with one bullet put an end to the outlaw and to outlawry.

That a boy in a brief life-span of twenty-one years should have attained his sinister preëminence on a lawless and turbulent frontier would seem proof of a unique and extraordinary personality. He was born for his career. The mental and physical equipment that gave his genius for depopulation effectiveness and background and enabled him to survive in a tumultuous time of plots and murders was a birthright rather than an accomplishment. He had the desperado complex which, to endure for any appreciable time in his environment, combined necessarily a peculiarly intricate and enigmatic psychology with a dextrous trigger-finger.

Billy the Kid doubtless would fare badly under the microscope of psychoanalysis. Weighed in the delicate balance of psychiatry, he would be dropped, neatly labelled, into some category of split personality and abnormal psychosis. The desperado complex, of which he was an exemplar, may perhaps be defined as frozen egoism plus recklessness and minus mercy. In its less aggravated forms it is not uncommon. There are desperadoes of business, the pulpit, the drawing room. The business man who plots the ruin of his rival; the minister who consigns to eternal damnation all who disbelieve in his personal creed; the love pirate, who robs another woman of her husband; the speed-mad automobilist who disregards life and limb, are all desperado types. The lynching mob is a composite desperado. Among killers there are good and bad desperadoes; both equally deadly, one killing lawlessly and the other to uphold the law. Wild Bill won his reputation as an officer of the law, killing many men to establish peace. The good "bad man" had a definite place in the development of the West.

But in fairness to Billy the Kid he must be judged by the standards of his place and time. The part of New Mexico in which he passed his life was the most murderous spot in the West. The Lincoln County war, which was his background, was a culture-bed of many kinds and degrees of desperadoes. There were the embryo desperado whose record remained negligible because of lack of excuse or occasion for murder; the would-be desperado who loved melodrama and felt called upon, as an artist, to shed a few drops of blood to maintain the prestige of his melodrama; and the desperado of genuine spirit but mediocre craftsmanship whose climb toward the heights was halted abruptly by some other man an eighth of a second quicker on the trigger. All these men were as ruthless and desperate as Billy the Kid, but they lacked the afflatus that made him the finished master. They were journeymen mechanics laboriously carving notches on the handles of their guns. He was a genius painting his name in flaming colours with a six-shooter across the sky of the Southwest.

With his tragic record in mind, one might be pardoned for visualizing Billy the Kid as an inhuman monster revelling in blood. But this conception would do him injustice. He was a boy of bright, alert mind, generous, not unkindly, of quick sympathies. The steadfast loyalty of his friendships was proverbial. Among his friends he was scrupulously honest. Moroseness and sullenness were foreign to him. He was cheerful, hopeful, talkative, given to laughter. He was not addicted to swagger or braggadocio. He was quiet, unassuming, courteous. He was a great favourite with women, and in his attitude toward them he lived up to the best traditions of the frontier.

But hidden away somewhere among these pleasant human qualities was a hiatus in his character—a sub-zero vacuum—devoid of all human emotions. He was upon occasion the personification of merciless, remorseless deadliness. He placed no value on human life, least of all upon his own. He killed a man as nonchalantly as he smoked a cigarette. Murder did not appeal to Billy the Kid as tragedy; it was merely a physical process of pressing a trigger. If it seemed to him necessary to kill a man, he killed him and got the matter over with as neatly and with as little fuss as possible. In his murders, he observed no rules of etiquette and was bound by no punctilios of honour. As long as he killed a man he wanted to kill, it made no difference to him how he killed him. He fought fair and shot it out face to face if the occasion demanded, but under other circumstances he did not scruple at assassination. He put a bullet through a man's heart as coolly as he perforated a tin can set upon a fence post. He had no remorse. No memories haunted him.

His courage was beyond question. It was a static courage that remained the same under all circumstances, at noon or at three o'clock in the morning. There are yellow spots in the stories of many of the West's most famous desperadoes. We are told that in certain desperate crises with the odds against them, they weakened and were no braver than they might have been when, for instance, the other man got the drop on them and they looked suddenly into the blackness of forty-four calibre death. But no tale has come down that Billy the Kid ever showed the "yellow streak." Every hour in his desperate life was the zero hour, and he was never afraid to die. "One chance in a million" was one of his favourite phrases, and more than once he took that chance with the debonair courage of a cavalier. Even those who hated him and the men who hunted him to his death admitted his absolute fearlessness.

But courage alone would not have stamped him as extraordinary in the Southwest where courage is a tradition. The quality that distinguished his courage from that of other brave men lay in a nerveless imperturbability. Nothing excited him. He had nerve but no nerves. He retained a cool, unruffled poise in the most thrilling crises. With death seemingly inevitable, his face remained calm; his steady hands gave no hint of quickened pulses; no unusual flash in his eyes—and eyes are accounted the Judas Iscariots of the soul—betrayed his emotions or his plans.

The secret of Billy the Kid's greatness as a desperado —and by connoisseurs in such matters he was rated as an approach to the ideal desperado type—lay in a marvellous coördination between mind and body. He not only had the will but the skill to kill. Daring, coolness, and quick-thinking would not have served unless they had been combined with physical quickness and a marksmanship which enabled him to pink a man neatly between the eyes with a bullet at, say, thirty paces. He was not pitted against six-shooter amateurs but against experienced fighters adept themselves in the handling of weapons. The men he killed would have killed him if he had not been their master in a swifter deadliness. In times of danger, his mind was not only calm but singularly clear and nimble, watching like a hawk for an advantage and seizing it with incredible celerity. He was able to translate an impulse into action with the suave rapidity of a flash of light. While certain other men were a fair match for him in target practice, no man in the Southwest, it is said, could equal him in the lightning-like quickness with which he could draw a six-shooter from its holster and with the same movement fire with deadly accuracy. It may be remarked incidentally that shooting at a target is one thing and shooting at a man who happens to be blazing away at you is something entirely different; and Billy the Kid did both kinds of shooting equally well.

His appearance was not unprepossessing. He had youth, health, good nature, and a smile—a combination which usually results in a certain sort of good looks. His face was long and colourless except for the deep tan with which it had been tinted by sun, wind, and weather, and was of an asymmetry that was not unattractive. His hair was light brown, worn usually rather long and inclined to waviness. His eyes were gray, clear, and steady. His upper front teeth were large and slightly prominent, and to an extent disfigured the expression of a well-formed mouth. His hands and feet were remarkably small. He was five feet eight inches tall, slender, and well proportioned. He was unusually strong for his inches, having for a small man quite powerful arms and shoulders. He weighed, in condition, one hundred and forty pounds. When out on the range, he was as rough-looking as any other cowboy. In towns, among the quality-folk of the frontier, he dressed neatly and took not a little care in making himself personable. Many persons, especially women, thought him handsome. He was a great beau at fandangos and was considered a good dancer.

He had an air of easy, unstudied, devil-may-care insouciance which gave no hint of his dynamic energy. His movements were ordinarily deliberate and unhurried.

But there was a certain element of calculation in everything he did. Like a billiardist who "plays position,"
he figured on what he might possibly have to do next.
This foresightedness and forehandedness even in inconsequential matters provided him with a sort of subconscious
mail armour. He was forearmed even when not fore-
warned; for ever on guard.

Like all the noted killers of the West, Billy the Kid was
of the blond type. Wild Bill Hickok, Ben Thompson,
King Fisher, Henry Plummer, Clay Allison, Wyatt Earp,
Doc Holliday, Frank and Jesse James, the Youngers,
the Daltons—the list of others is long—were all blond.
There was not a pair of brown eyes among them. It was
the gray and blue eye that flashed death in the days when
the six-shooter ruled the frontier. This blondness of
desperadoes is a curious fact, contrary to popular imagination and the traditions of art and the stage. The theatre
immemorially has portrayed its unpleasant characters
as black-haired and black-eyed. The popular mind
associates swarthiness with villainy. Blue eyes and
golden hair are, in the artistic canon, a sort of heavenly
hall mark. No artist has yet been so daring as to paint a
winged cherub with raven tresses, and a search of the
world's canvases would discover no brown-eyed angel.
It may be remarked further, as a matter of incidental
interest, that the West's bad men were never heavy,
stolid, lowering brutes. Most of them were good-looking,
some remarkably so. Wild Bill Hickok, beau ideal of
desperadoes, was considered the handsomest man of his
day on the frontier, and with his blue eyes and yellow hair
falling on his shoulders, he moved through his life of
tragedies with something of the beauty of a Greek god.
So much for fact versus fancy. Cold deadliness in West-

ern history seems to have run to frosty colouring in eyes, hair, and complexion.

Though it is possible that the record of twenty-one killings attributed to Billy the Kid is exaggerated, there is strong reason to believe it true. He was remarkably precocious in homicide; he is said to have killed his first man when he was only twelve years old. He is supposed to have killed about twelve men before he appeared in Lincoln County. This early phase of his life is vague. From the outbreak of the Lincoln County war, his career is easily traceable and clearly authentic.

It is impossible now to name twenty-one men that he killed, though, if Indians be included, it is not difficult to cast up the ghastly total. It may be that in his record were secret murders of which only he himself knew. There are rife in New Mexico many unauthenticated stories in which the names of his victims are not given. One tale credits him with having killed five Mexicans in camp near Seven Rivers. Another has it that a number of the twenty or more unmarked graves on the banks of the Pecos at the site of John Chisum's old Bosque Grande ranch contain the dust of men the Kid sent to their long sleep.

The Kid himself claimed to have killed twenty-one. He made this statement unequivocally a number of times to a number of men and he was never regarded as a braggart or a liar.

"I have killed twenty-one men and I want to make it twenty-three before I die," he said a little before his death to Pete Maxwell at Fort Sumner. "If I live long enough to kill Pat Garrett and Barney Mason, I'll be satisfied."

Sheriff Pat Garrett, who for several years was the Kid's close friend—and who killed him—placed the Kid's record at eleven.   John W. Poe, who was with Garrett at the Kid's death, accepted the Kid's own statement. In a letter written to me shortly before his death in 1923, Poe said:

> Billy the Kid had killed more men than any man I ever knew or heard of during my fifty years in the Southwest.   I cannot name the twenty-one men he killed; nor can any man alive to-day.   I doubt if there ever was a man who could name them all except the Kid himself. He was the only man who knew exactly.   He said he had killed twenty-one and I believe him.

Poe, who succeeded Pat Garrett as sheriff of Lincoln County and was at the time of his death president of the Citizens National Bank of Roswell, was a veteran man-hunter and knew the criminal element of the Southwest as few men did.   If Poe, with his first-hand knowledge of the Kid, had faith in the Kid's own statement, it would seem fair grounds for presumption that the statement is true.

So the matter stands.   With most of the actors in the old drama now dead and gone, it is safe to say the tragic conundrum of how many men fell before Billy the Kid's six-shooters will never be definitely answered.   Certainly the list was long.   And it is worth remembering that the Kid was only a boy when he died and, however his record is itemized, each item is a grave.

To realize the bizarre quality of Billy the Kid's character try to fancy yourself in his place.   Suppose, if you please, that under stress of circumstances you had killed several men.   Assume that you felt justified in these homicides.   Very well.   Would an easy conscience bring you peace of mind?   No.   If you did not regret the killings, you would regret profoundly the necessity for them.   The thought of blood on your soul would for ever

haunt you.   Your spirit would be shaken and shadowed
by remorse.

But that would not be all.   The relatives and friends of
those you had killed would hate you.   They would
hound you everywhere with their hatred.   They would
dog your footsteps and lie in wait to take your life.   They
would watch with jungle eyes for an opportunity for
revenge.

Nor would this fill the cup of your misery.   You would
have achieved the sinister reputation of a fighter and a
killer.   Men who had no cause of quarrel against you, to
whom your killings had meant nothing, would look upon
you as they might upon a dangerous beast, a menace to
society, a being outside the pale of human sympathy
and law.   The pack would be ready at any time to fall
upon you without mercy and tear you to pieces.   You
would approach every rock and tree with caution lest
some hidden foe fire upon you.   You would not dare sleep
in the same bed twice.   You would suspect every man of
treachery.   When you sat at meat, you would feel that
Death sat across the table with hollow eyes fixed upon
you.   Any minute you might expect a bullet or the plunge
of a knife driven by unutterable hatred.   Fear would
walk hand in hand with you and lie down with you at
night.   You could not smile; peace and happiness would
be denied you; there would be no zest, no joy for you this
side of the grave.   In your despair, you would welcome
death as an escape from the hopeless hell of your hunted,
haunted life.

But Billy the Kid was not of the stuff of ordinary men.
There must have been in him a remarkable capacity for
forgetfulness; he might seem to have drunk every morning
a nepenthe that drowned in oblivion all his yesterdays.

For him there was no past.   He lived in the present from minute to minute, yet he lived happily.   He killed without emotion and he accepted the consequences of his killings without emotion.   His murders were strong liquor that left no headache.   Surrounded by enemies who would have killed him with joy, breathing an atmosphere of bitter hatred, in danger of violent death every moment, he went his way through life without remorse, unracked by nerves or memories, gay, light-hearted, fearless, always smiling.

If you would learn in what affectionate regard the people of New Mexico cherish the memory of Billy the Kid to-day, you have but to journey in leisurely fashion through the Billy the Kid country.   Every one will have a story to tell you of his courage, generosity, loyalty, light-heartedness, engaging boyishness.   More than likely you yourself will fall under the spell of these kindly tales and, before you are aware, find yourself warming with romantic sympathy to the idealized picture of heroic and adventurous youth.

Sit, for instance, on one of the benches under the shade trees in the old square at Santa Fé where the wagon caravans used to end their long journey across the plains. Here the rich and poor of this ancient capital of the land of mañana and sunshine come every day to while away an hour and smoke and talk politics.   Mention Billy the Kid to some leisurely burgher.   Instantly his face will light up; he will cease his tirade against graft and corruption in high places and go off into interminable anecdotes. Yes, Billy the Kid lived here in Santa Fé when he was a boy.   Many a time when he was an outlaw with a price on his head, he rode into town and danced all night at the dance hall over on Gallisteo Street.   The house is still there; the pink adobe with the blue door and window shutters. Did the police attempt to arrest him? Not much. Those blue-coated fellows valued their hides. Why, that boy wasn't afraid of the devil. Say, once over at Anton Chico . . .

Or drop into some little adobe home in Puerta de Luna. Or in Santa Rosa. Or on the Hondo. Or anywhere between the Ratons and Seven Rivers. Perhaps the Mexican housewife will serve you with frijoles and tortillas and coffee with goat's milk. If you are wise in the ways of Mexicans, you will tear off a fragment of tortilla and, cupping it between your fingers, use it as a spoon to eat your frijoles that are red with chili pepper and swimming in soup rich with fat bacon grease. But between mouthfuls of these beans of the gods—and you will be ready to swear they are that, else you are no connoisseur in beans —don't forget to make some casual reference to Billy the Kid. Then watch the face of your hostess. At mention of the magic name, she will smile softly and dreamlight will come into her eyes.

"Billee the Keed? Ah, you have hear of heem? He was one gran' boy, señor. All Mexican pepul his friend. You nevair hear a Mexican say one word against Billee the Keed. Everybody love that boy. He was so kindhearted, so generous, so brave. And so 'andsome. *Nombre de Dios!* Every leetle señorita was crazy about heem. They all try to catch that Billee the Keed for their sweetheart. Ah, many a pretty *muchacha* cry her eyes out when he is keel; and when she count her beads at Mass, she add a prayer for good measure for his soul to rest in peace. Poor Billee the Keed! He was good boy —*muy valiente, muy caballero.*"

Or ask Frank Coe about him. You will find him a

white-haired old man now on his fruit ranch in **Ruidosa Cañon.** He fought in the Lincoln County war by the Kid's side and as he tells his story you may sit in a rocking chair under the cottonwoods while the Ruidosa River sings its pleasant tune just back of the rambling, one-story adobe ranch house.

"Billy the Kid," says Coe, "lived with me for a while soon after he came to Lincoln County in the fall of 1877. Just a little before he went to work for Tunstall on the Feliz. No, he didn't work for me. Just lived with me. Riding the chuck line. Didn't have anywhere else special to stay just then. He did a lot of hunting that winter. Billy was a great hunter, and the hills hereabouts were full of wild turkey, deer, and cinnamon bear. Billy could hit a bear's eye so far away I could hardly see the bear.

"He was only eighteen years old, as nice-looking a young fellow as you'd care to meet, and certainly mighty pleasant company. Many a night he and I have sat up before a pine-knot fire swapping yarns. Yes, he had killed quite a few men even then, but it didn't seem to weigh on him. None at all. Ghosts, I reckon, never bothered Billy. He was about as cheerful a little hombre as I ever ran across. Not the grim, sullen kind; but full of talk, and it seemed to me he was laughing half his time.

"You never saw such shooting as that lad could do. Not a dead shot. I've heard about these dead shots but I never happened to meet one. Billy was the best shot with a six-shooter I ever saw, but he missed sometimes. Jesse Evans, who fought on the Murphy side, used to brag that he was as good a shot as the Kid, but I never thought so, and I knew Jesse and have seen him shoot. Jesse, by the way, used to say, too, that he wasn't afraid of Billy the Kid. Which was just another one of his brags.

He was scared to death of the Kid, and once when they met in Lincoln, Billy made him take water and made him like it. Billy used to do a whole lot of practice shooting around the ranch, and had the barn peppered full of holes. I have heard people say they have seen him empty his shooter at a hat tossed about twenty feet into the air and hit it six times before it struck the ground. I won't say he couldn't do it, but I never saw him do it. One of his favourite stunts was to shoot at snowbirds sitting on fence posts along the road as he rode by with his horse at a gallop. Sometimes he would kill half-a-dozen birds one after the other; and then he would miss a few. His average was about one in three. And I'd say that was mighty good shooting.

"Billy had had a little schooling, and he could read and write as well as anybody else around here. I never saw him reading any books, but he was a great hand to read newspapers whenever he could get hold of any. He absorbed a lot of education from his newspaper reading. He didn't talk like a backwoodsman. I don't suppose he knew much about the rules of grammar, but he didn't make the common, glaring mistakes of ignorant people. His speech was that of an intelligent and ·fairly well-educated man. He had a clean mind; his conversation was never coarse or vulgar; and while most of the men with whom he associated swore like pirates, he rarely used an oath.

"He was a free-hearted, generous boy. He'd give a friend the shirt off his back. His money came easy when it came; but sometimes it didn't come. He was a gambler and, like all gamblers, his life was chicken one day and feathers the next, a pocketful of money to-day and broke to-morrow. Monte was his favourite game; he banked the game or bucked it, depending on his finances. He was as slick a dealer as ever threw a card, and as a player, he was shrewd, usually lucky, and bet 'em high—the limit on every turn. While he stayed with me, he broke a Mexican monte bank every little while down the cañon at San Patricio. If he happened to lose, he'd take it like a good gambler and, like as not, crack a joke and walk away whistling with his hands rammed in his empty pockets. Losing his money never made him mad. To tell the truth, I never saw Billy the Kid mad in my life, and I knew him several years.

"Think what you please, the Kid had a lot of principle. He was about as honest a fellow as I ever knew outside of some loose notions about rustling cattle. This was stealing, of course, but I don't believe it struck him exactly that way. It didn't seem to have any personal element in it. There were the cattle running loose on the plains without any owner in sight or sign of ownership, except the brands, seeming like part of the landscape. Billy, being in his fashion a sort of potentate ruling a large portion of the landscape with his six-shooter, felt, I suppose, like he had a sort of proprietary claim on those cattle, and it didn't seem to him like robbery—not exactly—to run them off and cash in on them at the nearest market. That's at least one way of figuring it out. But as for other lowdown kinds of theft like sticking up a lonely traveller on the highway, or burglarizing a house, or picking pockets, he was just as much above that sort of thing as you or me. I'd have trusted him with the last dollar I had in the world. One thing is certain, he never stole a cent in his life from a friend."

The history of Billy the Kid already has been clouded by legend. Less than fifty years after his death, it is not

always easy to differentiate fact from myth. Historians
have been afraid of him, as if this boy of six-shooter deadliness might fatally injure their reputations if they set
themselves seriously to write of a career of such dime-
novel luridness. As a consequence, history has neglected
him. Fantastic details have been added as the tales
have been told and retold. He is already in process of
evolving into the hero of a Southwestern Niebelungenlied.
Such a mass of stories has grown about him that it seems
safe to predict that in spite of anything history can do
to rescue the facts of his life, he is destined eventually to
be transformed by popular legend into the Robin Hood
of New Mexico—a heroic outlaw endowed with every
noble quality fighting the battle of the common people
against the tyranny of wealth and power.

Innumerable stories in which Billy the Kid figures as a
semi-mythical hero are to be picked up throughout New
Mexico. They are told at every camp fire on the range;
they enliven the winter evenings in every Mexican home.
There is doubtless a grain of truth in every one, but the
troubadour touch is upon them all. You will not find
them in books, and their chief interest perhaps lies in the
fact that they are examples of oral legend kept alive in
memory and passed on by the story-tellers of one genera-
tion to the story-tellers of the next in Homeric succession.
They are folklore in the making. As each narrative adds
a bit of drama here and a picturesque detail there, one
wonders what form these legends will assume as time goes
by, and in what heroic proportions Billy the Kid will
appear in fireside fairy tales a hundred years or so from
now.

CHAPTER VI

CHILD OF THE DARK STAR

THROUGHOUT his life of lurid adventure, Billy the Kid's name was lost in his pseudonym. His name really doesn't matter much; by any other, he would have shot as straight; but it happened to be William H. Bonney, and he was born in New York City, November 23, 1859. William H. and Kathleen Bonney, his parents, both of unknown antecedents, emigrated in 1862 to Coffeyville, Kansas, taking with them three-year-old Billy and a baby brother named Edward.

When little Billy Bonney was toddling about its streets, Coffeyville was a mere collection of shacks on an obscure frontier, safely to one side of the fighting in the Civil War, which was then in full swing. All that is known of the Bonneys in the little Kansas town is that Billy's father died and was buried there. Soon afterward, the widow with her two children moved to Colorado.

Colorado in those days was the ultimate West, lying beyond the Great American Desert, vaguely celebrated as a land of gold through the Pike's Peak mining stampede of a few years before; Denver, the principal town, contained only two or three thousand people, and communicated with the outside world by pony express which carried the mail at twenty-five cents an ounce to Leavenworth in ten days. How Mrs. Bonney made the trip across the plains, or in what town in Colorado she located, is not of record; but in whatever town it was, she married a man named Antrim and soon set out for Santa Fé, the centre of the ancient Spanish civilization along the upper reaches of the Rio Grande.

By wagon the little family must have gone, following the mountain route of the Sante Fé trail, through the Mexican adobe village of Trinidad on the River of the Lost Souls, over Raton Pass into New Mexico; and it is easy to fancy little Billy opening his eyes in amazement as almost over his head towered the four-square battlements of Fisher's Peak, uniquely beautiful among mountains, with the flat-topped Ratons stepping down the horizon in a series of tablelands.   Yonder in the north rose the twin summits of the Spanish Peaks; and along the southwestern sky tumbled the white chaos of the Sangre de Cristo, Blood of Christ Mountains, named by the early padres when their eyes visioned the eternal snows crimsoned by the sunset. Pine forests clothed the slopes; the valleys were deep bowls of misty purple; and the rough wagon road hung against granite walls and skirted precipices, with a thousand-foot drop a few inches to one side, just as the broad motor boulevard over the pass does to-day.

Billy and his mother come out a little more definitely on the canvas after their arrival in Santa Fé.   The boy was five years old then and lived in the quaint old city three years, during which time his mother kept a boarding house.   A few old-timers remember the child to this day, a lively gamin playing in the streets with the Mexican children, shooting marbles in the purlieus of the haunted old Palace, spinning tops on ground hallowed by pioneer padre and conquistador; trailing Kit Carson about the streets with other little ragamuffin hero-worshippers whenever the famous old scout and Indian fighter rode into town from his home at Taos, ninety miles away;

feasting his eyes on the solemn pomp of religious fiestas and processions, and thrilling to the prairie-schooner caravans that drove in every summer over the Santa Fé trail to fill the ancient plaza with the stir and excitement of strange romance.

The Antrims moved in 1868 to Silver City in south-western New Mexico, a silver camp in its raw boom days. Here Antrim worked in the mines; his wife opened another boarding house. Billy, who was eight years old upon their arrival, went to school. Ash Upson, one of Mrs. Antrim's boarders, has left his testimony that Billy was bright at his lessons and stood well in his classes. "He had as a little boy," says Upson, "a happy, sunny dis-position but also a fiery temper, and when he was in one of his rages nobody could do anything with him."

For four years Billy lived here in Silver City, growing into precocious youth. The town was uncouth and law-less, filled with saloons and gambling houses, bad Mexicans, and worse white men. It was the devil's own school for any boy, and Billy learned its lessons well. He associated on familiar terms with the wild spirits of the place, hung about saloons, watching the gamblers at their games, and soon displayed a natural and uncanny facility at cards. To a boy of such talent, gamblers good-naturedly condescended to teach their tricks. Under their expert coaching, Billy became an adept at dealing stud poker and monte, learned to stack a deck, deal from the bottom, palm a card, and cheat a fellow gamester's eyes out with-out detection. In a little while he was master of all the dextrous stratagems of the crooked short-card gambler. This at an age when boys in less strenuous communities are still at tops and marbles.

It was at Silver City, when twelve years old, that Billy

killed his first man.   His mother with Billy at her side was on her way from home into the business section to do some shopping.   Picture the couple if you will: the mother in her plaid gingham and sunbonnet, her face kindly, honest, rather sad, according to descriptions; the lad slender, alert, swinging along with brisk, vigorous step, looking like a happy, careless infant, except for his prematurely wise gray eyes.   A group of men lounged in front of a saloon, a young blacksmith among them, with some reputation in town as a rough character and bully. As Billy and his mother passed, the smith perhaps half-tipsy, dropped some light remark, directed, possibly with flirtatious intent, at Mrs. Antrim.   In his eyes, the boy was negligible.   But Billy flamed at once into violent passion and resentment, picked up a stone, hurled it with all his might at the head of the insulter of his mother. The missile knocked off the blacksmith's hat; an inch or two lower and it would have caught him full in the forehead and probably have killed him.   Unhurt but blazing with anger, the fellow rushed at Billy, who dodged away into the street.   A man named Moulton was standing at the curb; as the blacksmith lurched past, Moulton knocked him down with his fist, and when he arose, knocked him down again.   Which rough chivalry, in keeping with the spirit of the mining camp, saved Billy from chastisement and, for the time being, closed the incident.

On an evening a few weeks later, Moulton was refreshing himself with a glass of beer in Dyer's saloon on the main street.   It was a quiet night; a few stragglers at the bar; the faro games and monte layouts along the opposite wall doing a fair business.   The young blacksmith was sitting in at a poker game in a corner; Billy Bonney was leaning against the ice box, idly observant.

Two drunken fellows blundered in off the street through the swinging doors and one, in drunken humour, with a full-arm swing, knocked Moulton's hat off his head. There was doubtless merry intent in the joke, but Moulton, bent upon the quiet enjoyment of his beer, failed to enter into the spirit of it and with a blow of his fist stretched the jester on the floor. Thereupon the other man took up the quarrel and in a moment the prostrate fellow having regained his feet, a furious three-cornered fight was in full swing, with Moulton hard-pressed but holding his own.

The blacksmith saw in the situation an opportunity for revenge. Still smarting from the drubbing he had previously received, he sprang from his seat, raised his heavy chair high in air, and aiming at the back of Moulton's head, brought it down with smashing force. The blow failed of its target; struck glancingly against Moulton's shoulder. With this new adversary in action, Moulton, fighting one against three, was in danger. But Billy Bonney no longer leaned idly against the ice box. He, too, saw an opportunity for revenge and an opportunity also to render assistance to a friend in distress—a friend who had been his champion when he had needed aid and to whom he owed a debt of gratitude. Whipping out his pocketknife, he rushed upon the blacksmith just as that ruffian, again swinging the chair aloft, was in the act of delivering a second blow at Moulton. Three times the boy struck with his blade; down fell the chair clattering against the bar; the blacksmith, staggering back, clutched at his heart, pitched headlong.

So, for the first time, the wolf cub tasted blood.

It is perhaps worth noting that this unpretty barroom tragedy—the first murder in Billy the Kid's long list—was hall-marked by a native expertness in deadliness. No veteran of crime could have done the thing more deftly. Here was a child, at least in years, who had never taken human life before and probably had never remotely considered such a contingency. But when a problem arose which, it seemed to him in an instinctive flash, only murder could solve, he solved it with murder without a moment's hesitation. The soul of this infant, only just out of swaddling clothes, seemed plainly no boy's soul, but rather that of a man with a background of crime already achieved; a soul out of the frozen dark of ages, charged with a heritage of sinister sophistication.

With his victim dead at his feet, Billy darted out the door and, slinking through back streets and alleys, made his way home, his only thoughts now upon escape. Possibly a vague vision of the gallows or prison arose before him. He would not wait for arrest; he would take no chances on suffering any penalties for his deed. His mind was made up. He would flee from Silver City, hide out in the mountains, put distance between him and the law, find refuge beyond the horizon, somewhere, anywhere. He went to his mother's room, told her he had killed the man who had insulted her; not boastfully, nor yet regretfully, dealing coldly with a fact. Heretofore we have had dim pictures of this mother in the humdrum of prosaic existence. Here was her crisis, and in the revealing light of it she stands out a Spartan. She shed no tears; it was no time for tears. She thought only of the safety of her first-born. She agreed with his plan to dodge arrest; gave him the few dollars she had on hand; drew him to her bosom for the last time and kissed him goodbye. The boy slipped out into the night, his mother's eyes straining after the slight, furtive figure hurrying away, growing dimmer and dimmer, fading out at last in the darkness. It was the final parting on earth; mother and son never saw each other again.

For the next four years we know little of the details of Billy Bonney's career. He got finally into Arizona where he evolved through hard experience into an expert cowboy. He worked on various cattle ranches and for various cattle outfits between the Mogollon Mountains and the Mexican boundary and at odd times was in and out of Bowie, Tucson, Benson, Douglas, Nogales, Bisbee, and Gila River villages. It was a sparsely settled country of mountains, deserts, and open range; a dangerous country, too, with the Apaches murdering and raiding at will; and as wild and turbulent as could be found in all the West even in that early day.

Billy reappears definitely upon the stage at the age of sixteen. From this time on, his career gallops swiftly. He was now a well-grown boy, almost as tall as he ever became, lean, full of restless energy; a happy-go-lucky youth, good-naturedly conscienceless, laughingly reckless, utterly irresponsible, unhampered by moral scruples of any kind, capable of smiling murders; in appearance and manner, as innocuous as a sucking dove, but as poisonously dangerous as a bull rattlesnake.

While hanging about Fort Bowie in southeastern Arizona, dealing monte and living precariously, he picked up a partner of unknown name but who, doubtless, in dodging the law here and there about the country, had borne many names and who at this time passed under the suggestive nickname of "Alias." Bound for the San Carlos reservation, three Indians camped at the military post, fresh from a hunting and trapping expedition in the Chiricahui Mountains. They had in their possession eight valuable packs of fur pelts, twelve ponies, good saddles, firearms, and blankets, which aroused the cupidity of Billy and Alias, the cards having run against these two of late, leaving them practically penniless.

Learning the trail the Indians would take out of the fort, Billy and his partner went ahead on foot a few miles and lay in ambush. When the redmen came jogging along on their ponies, Billy stepped out and with three shots toppled them out of their saddles dead in the road. Stopping only long enough to drag the bodies out of sight into the underbrush, Billy and his companion, now well armed and mounted, headed to the south with their plunder. They sold everything except the horses they were riding and the weapons they had appropriated for their personal accoutrement to a party of freighters in the Dragoon Mountains, and, with well-filled pockets, made their way to Tucson, where they enjoyed themselves on the proceeds of their adventure. Alias steps out of the story here; Billy remained in Tucson for an undetermined period, living by his wits and his nimble fingers at cards and becoming a familiar figure in the sporting element of the town, which at that time was the dominant portion of the population.

While in Tucson, Billy killed another man over a card game. Nothing more is known about it: neither the name of the man nor any single circumstance. Doubtless, the tragedy at the time rang through the town; the picture of it grips the imagination: the electric hush that broods over a card game; a sudden quarrel; anger flaming into high words; a shot; a dead man sprawled on the floor; something dark slowly spreading about him. Who knows what human history was behind this man? Here was the end of ambition, passion, striving; some mother had loved him; the tenderness of home was in his story some-where.   A big thing in its moment, this old-time tragedy; now it is forgotten, every detail of it lost in dead, hopeless silence.   "Billy killed another man" is all the history of it; an epic of life and death packed in four words.

Also Billy killed a Negro soldier in these early days. This seems rather definitely established.   According to the story, Billy caught the Negro cheating at cards.   But no more is known of this murder than of the other in Tucson; not even where it occurred.   It is supposed to have been at an army post, but at which one remains a question.   Some of the stories locate it at Fort Union, New Mexico.   This seems improbable, as, except for this vague ascription, there is nothing to indicate that Billy at this phase of his career was ever anywhere near Fort Union, which was up in the Mora country northeast of Las Vegas.

Billy slipped across the border after these affairs into old Mexico.   While knocking about Sonora, he fell in with Melquiades Segura, a young gambler as ready as he for any escapade.   These two, pooling their capital, opened a monte bank in Agua Prieta.   Bucking the game, José Martinez quarrelled with Billy, who was dealing. Both reached for their guns, Billy was the quicker and Martinez fell dead across the gambling layout.

Behold thereafter Billy and Segura galloping by moon-light over Sonoran sagebrush steppes, across the Sierra Madre ranges into Chihuahua.   Southward past Casas Grandes they rode through the same country which in years later saw Pancho Villa and his bandit raiders go up to the sack of Columbus.   Their destination was Chihuahua City, painted alluringly by Segura as a good gambling town, offering fat pickings, and here the two adventurers finally fetched up.   Chihuahua, living up to its reputation, proved such a good gambling town that Billy and Segura soon lost their bank roll.

Followed then a series of street robberies which set the old town buzzing. Prosperous Mexican gamblers were accustomed toward morning to take home the receipts of the night's play in buckskin bags carried by their mozos. Billy and Segura found it child's play to step from some dark doorway and at the point of their revolvers relieve the gamblers of their bags of dollars and doubloons. One gambler, however, resisted, and Billy took his life as well as his money; and before daybreak, on stolen horses, Billy and Segura were riding hard for the Rio Grande, three hundred miles away.

Once more in New Mexico and parted from Segura, Billy met Jesse Evans, a few years older than himself, living also by his wits and his six-shooter. Though later to fight with the Murphy faction against Billy in the Lincoln County war, Jesse Evans seems to have held the highest place in Billy's esteem of all the comrades of these early years. Quite worthy, too, of the young daredevil's friendship, this dashing Texas cowboy might seem to have been. He was a crack rider, crack shot, gambler, rustler, highwayman, heading as straight as might be for the penitentiary where he eventually landed, but on the way, taking life merrily, worrying not at all about the future, and riding "high, wide, and handsome."

These two scapegrace men-at-arms wandered together through the border country, rustling stock occasionally, taking a whirl at cards, sharing the luck of fat and lean days. If perchance their fortunes were at low ebb, they had but to drive a few stolen steers to market. Then logically to a faro bank where they might heel a bet from the queen to the ace or copper a stack on the deuce. If they won, the world was theirs for at least twenty-four hours; if they lost, there were plenty of steers on the range. Of the adventures that befell them only one has survived in dubious tradition. Somewhere between the San Andreas Mountains and the Guadalupes, it is said, they broke bread one day with a party of immigrants, three men, three women, and several children. After they had taken their departure, a band of Apaches swooped out of the hills and attacked the camp. Riding back, Billy and Jesse opened fire with their rifles upon the savages, who were finally driven off, leaving eight dead on the field. During the fight, an Indian bullet shattered the stock of Billy's rifle and another knocked off the heel of one of his boots. One of the immigrants received a wound through the stomach from which he died and two others were shot, though not dangerously.

Billy and Jesse joined fortunes with Billy Morton, Frank Baker, and Jim McDaniels, cowboy friends of Evans, in the summer of 1877 around Mesilla, and remained with them for a time. In camp-fire talk, McDaniels once made passing allusion to Billy.

"Who?" asked Evans, not hearing the name.

"Billy," replied McDaniels and added by way of indubitable identification, "the Kid."

There was a certain hard staccato music in the words that appealed to McDaniels and he rolled the name he had inadvertently coined over his tongue again and again—"Billy the Kid, Billy the Kid."

So a famous name was born casually. Nothing original about it; but it had a quaint ring that caught the fancy of the other cowboys, and from that time on Billy Bonney was Billy the Kid to them and the rest of the world.

Mexicans sometimes changed the epithet into the Spanish equivalent, "El Chivato." But they usually took no more liberties with the name than with the Kid himself; it remained with them and their descendants "Billee the Keed. "Thousands of youngsters have been called "Billy" since then in that part of the country, and thousands have been referred to as "the Kid." But in combination, the words have a single connotation. For the Southwest there has never been but one Billy the Kid.

When his four companions set off eastward for the Pecos, Billy remained in Mesilla; there was a little matter which required his personal attention. It was as well for Morton and Baker, as they shook his hand in parting, that they could not read the future. Within less than a year, Billy the Kid was to snuff out both their lives.

Word had reached Billy that his former comrade, Segura, was in jail in San Elizario in Texas, eighty miles away, and he determined on a daring coup to save him. With plans carefully laid, he set out on his pony late in the afternoon for a Paul Revere dash to the Rio Grande. It was fifty-five miles from Mesilla to El Paso; Billy had covered the distance before midnight. By three o'clock in the morning, he was in San Elizario. The little town on the river bank was asleep. Hiding his pony in an alley, Billy slipped through the dark streets to the jail. He thumped boldly on the door. A fat Mexican jailer, startled from slumber on an office cot, shuffled across the floor.

"*Quién es?*" he called gruffly.

"Texas Rangers," answered Billy in Spanish. "Open up. We have two American prisoners."

There was a rattling of keys on the inside; the door swung cautiously open. Billy pushed in; at the same time shoving the barrel of his six-shooter into the paunch of the astonished Mexican official.

"Hands up!" he commanded.

Up went the Mexican's arms at full length above his head. Billy had no sooner disarmed him and taken possession of the keys than a Mexican guard, aroused by the hubbub, came in from a rear room, rubbing his eyes drowsily. He, too, was quickly disarmed. Marching jailer and guard before him, Billy hunted out the cell in which Segura was confined.

"*Como le va, amigo?*"

"*Ola, compadre!* It is you."

Releasing his old side-partner, Billy pushed the two Mexicans into the cell and locked the iron-barred door upon them. Billy and Segura hurried out of the little prison and, both mounted on Billy's pony, were soon splashing across the Rio Grande. Safe in old Mexico, they made for the ranch of one of Segura's friends. Here they lay in hiding for a few days, resting up. Then Segura headed southward and Billy made his way back to Mesilla.

Bound now for the Pecos country to rejoin Jesse Evans and his cowboy friends, Billy set out from Mesilla in company with Tom O'Keefe. While crossing the Guadalupe Mountains, they were attacked by Apaches. During a running battle, the two boys became separated; the main band of the Indians riding hard on the flying traces of O'Keefe, the others pursuing Billy and making the cliffs ring with their war-whoops. When his horse was shot under him, Billy scrambled up a steep hillside, dodging among giant boulders and working gradually toward the crest of the ridge. Dismounting, the Indians charged after him. Billy killed two in their first rush. Sheltering themselves behind rocks and trees, the savages rained bullets about him. As one peeped over a boulder and shifted his gun into position, Billy planted a shot between his eyes. As another was slinking from one ambush to another, Billy dropped him in his tracks. Another, who drew himself over a ledge within twenty feet of Billy, fell with a bullet through his heart and, tumbling down the hill, lodged in the branches of a tree, where he hung suspended. With his score at five, the Indians gave up the fight, and Billy, slipping over the ridge, found safety in flight.

This is the story of his adventure that Billy himself told when, after wandering for three days and subsisting on wild berries, he found his way into Murphy's cow camp on Seven Rivers and was welcomed by Evans, Morton, Baker, and McDaniels O'Keefe, it may be added, also escaped the Indians and got back unhurt to Mesilla.

Billy struck the Pecos Valley in the fall of 1877 a few weeks before he was eighteen years old. Staked to a pony by his cowboy friends, he arrived a little later at Frank Coe's place on the Ruidosa where, as we have seen, he spent most of the following winter, eventually taking employment at Tunstall's ranch on the Rio Feliz to remain there until the murder of the Englishman launched the Lincoln County war.

The foregoing tales may be regarded, as you please, as the apochryphal cantos of the saga of Billy the Kid. They are not thoroughly authenticated, though possibly they are, in the main, true. Most of them are perhaps too ugly to have been inventions. If you are skeptical, your doubt may be tempered by the fact that they have at least always gone with the legend and have such authority as long-established currency may confer.

CHAPTER VII

AN EYE FOR AN EYE

BITTERNESS of years flamed into war with the murder of Tunstall. The unprovoked killing was Murphy's challenge to both Chisum and McSween. For all his unsophistication and gentleness of soul, McSween must have foreseen the impossibility of avoiding further violence. But he laid his plans seemingly for justice rather than revenge.

His problem was as delicate as it was dangerous. Justice seemed chimerical at that wild moment. The situation was inflammable. The mood of his men was lawless. They cared no more for law just then than did Murphy's followers. They were restlessly eager for vengeance; their trigger fingers itched to pay off the score against their enemies with blood. Plainly there was no hope in Sheriff Brady for the maintenance of law. His posse had committed the murder; that he would arrest the murderers was not to be expected. If they were to answer the law for their crime, McSween himself must bring them to book. There was no other way.

In a crisis in which law was a dead letter, McSween was still the lawyer to whom law was both theory and practice. His enemies had acted under the guise of law and he did not propose that his own actions should lack colour of legal authority. His course was made easy by Justice of the Peace John P. Wilson of Lincoln, who found it convenient to trim his sails to factional winds and managed with diplomatic shrewdness to steer a safe and neutral course between Scylla and Charybdis. Through his influence with this accommodating official, McSween brought about the appointment of Dick Brewer, the leader of the field forces, as special constable; and Brewer, having assembled a legal posse of deputies and obtained legal warrants for the arrest of Tunstall's murderers, set off for the Seven Rivers country to fulfil his legal mission.

McSween's explicit instructions were to serve the warrants without bloodshed and bring back the prisoners for trial. It is possible that, with his faith in the goodness of men, McSween expected the posse to carry out his orders. He may, perhaps, be given the benefit of the doubt. But whatever his intentions, it is certain the possemen themselves were inspired with no such pacific purpose. They rode out of Lincoln not as champions of law but as personal avengers; their warrants were mere scraps of paper and their dearest wish was for the opportunity to serve them from the muzzles of their guns.

With Special Constable Brewer on his expedition were Billy the Kid, Charlie Bowdre, Doc Skurlock, Hendry Brown, Jim French, John Middleton, Fred Wayt, Sam Smith, Frank McNab, and a man named McCloskey. The very personnel of the posse was fair earnest of its designs. It would have been difficult to rake together even in that country more desperate and lawless men. But they were bold fellows, whatever else they were, and they rode straight for the heart of the enemy's country, undoubtedly prepared neither to give nor to take quarter. The region of the Seven Rivers was a Murphy stronghold; in the midst of it was the Murphy ranch with its "miracle herd"; it had served as a base for forays against Chisum's cattle; its people were either Murphy sympathizers or active Murphy partisans.

The posse travelled down the Bonito and Hondo cañons and turned south in the Pecos Valley. At the lower crossing of the Peñasco, six miles from its confluence with the Pecos, they caught sight of five horsemen, dismounted and resting under a clump of trees near the ford, who, when they saw the posse approaching, hurriedly climbed into their saddles, drove the spurs into their ponies, and went careering away in a cloud of dust, Brewer's men tearing pellmell after them, firing at every jump. After several miles of this mad race, two of the fugitives separated from the other three and headed for the hills to the west. Billy the Kid recognized these two for his former friends of Mesilla days, Billy Morton and Frank Baker; both Morton, as leader of the Tunstall murder posse, and Baker, as a member of it, in at Tunstall's death and participants in the orgies over his dead body. These two and any others of that murderous band he might chance to meet the Kid had sworn to kill.

The Kid wheeled his horse off after Morton and Baker, and the remainder of the posse followed his lead. The pursuers gained gradually; their bullets began to sing close about the ears of the fugitives and knock up spouts of earth around them. Turning in their saddles, Morton and Baker returned the fire. A sudden change in their course brought them broadside to the posse and both their horses were killed under them. On foot, their case seemed hopeless. It chanced there was a deserted dugout not far off, with low sod walls and dirt roof, offering protection. They made this on the run and found refuge in the cavernous interior.

The dugout was in open land, and behind its bullet-proof

walls Morton and Baker were fairly safe as long as their
ammunition held out, their enemies not daring to venture
too close to their rude fortress. The fight turned into a
siege with only desultory firing on either side. For two
days and nights, the posse held the two men penned up
in the dugout and then, seemingly facing death from starvation and thirst and their ammunition almost exhausted,
Morton and Baker stuck a white rag out the door on the
point of a rifle in token of their desire for an armistice.
The possemen drew near and a parley was opened.

"We'll surrender," called out Morton, "if you'll give
us your word we won't be killed."

There was silence for a moment.

"All right," said Brewer at length. "Come on out.
We'll guarantee you won't be harmed."

"Not now nor later either," argued Morton.

"We'll promise you protection," answered Brewer.

Then the two men marched out with their hands in the
air. When their guns had been taken from their belts,
they spied Billy the Kid leaning on his rifle.

"Hello, Billy," said Morton.

"Howdy, Kid," said Baker.

They extended their hands. This boy had chummed it
with them at their camp fire at Mesilla.

Billy regarded them with a look of cold deadliness.

"I don't know you and don't want to know you," he
said with an oath and turned away.

The posse arrived late that same day at John Chisum's
South Spring Ranch and put up for the night.

"I gave up my own bedroom to the two prisoners that
night," said Mrs. Sallie Roberts, then Miss Chisum, in
recalling her memories of the incident. "I don't think
either of them got much sleep. Several of the possemen,

armed to the teeth, sat up with them all night long to prevent any possibility of escape. These poor boys—both nice-looking fellows, too—knew they were doomed and didn't have a chance on earth. Nobody told me but I knew it, too, and everybody at the ranch knew it. We sensed it in the grim looks and the silence of the possemen.

"Morton and Baker were as pale as corpses when they came out of the prison room for breakfast in the morning. When they had eaten, Baker came to me and gave me his gold watch, his horsehair bridle, and a letter he had written in the night to his sweetheart.

"'I want to make my last request on earth to you, Miss Chisum,' he said. 'I will never live to get to Lincoln. When you hear of my death, I wish you would send my watch and bridle, which I plaited myself, to my sweetheart and mail this letter to her.'

"The letter was addressed to Miss Lizzie N. Lester, Syracuse, New York. I mailed it to her a little later and sent her the watch and bridle, and we kept up a correspondence for quite a while. I never saw her and never learned a great deal about her, but from her letters she must have been a sweet, fine, educated girl. When Morton told me good-bye, he merely gripped my hand hard: he couldn't talk."

The posse set out for Lincoln with their prisoners that morning. They halted in Roswell, then a straggling village, five miles away, to allow Morton an opportunity to write a letter to his cousin, H. H. Marshall of Richmond, Virginia, a lawyer, and a wealthy man, according to report, of an old and aristocratic family of which Morton had turned out to be the black sheep. In the letter, as was learned afterward, Morton informed his relative he was on his way to death and bade him a last farewell.

Ash Upson, who a few years before had lived at the boarding house of Billy the Kid's mother in Silver City, was postmaster of Roswell at this time.

"I wish," said Morton to Postmaster Upson in turning the letter in to him, "you would write my cousin the full particulars of my death when you hear of them."

Posseman McCloskey, an old buffalo hunter, and according to all accounts a brave, decent man, was standing near by.

"If they kill you two men," he said to Morton within hearing of several others of the posse, "they will have to kill me first."

When the posse started out from Roswell, they took the main road to Lincoln which ran westward across the Pecos Valley, over Pecacho Hill and by way of Hondo and Bonito cañons. Martin Chavez of Pecacho, later merchant and politician in Santa Fé, riding toward Roswell, saw them turn from the travelled highway and head for Agua Negra by a dim, unfrequented trail.

Agua Negra is a spring at the eastern foot of Capitan Mountain in an uninhabited country through which few travellers pass. It gushes from a cliff a little way inside the wide mouth of Agua Negra Cañon. Steep hills dark with piñons rise above it and the great peak towers beyond. The spring pours through lichened boulders into a spacious basin where cattle and sheep sometimes come to drink and where the still, clear waters lie so dark in the shadows of trees that the pool has been named Agua Negra—the Black Water. A haunted, lonely spot it is, fit scene for crime. When Chavez reached Roswell, he reported this strange turning aside from the main travelled road to Ash Upson, who read sinister meaning in it.

"It's all over with those poor boys," said Upson.

"Billy the Kid has taken them there to that deserted spot to murder them."

It turned out as Ash Upson prophesied. Morton and Baker were murdered at Agua Negra but the details of the tragedy are still an enigma. There was a story generally believed in those days and widely believed now that when the posse reached Agua Negra, Billy the Kid marched Morton and Baker a little apart from the posse and, on the margin of the water hole, while they begged on their knees for their lives, blew out their brains. Billy the Kid and the members of the posse, however, stoutly denied this and gave their own account of the affair, which at least seems plausible and may be true.

As the posse approached Black Water Spring, according to Billy the Kid's account, the Kid and Charlie Bowdre were riding in the lead, McCloskey and Middleton were jogging beside the two prisoners, and the other possemen were strung out in the rear. Suddenly Frank McNab and Hendry Brown spurred up their horses and drew rein alongside of McCloskey and Middleton.

"So you are the brave hero," roared McNab to McCloskey, "who will die before he sees these two fellows killed. All right. We'll send you to hell along with them."

He stuck his six-shooter into McCloskey's face and pulled the trigger. The flame leaping from the muzzle burned McCloskey's eyebrows and blackened his skin with powder burns and he fell out of his saddle dead.

When he heard the shot, so the tale goes, Billy the Kid turned to see Morton and Baker spurring their ponies in a breakneck dash for liberty. He made no attempt to pursue but, sitting still on his horse, fired twice. Morton and Baker threw up their hands and, toppling over backward, plunged lifeless to the ground.

Once again on the road to Lincoln, Billy the Kid rode in silence, and his companions left him to his thoughts.

"Say, Hendry," he said at length to Hendry Brown, who rode beside him.

"Yes, Billy."

"Do you know what?"

"No, Billy, what?"

Brown had an idea the Kid's memories were still grimly on the murders and the corpses left lying to stare at the sky.

"Well, I'll tell you what," said Billy. "Juan Patron's beer is as good as any ever served across a bar in these mountains and I aim to have two or three cold glasses as soon as I get back to Lincoln."

Some sheep herders driving their flock to water at the lonely pool a week later found the three corpses and buried them. But where their graves are no one knows to-day; how they died and where they sleep are alike secrets of the Black Water. The spring gurgling among the boulders sings their requiem. Capitan Mountain is their only headstone.

CHAPTER VIII

THIRTEEN TO ONE

BILL ROBERTS didn't amount to much. He was just a nobody, people said. He was a stocky, square-cut, homely little man of middle age, illiterate, commonplace, poorly dressed. He used to ride an old bay mule, and Lincoln County folks could hardly conceal their smiles when he jogged along the road, kicking the patient beast in the ribs with his heels, his elbows flapping up and down. He kept to himself, never had much to say, had few friends. The question of his courage was never discussed; nobody thought Bill Roberts worth discussing from any angle.

But Bill Roberts had courage; not the ordinary courage of ordinary men, but the courage that nothing can daunt and nothing conquer and that does not know the meaning of fear. Bill Roberts's courage rose above his ignorance and homeliness, the ridiculousness of his sorry figure on his old bay mule, above life, above death, to heights of supreme heroism. His battle at Blazer's sawmill in the Mescalero Apache Indian reservation with odds of thirteen to one against him, and the thirteen the most desperate professional fighters of the McSween faction, including the redoubtable Billy the Kid, is rated in the Southwest as one of the gamest single-handed fights in the history of the frontier. He lost his life in the fight but death did not rob him of victory.

Roberts was a Texan. He had served for years in the

army and rose to the rank of sergeant; as a soldier he took part in campaigns against the Kiowas and Comanches and was badly shot in an Indian battle. He had been a member of the Texas Rangers and saw hard service with them along the Rio Grande. He had killed a man somewhere in Texas, it was said, and when twenty-five Rangers came to arrest him, he turned at bay and they riddled him with bullets before they took him. He carried a considerable quantity of lead in him for the rest of his life. Wherefore he was known as "Buckshot Bill" Roberts. These old wounds had left him so badly crippled he could not raise a rifle to his shoulder. Inability to raise a rifle to his shoulder was a serious handicap in that part of the country. He overcame his handicap by learning to shoot from his hip with remarkable accuracy.

Roberts was settled on a little ranch in Ruidoso Valley when the Lincoln County war broke out. There are two stories as to his attitude toward the feud. While he had been a friend of Murphy he had been no enemy of Mc-Sween and, it is said, he declared his intention of remaining neutral. Neutrality was not regarded just then as a crowning virtue. War was in the air and no pacifist was tolerated. A man had three choices: he had to be either against Murphy or against McSween or against public sentiment; and one choice was about as dangerous as another. When one of his neighbours asked him about this report of his neutrality, Roberts, it is said, replied in his slow way: "I don't aim to take sides. I've seen enough fighting. All I ask is to be let alone. My fighting days are over."

This is one story.

But, according to the other, Roberts allied himself with the Murphy faction. When, as the tale goes, Murphy offered a reward of one hundred dollars apiece for the scalps of McSween men, Roberts, his enemies say, went gunning for Murphy's foes with the design of feathering his nest with some of this blood money.   Frank Coe, who was at Blazer's sawmill when Roberts made his last fight, still alludes to him as "one of Murphy's scalp hunters."   But the fact that he never took any scalps and never shot anybody and never got any blood money might seem to discredit this story.   There was, too, a rumour that Roberts was a fugitive from justice and was wanted in Texas for murder.   There was another that he was a deserter from the army.   So a certain mystery still clings to Roberts. But nobody cared about his past.   Neither did his sympathies in the vendetta, one way or the other or neither way, arouse any special interest or comment.   Bill Roberts was generally regarded as a man of no consequence.

Soon after the murder of Morton and Baker at Black Water Spring, Billy the Kid and Charlie Bowdre had a brush with Roberts in the neighbourhood of San Patricio on the Ruidoso.   Roberts is said to have fired on them without warning, and in the little battle that followed a number of shots were exchanged without injury to any of the combatants.   The details of this fight are vague. How or why an encounter between such desperate fighting men ended ingloriously without bloodshed, nobody to-day seems to know.   It may have been this skirmish that caused the McSween faction to swear out a warrant against Roberts.   On what charge the warrant was based is not known, but there was such a warrant, and it was in the hands of Special Constable Dick Brewer when he set out from Lincoln for the lower country on his second scouting expedition after McSween's enemies.

Brewer had with him on this man-hunt Billy the Kid,

Frank and George Coe, Charlie Bowdre, John Middleton, Hendry Brown, Tom O'Folliard, Jim French, Stephen Stevens, Bill Scroggins, and two others whose names have been forgotten, thirteen in all. They did not find Roberts but Roberts found them. While they were nooning at Blazer's sawmill, Roberts came splashing across Tularosa River on his old bay mule to meet his heroic death.

Frank Coe attempted to act as peacemaker and tried to save Roberts, but Roberts was as stubborn as he was brave and refused to be saved. Coe told the story of the fight in detail years afterward when he and his cousin, George Coe, were the only surviving eyewitnesses. It was a plain, unvarnished tale, seeming somehow to lack any special dramatic interest. But then Roberts was not in any way dramatic; only an illiterate, homely, commonplace fellow, looking as little like a hero as any one could imagine. The man who didn't amount to much simply fought his fight against desperate odds, did the best he could, and died. That's all there was to it.

"Brewer had heard that several men we were looking for were in Rinconada in the Mescalero reservation," said Coe, "and we went there but found nobody. We camped for the night in Rinconada and next day rode to Blazer's mill on Tularosa River. We got there about ten o'clock in the morning and Brewer ordered dinner. While we were eating, Middleton, who had been left outside to guard our saddle horses, came and reported to Brewer that 'a mighty well-armed man' had just ridden from across the river on a bay mule and was hitching down at the corral. That didn't excite anybody much, as well-armed men were common in the country just then, and we went on eating. I happened to get through first and went out into the yard. Roberts, with a rifle in his hand, was coming up from the corral.   I knew him well and he and I had been friendly; he had frequently stopped at my place on the Ruidoso; and we said 'Hello' and shook hands.   Then we went around the house and sat down in a side door to talk.

"'We've got a warrant for you, Bill,' I said.

"'The hell you have,' said Bill.

"'Yes, and I'm glad you rode up because now we won't have the trouble of hunting for you.   You better come on in the house and see Brewer and surrender.'

"'Me surrender?' said Bill.

"'Why, of course.   There ain't any way out of it now.'

"'Well, we'll see about that.'

"'There are thirteen in the gang, Bill,' I said, 'and if you don't surrender peaceable, it means simply they'll kill you.   You wouldn't have a chance on earth.'

"'As long as I've got a load in old Betsy here,' replied Roberts, patting the butt of his Winchester, 'there ain't nobody going to arrest me, least of all this gang.'

"'Now, don't be foolish, Bill,' I argued. 'There ain't no sense in resisting and getting yourself killed.'

"'I'd be killed if I surrendered.'

"'What makes you think that?'

"'Didn't I try to kill Billy the Kid and Charlie Bowdre last week?   If those two fellows got their hands on me now, they'd kill me sure.'

"'No, they wouldn't.   You surrender and nobody will hurt you.'

"'Yes,' said Bill, 'that's what they told Morton and Baker.   I know this gang.'

"Well, I must have talked to Roberts nearly half an hour, trying to persuade him to surrender, but I might as well have talked to his mule; there wasn't any surrender in that fellow.   I knew if he didn't give up what the fellows would do to him, and as he and I had been friends I didn't want to see him get hurt. It seemed funny while we were sitting there that he didn't make a break to get away, knowing that thirteen men who were looking for him were just inside the house and believing in his heart they meant to kill him. But he didn't make a move; didn't seem the least disturbed; just went on talking quietly.

"When the gang got through eating dinner, they walked out the front door and in a moment here they all came around the corner of the house, Charlie Bowdre in advance. Roberts rose in a leisurely sort of way from where he had been sitting in the door and stood facing them at a distance of not more than fifteen feet. As soon as Bowdre saw Roberts he cracked down on him with a six-shooter.

"'Throw up your hands, Roberts,' he said, 'or you're a dead man.'

"'Not much, Mary Ann,' replied Roberts, still as cool as you please; and he brought his rifle to a level at his hip.

"Bowdre and Roberts fired point-blank at each other and at the same time. Bowdre's bullet struck Roberts in the chest and went clear through him, giving him a death wound. Roberts' shot cut Bowdre's gun belt from around his waist so it fell to the ground, and Bowdre jumped back around the corner. The others opened fire now. But wounded to the death, Roberts did not retreat an inch. There were a dozen of the most desperate fighters in the Southwest blazing away at him at close range; but the little man only staggered up against the wall and went on pumping lead.

"He bored Middleton through the body just above the heart; Middleton stumbled around the corner and fell unconscious. Another bullet tore off George Coe's trigger finger and knocked the six-shooter out of his hand; and he, too, jumped out of sight. Fighting like a tiger at bay, Roberts, in less time than it takes to tell it, had the field to himself and not a foe in sight; every man in the crowd had disappeared around the corner.

"In this lull in the battle, he backed into the shelter of the door. Just then Billy the Kid, late in getting into action, came into view between the house and a road wagon standing near. He fired twice, but Roberts being inside the door, the Kid could not get a bead on him. From where I stood back along the wall, I yelled to the Kid to get back and motioned to him with my hand, and he ducked out of sight just as Roberts fired a shot that, I'll bet, didn't miss the Kid by an inch.

"Roberts was sick from his wound; I could hear him groaning. But his fighting spirit was as brave as ever. He slammed and locked the side door and went through the house into the front room and, firing again through the front door, sent his enemies rushing around the house out of range. He had churned all the shots out of his Winchester by this time; so he threw the gun aside and got a heavy Sharp's rifle—an old buffalo gun—which he found standing in a corner. Then he pulled a mattress off the bed and, dragging it across the floor under the open front window, lay down on it and prepared to keep up the fight. Nobody was ever able to figure out how, shot through and through as he was, he managed to do all this; his vitality was as marvellous as his nerve.

"Brewer and the rest of us now held a council of war. Billy the Kid wanted to rush the front door. Some of the others agreed to this. But I told them Roberts couldn't live three hours, was as good as dead already, and there wasn't any sense in any more of us getting shot up or perhaps killed by any such daredevil foolishness. An argument arose as to who had shot him. Billy the Kid and George Coe both claimed the credit; but they were both wrong; Bowdre shot him. 'I dusted him on both sides,' said Bowdre. That was a way those fellows had of talking; he meant his bullet had knocked dust out of Roberts' clothes where it went in and where it came out.

"Brewer was determined to have Roberts dead or alive. He called to Doctor Blazer to bring Roberts out of the house. Doctor Blazer wouldn't do it. Brewer threatened, if he didn't, he would burn the house down. Still Doctor Blazer refused. This made Brewer mad clear through; he didn't want to give Roberts time to die but was bound to kill him at once, if possible, and have it over with. He crept down around the barn and outhouses and, keeping under cover, got into position behind a pile of saw logs near the mill and a hundred yards directly in front of the house. From this ambush he sneaked over two or three shots which went through the window beneath which Roberts was lying and knocked the plaster off the back wall of the room but drew no answering fire. I suppose Brewer thought Roberts was nearly done for and he became a little careless. He raised his head above the logs to have a look. Roberts happened to have his Sharp's rifle resting at a level on the window sill at that exact moment, and he let fly a ball that struck Brewer square in the middle of the forehead and tore off the top of his head. It was a long shot and slightly downhill and a great piece of marksmanship, though I figure the shot was to a certain extent accidental and Roberts couldn't have done it again once in a hundred trys. But once was enough, and Brewer simply slumped over dead where he lay at full length behind the logs and never made another move.

"With Brewer dead, the rest of us decided to go away from there. We knew it was only a question of a short time when Roberts would cash out, and there was nothing we could gain by hanging around. Besides, our own wounded required attention: Middleton dangerously hurt, Coe with his finger shot off, and Bowdre with a sharp pain in his side where Roberts' rifle bullet had struck his cartridge belt. We got a government ambulance and, placing the wounded men in it, drove over to my Ruidoso ranch where we passed the night and then on to Roswell where we found a surgeon. It was several weeks before Middleton recovered. Doctor Blazer, we afterward learned, sent to Fort Stanton for the army surgeon to come and see what could be done for Roberts, but Roberts died before the doctor got there."

They buried Roberts and Brewer the day after the fight in a little private burial plot on a knoll near the mill. John Patten, an old trooper of the Third Cavalry, mustered out at Fort Stanton in 1869, and at that time boss sawyer at Doctor Blazer's mill, and who lived in that country long afterward, said they were buried in the same coffin and the same grave. According to Patten's story, he made the coffin h mself out of rough mill lumber, and he ought to have known. Emil Blazer, Doctor Blazer's son, however, declared they were buried close together and side by side but in separate graves.

But whether in one grave or two is no matter now. Their last resting place is unmarked by any headstone and overgrown with grass and weeds; and there they still lie, these two desperate men who died hating each other, fighting each other to the death, and sleeping together through all eternity.

CHAPTER IX

THE SHERIFF'S MORNING WALK

SHERIFF BRADY was annoyed. His plans for a quick and decisive Murphy victory had miscarried. The savage fighting spirit of Murphy's enemies had surprised him. The McSween faction was sweeping all before it and seemed in a fair way to overthrow Murphy's power and rise itself to supremacy.

Sheriff Brady was up to his eyes in the feud. With frankness and enthusiasm he had thrown the power of his office on the Murphy side. Why not? Murphy was his friend. He owed to Murphy not only his personal fortunes but his office. As honest as most men, he honestly believed Murphy represented whatever law and justice were in the vendetta. Defeat for Murphy meant ruin for himself. In fighting for Murphy, he was fighting for his own interests. His attitude, it must be admitted, was incompatible with the impartial performance of his duties as sheriff; it was neither fair nor legal; but at least it was fundamentally human.

When Murphy had decided that Tunstall should be killed, Sheriff Brady organized the posse and dispatched it on its tragic mission. Thus he launched the war, though in the episode he served only as the cat's-paw to pull Murphy's chestnuts out of the fire. Whether he knew in advance the posse's purpose was murder may not now be definitely determined; but it is logical to assume that he did. Certainly he condoned the murder and shielded the murderers. Though he regarded with cool detachment the killing of Tunstall by Murphy men, the killing of Morton and Baker by McSween men stirred his bitter resentment. Both crimes were equally atrocious, but he took no steps to apprehend the murderers of Tunstall while he planned to hunt to the death all who had had part in the murder of Morton and Baker.

Billy the Kid, by whose hand Morton and Baker had died, was the special target of Sheriff Brady's wrath. The sheriff had procured the offer of a reward for this young outlaw dead or alive, which, according to popular interpretation, meant preferably dead. But if Sheriff Brady hated the Kid, the Kid hated him with equal fervour. While Sheriff Brady sought to compass the Kid's death as the murderer of his friends Morton and Baker, the Kid determined upon the sheriff's death as the man responsible for the murder of his friend Tunstall. So the sheriff sought personal vengeance against the Kid, and the Kid sought personal vengeance against the sheriff. But these deadly quests differed according to the characters of the two men. Sheriff Brady relied upon his deputies to carry out his design; the Kid depended upon himself.

Sheriff Brady, Deputy Sheriffs George Hindman and "Dad" Peppin, and Circuit Court Clerk Billy Matthews foregathered in front of Murphy's store in Lincoln at ten o'clock on the morning of April 1, 1878. All were men of mature years except Matthews, who was a brisk, smart fellow in early manhood.

"Judge Warren Bristol of Mesilla has sent me word," said Sheriff Brady, "that he will not hold the regular term of the Circuit Court in Lincoln this April. He has been informed there is a plot among the McSween men against his life in which Billy the Kid is the ringleader, and if he attempts to hold court here, these McSween assassins will shoot him down as he sits on the bench.   The judge does not propose to risk his life in such a dangerous community, and he has ordered me, as a matter of routine form, to open and adjourn court this morning.   That's why I have asked you boys to meet me here.   We will go to the court-house now and carry out Judge Bristol's orders."

So the four men started out for the courthouse near the other end of town.   All were armed with Winchesters and six-shooters; unusual equipment, it might seem, for men whose purpose was to open court, but hardly amenable to criticism in that place and time.   They walked at moderate pace, indulging in casual converse, carrying their rifles in their hands, as soldiers would say, at trail.

The morning was unclouded and the sun was bathing Bonito Valley in brightness and warmth.   So clear was the air, they could almost count the blades of new grass springing up among the piñons on the mountain walls of the cañon.   They could see from one end of the town to the other; the grove of shade trees about Bonito Inn where the road makes a slight bend and which now obstructs the view was not in existence, and Jimmy Dolan's residence which evolved into the little hostelry directly across from the McSween store had not yet been built.   The McSween home, the McSween store, the Church of San Juan, and the adobe homes in their flower gardens along the quiet street stood sharply etched in every detail in the bright sunshine.   Just beyond the church was the building used as the courthouse, perhaps a quarter of a mile away.   A few villagers were abroad; a Mexican shouted now and then to his plough team turning up the earth in black furrows in a field back of the church.

"Billy the Kid, I hear, has picked up a new fellow for his gang," remarked Billy Matthews.

"Yes?" said Sheriff Brady.

"Name's Tom O'Folliard," Matthews went on. "Hails from Texas somewhere. Wandered into the Kid's camp over on the Ruidoso on foot, they say. How he got there nobody knows. Didn't have a gun; didn't have a horse; didn't have nothing. Just wanted to fight."

"He'll get his fill of fighting if he fools around in this country long," observed Hindman.

"They say McSween keeps his fighting men on good pay," cut in Peppin.

"If our boys run into him, his money won't do him much good," said Brady.

"Well," continued Matthews, "when the Kid saw this big, gawky, solemn-looking fellow, he thought somebody had put up a joke on him. But the cuss was so earnest, Billy decided to take a chance and rustled up an old buffalo gun and a crow-bait pony for him, and now the recruit is a regular warrior. Worships the Kid, they say, and is ready to fight a buzz-saw if the Kid bats his eye."

"The Kid thinks he's some pumpkins since the Morton and Baker murder," said Brady. "That little horse thief is working to the end of his rope. He's just about due, and it don't matter to me much how he's got, so he's got. Hanging's too good for him."

So they talked as they strolled along the dusty road.

They passed the McSween house; it was silent; Mr. and Mrs. McSween were away on a visit to John Chisum, McSween's partner, at South Spring Ranch. Captain Saturnino Baca was sitting on his front porch across the street; he waved to them in greeting and they waved back to him. As they came to the McSween store, they nodded to a few Mexican loungers smoking cigarettes on the long porch.

They reached a point in the road fifty feet, perhaps, beyond the McSween store. Still walking leisurely and interested in their gossipy talk, they did not see six heads lift furtively and six pairs of eyes peep dangerously above the top of a low adobe wall that came out flush with the street at the east end of the McSween store, forming a corner of the side and back yard. Billy the Kid, Charlie Bowdre, Tom O'Folliard, Jim French, Frank McNab, and Fred Wayte suddenly straightened up with cocked rifles in their hands from the ambush where they had been lying in wait.

"Billy the Kid," Sheriff Brady was saying, "will never——"

A volley of rifle bullets from the adobe wall cut short his sentence. The sheriff threw up his arms wildly, flinging his rifle ten feet away; he staggered forward a few steps and crashed to the ground. His three companions took to their heels, bullets singing around them. Billy Matthews and "Dad" Peppin reached a little Mexican house close by on the south side of the road and dashed to safety through the door. Hindman kept to the road in his flight. A rifle ball struck him in the back between the shoulders; he stumbled on a little farther and fell in front of San Juan Church.

"Dammit," said Billy the Kid in business-like tones as he pumped another cartridge into his Winchester, "I didn't care so much about old 'Dad' Peppin but I'm sorry we didn't get Matthews."

However, all things considered, it was a fairly good workmanly job in the Kid's critical estimation. Though he had failed to "get" Matthews, there was at least something else that appealed to him as worth getting—Sheriff

Brady's rifle and six-shooter, both new and brightly fur-
bished. The Kid was canny even in assassination.

"I think I could use those guns," he said. "Come on,
Wayte, let's get 'em."

He and Wayte vaulted over the wall and walked out
into the road to where Brady lay. Wayte gathered up
the rifle; Billy was stooping over the prostrate form un-
buckling the cartridge belt with the six-shooter in its holster, when Billy Matthews, from the Mexican house in
which he had found refuge, opened fire. His first bullet
cut through the flesh of the Kid's hip and wounded Wayte
in the thigh. These two hustled back to the shelter of
the adobe wall, carrying with them, however, both the
sheriff's rifle and his six-shooter; the Kid, taking time, it is
said, to fire a bullet into Brady's head by way of grace
shot to make sure of the death of his enemy.

For nearly half an hour Hindman lay in the hot sun
where he had fallen, no one in the village daring to venture
to his side. He was dying. He called for water. Still
the panic-stricken people remained in their houses. At
last, Ike Stockton, saloon keeper, bad man, killed later
in Durango, Colorado, bravest of all in Lincoln town,
dipped up water in his hat from an asequia and took it to
the dying man. Hindman, supported in Stockton's arms,
took a deep drink and fell back dead.

Sheriff Brady had been riddled with eight or ten bullets,
some of which had passed entirely through him. Hindman was shot only once. It is impossible to say who
killed either. Hindman's death was by some attributed
to Billy the Kid; by others, to Frank McNab.

Billy Matthews's shot at the Kid, it may be mentioned,
had been winged with hatred. Only a few days before,
Matthews, a staunch Murphy partisan, had met the Kid

in Lincoln street; the Kid had taken a snap shot at him, his bullet missing him by inches and splintering the jamb of a door into which Matthews dodged. The wound Matthews gave the Kid was not serious; the Kid, as Frank Coe expressed it, "did not stop riding," indicating a trifling injury, riding being his customary locomotion. Wayte's thigh wound was likewise superficial.

Mrs. McSween, who at this writing, 1924, is Mrs. Susan E. Barber of White Oaks, had this to say of the incident:

"The murder of Sheriff Brady was Billy the Kid's own doing and was without excuse or palliation. McSween had had no inkling that such a plot was in the wind. If he had known, it is doubtful if he could have prevented it. He was not the man to 'ride the whirlwind and direct the storm' of the Lincoln County war. He found himself helpless to control the wild and lawless forces by which he was surrounded and his principles of humanity and religion weighed as nothing against the ferocity of Billy the Kid and his followers.

"Leaving moral considerations out of the question, the murder was bad diplomacy. It was worse than a crime; it was a blunder. It flouted public opinion and gave the McSween cause a blow from which it never recovered. McSween upbraided Billy the Kid when he next saw him. In my presence, he said:

"'Your crime, Billy, was not only cold-blooded but foolish. You could have done nothing more serious against my interests if you had tried deliberately to injure me. I cannot afford to appear to uphold you in the perpetration of such outrages. I propose to have you indicted and brought to trial for this assassination. This is a duty I owe to my conscience and to the public.'

"These were McSween's words as nearly as I can remember them," added Mrs. Barber, "and I believe, if he had lived, he would have done exactly as he said and procured the Kid's indictment for this infamous murder."

The murder of Sheriff Brady left the law in Lincoln County without even a figurehead. Through Brady, the Murphy faction had controlled the county's legal machinery. This had enabled it to make legal gestures with a certain flourish of good theatre and to give its actions legal verisimilitude in the public mind. To save its face, the McSween faction meanwhile had had recourse to the accommodations of sail-trimming Justice of the Peace Wilson and the appointment of special constables. Now that the McSween faction had swept into power on Billy the Kid's rifle volley, it hastened to consolidate its position by acquiring a sheriff of its own; and staging what may be regarded as a mock election, dominated by its gunmen, it placed John Copeland of Lincoln in the sheriff's office. Copeland was an honest, complacent man of little force. As sheriff, he served his purpose as a simulacrum, lived at the McSween home, and pursued an innocuous course under McSween's mild, religious despotism. He did nothing of consequence during his brief term of office and remains a mere name in the story of the Lincoln County war.

Billy the Kid—eighteen years old, if you please—was now the dominant figure in the situation. When Special Constable Dick Brewer lost his life in the fight with "Buckshot Bill" Roberts at Blazer's sawmill, his mantle as leader of the McSween fighting forces descended upon the shoulders of Billy the Kid. The prestige of this youthful desperado as fighter and killer was by this time firmly established. His will, backed by his six-shooter, was the law of the land. He ruled by terror, balked at nothing, and was recognized by friends and enemies alike as the personification of deadliness.

But the Kid's ascendancy proved a powerful weapon in the hands of his foes. The Murphy faction refused to surrender without a struggle the power that went with the control of the shrievalty and carried its case before Governor Samuel B. Axtell at Santa Fé. The fame of the Lincoln County war had spread far beyond the confines of New Mexico; it had given New Mexico a reputation for lawlessness and violence at a critical time when emigration westward was at flood tide, and such a reputation was bound to have a serious, if not disastrous, effect on the settlement of the territory. The territorial authorities had pondered ways and means to end the reign of terror, but had been unable to devise effective measures. In urging Governor Axtell's intervention, the Murphy leaders, while pointing out the illegality of Sheriff Copeland's election, presented as their most telling argument the deplorable condition of a vast region helpless in the power of such a murderous young outlaw as Billy the Kid. Though they left the tale only half told, there was a logic in their plea and Governor Axtell removed Copeland from office and appointed in his stead George W. Peppin, familiarly known as "Dad" Peppin, as sheriff of Lincoln County.

Thus, at one stroke, Governor Axtell reëstablished the Murphy faction in power, placed the shrievalty again in its control, and, in a manner, gave it the prestige of executive endorsement.

Though doubtless Governor Axtell was actuated by what he regarded as the best interests of New Mexico, his action was fatal to his own political fortunes. U. S. Commissioner Angell—the same who, by counting Indian noses on the Mescalero reservation, had once uncovered

Murphy's dishonesty in the matter of government contracts—took exception to the governor's partisanship and carried the war to Washington. There he laid the whole Lincoln County embroglio before President Rutherford B. Hayes. Convinced that Governor Axtell had been influenced by his friendship for leaders of the Murphy faction, that his method of intervention was unwise and unwarranted, and that, in the removal of Sheriff Copeland and the appointment of Sheriff Peppin, he had exceeded his authority, President Hayes removed the executive from office and sent out General Lew Wallace as governor with "extraordinary powers" and instructions to bring to an end as speedily as possible the bloody vendetta that had brought disgrace upon the territory and reëstablish law and order.

So the echoes of Billy the Kid's six-shooters were heard two thousand miles away and reverberated in the White House and the legislative halls of the national capital.

Sheriff Peppin burned some gunpowder in honour of his new job. Having organized a posse of twenty men in the lower Pecos Valley, he started back for Lincoln, where Billy the Kid and a number of McSween men were in quarters. He was halting for early supper at the Fritz ranch in Bonito Cañon, a few miles south of Lincoln, when Frank McNab, Frank Coe, and Jim Saunders, riding by, stopped for a drink at the Fritz spring, which comes gushing from a rocky cliff by the road in such volume of crystal-clear water that it was used then, and is still used, to irrigate the farm. The three men had their first intimation of the proximity of enemies when bullets began to knock up dust about them. Springing into their saddles, they dashed down the cañon with the Peppin men in pursuit, eager to kill McNab, an old Chisum foreman who had taken part in Sheriff Brady's assassination and had been with Billy the Kid when Morton and Baker were murdered. McNab's mount was shot early in the chase and Saunders's saddle turned at about the same time, unhorsing him. They struck for the side hills of the cañon on foot but were shot down before they reached shelter. McNab crawled into some underbrush and died. Saunders was disabled by bullets which broke his ankle and gave him a bad wound in the hip. Coe seemed on the point of escaping when his horse was killed by a marvellous shot at twelve hundred yards. As Coe dragged himself free of his fallen steed, Bob Ollinger rode up and leaped from his horse, and the two men emptied their six-shooters at each other. Coe took refuge in an arroyo as the other possemen closed in. Following a parley he threw his revolver out of the ditch and surrendered.

"The Peppin men told me McNab was dead and Saunders dying," said Coe in telling the story. "I begged them to go and get Saunders. 'He's a good man,' I said, 'and it's a shame to let him die out there alone.' They sent a buggy out for him and put him to bed in the Fritz ranch house. Then they started for Lincoln, taking me along as prisoner, and camped at the edge of town for the night.

"About a dozen McSween men were garrisoning the Ellis House. George Coe, my cousin on picket duty next morning at sun-up, saw Bill Campbell, of the Peppin posse, scouting a quarter of a mile off, down by the Bonito. George was a crack rifle shot and at that distance he broke Campbell's leg, bringing him down. His shot opened the battle, which lasted half the day. The Peppin men shot from the cover of outlying houses, the McSween men keeping up a steady answering fire. McSween bullets

were soon pattering all around me and I hinted delicately
to Wallace Ollinger, Bob's brother, who was guarding me,
that I wouldn't seriously object to being somewhere else.
He wasn't any too comfortable himself, and he took me
across the river and, skirting through the hills, brought me
to the Murphy store in the other end of town.   A half-
dozen Murphy men were there and they put me, for safe
keeping, upstairs in the same room Billy the Kid occupied
later when he was a prisoner under sentence of death.

"The firing was growing heavy down at the Ellis House.
Wallace Ollinger wanted to get into the fighting; he was
tired of guarding me.   He tossed me a six-shooter. 'Take
care of yourself,' he said, and walked out of the room.
When the other Murphy men asked him where I was, he
said, 'Upstairs,' and some of them started up to get me.
I stood at the head of the passageway with the gun Ollinger had given me and told them, if they came up, I would
kill them.   They decided they didn't want me bad enough
to take that chance and all of them went away and joined
in the battle.   I strolled down street to the McSween
home where I was safe among my friends.

"The battle ended with nobody killed when the Murphy
forces drew off into the hills.   Saunders and Bill Campbell
were sent to the military hospital at Fort Stanton, where
they occupied adjoining cots and had terrific quarrels
every day until they recovered from their wounds."

The late spring and early summer of 1878 were busy
times for Sheriff Peppin.   With the moral support of the
territorial government, he spent his time in strengthening
his forces for the decisive battle which both sides realized
was now near at hand.

His scouts kept a sharp watch on the movements of the
Kid, and when they located the McSween leader with

half-a-dozen followers at Chisum's South Spring Ranch in Pecos Valley, Deputy Sheriff Marion Turner with a large posse surrounded the place. A desultory fire was kept up on both sides for hours. At last one of the ranch hands rode away under a shower of bullets and brought back twenty-five cowboys from one of Chisum's camps a few miles distant. When these reinforcements came galloping over a hill, Turner and his men got on their horses and hurried back to Roswell. The Kid and his men left for Lincoln next day.

The Turner posse trailed the Kid at a safe distance all the way to Lincoln, making no effort to come to close quarters, and rode into town an hour or so after the Kid and his followers had gone into quarters in the McSween home. The bloodless little skirmish at Chisum's headquarters ranch served as a curtain-raiser to the big battle that practically ended the Lincoln County war.

CHAPTER X

THE hush of a July night lay upon Lincoln. The dark, silent town seemed asleep under the peaceful stars.

But behind the bastion-like walls of the Murphy store warlike preparations were toward. Within the deep seclusion of Murphy's old office Sheriff Peppin held council with Jimmy Dolan, Marion Turner, John Kinney, Andy Boyle, Old Man Pearce, and other leaders of the Murphy faction.

"We've got the Kid at last," declared Peppin. "There ain't no way for him to get away. We'll get him this time, dead or alive."

The Kid, with half-a-dozen other McSween partisans, fresh from the fight at Chisum's South Spring Ranch, had ridden in a few hours before and taken refuge in the McSween residence. Deputy Sheriff Turner, with twenty-five men, having trailed him all the way from the Pecos, had arrived in Lincoln a little later.

"With Turner's posse, we've got sixty men in all," said Peppin. "Nineteen Americans, the rest Mexicans. All good fighters. The Kid ain't got no idea how many of us he's got to fight. He thinks he'll have easy picking. But he's in a trap. We'll spring it on him."

"There's enough of us to rush the McSween house," advised Dolan.

"No use in that," cautioned Kinney. "We got the Kid dead to rights without takin' no chances."

"The Kid's a wise hombre," reflected Peppin. "If we propose that he surrender, I believe, under the circumstances, he'll listen to reason."

"That's right," cut in Old Man Pearce. "He's liable to get some of us if we shoot it out with him."

But how to open negotiations with the Kid was a problem. The man who attempted a parley might acquire a bullet.

"I think I know how," said Turner.

With Dolan and Kinney, Turner slipped into the bottom land along the Bonito River and crept up behind the McSween barn. There, standing sheltered from possible shots, he set up a lusty hailing cry. To this halloo, the Kid responded through a crack in the kitchen door.

"We've got you surrounded, Kid," shouted Turner. "If you make a fight, we'll kill you all to the last man. If you'll surrender, we'll promise you won't be hurt."

Something that sounded suspiciously like laughter came from the crack in the kitchen door.

"It's no joke, Kid. You better surrender."

"Surrender to a bunch of hounds like you? What six kinds of a fool do you think I am?"

"We'll guarantee you protection."

"I'll stay where I am and protect myself. If you want me, come and get me. Go back to your gang and tell 'em to turn on the fireworks. We're ready for you."

Out of the east end of town came a rumble of horses' hoofs, a chorus of zipping yells, scattered shots. Turner and his companions did not wait to learn the cause but, breaking short the conference, rejoined Sheriff Peppin. Faction Leader McSween had ridden into town from his camp on the Ruidosa with a tail of thirty-five Mexican fighting men at his back.

When Turner and his posse rode in from Roswell, Martin Chavez, deputy under Sheriff Copeland and a McSween partisan, had spurred hard for McSween's camp to carry the news of the Kid's perilous predicament. Forthwith, McSween and his henchmen had mounted in haste and come to Lincoln on the run. This strong reinforcement materially altered the situation, which thereafter did not look so dark. Under cover of the night, McSween and several of his Mexican allies slipped into the McSween home without drawing enemy fire and joined the Kid, who welcomed them with no little enthusiasm.

The Murphy forces held the Murphy store and hotel. The buildings were in the west end of town within fifty yards of the McSween house, the hotel on the same side of the street, the store on the other. High on the hillsides on the south side of the cañon, Murphy sharpshooters commanded the entire village.

The McSween men under Chavez garrisoned the Montaña and Patron houses in the east end of Lincoln. Charlie Bowdre, George Coe, and Hendry Brown were posted in the McSween store, a little to the west of the McSween house. With McSween in his home were Billy the Kid, Tom O'Folliard, Jim French, Doc Skurlock, Harvey Morris, Francisco Semora, Ignacio Gonzales, Vincente Romero, José Chavez y Chavez, and Ighenio Salazar. Three women also were in the house—Mrs. McSween, Mrs. Elizabeth Shield, her sister, and Mrs. Ealy, wife of the Presbyterian minister whom McSween had brought out to Lincoln from the East and who held services every Sunday in the McSween store.

With the long vendetta about to break in murderous

battle climax, McSween still leaned upon the Lord for divine intervention that would avert the tragedy that was now inevitable. He spent the night in prayer. On his knees in his room, he talked with God as if face to face and pleaded for the miracle. "Touch, O Lord, the hearts of our enemies with Thy goodness and mercy. . . . Guide them in the better way. . . . Send down Thy blessing of peace."

When Billy the Kid and the others gathered for breakfast next morning they were in high spirits and ready for battle. With witty sallies and gay bantering talk they inspected their rifles and six-shooters. Mrs. McSween, Mrs. Shield, and Mrs. Ealy bustled between kitchen and dining room loading the table with steaming dishes. McSween entered with his Bible in his hand.

There was in his appearance the solemnity and austerity of an ancient prophet. His tall, spare form was erect with the serene courage of one who fancies himself panoplied by angels. His face, pale from his sleepless vigil, shone with supreme and abiding faith. In his eyes was a look of apocalyptic vision as of one who sees beyond earthly horizons the loom of "opal towers and battlements adorned of living sapphire." Taking his place at the head of the table, he bowed his head in his hand and said grace.

Came a crash of rifles from the Murphy clan shooting from the windows of the Murphy store and hotel. The balls thudded against the adobe walls of the McSween house and tore ragged holes through the window shutters, bursting the panes and scattering fragments of glass over the floor.

A look of pained surprise for an instant swept McSween's face. He had prayed for peace. Bullets were his answer.

"Where's your gun, Mr. McSween?" queried the Kid.

"I have no gun," replied McSween. "I have never owned one. I have never fired one in my life."

"But you'll lend a hand and do some fighting now?"

"God forbid."

"But we're in for it good and plenty. We've got to fight for our lives. Every man will count."

"I would rather die than stain my soul with the blood of my fellow man," replied McSween with deep solemnity. "I have no need to commit that great sin. God is my refuge and strength. He will protect me."

A cynical smile twisted a corner of the Kid's mouth.

"All right, governor," he returned good-naturedly. "Go ahead and trust in the Lord. The rest of us'll trust in our six-shooters."

He threw open the shutters, useless for defense. Through the open windows, he and his men replied to the volleys of the enemy.

The battle developed quickly all along the line. While the Murphy forces hidden in store and hotel concentrated their fusillades on the McSween home, their sharpshooters, ranging along the hills at the south side of the cañon, poured an incessant fire upon Chavez's men in the Montaña and Patron houses.

"Kind of a tame fight," remarked the Kid as the day of random firing drew toward a close. "Those Murphy fellows stay under cover. I can't get a good, square crack at anybody. We better sneak out of here to-night and join up with Chavez. Then we can chase the Murphy gang out of town."

"We will stay where we are," said McSween. "We must free our hearts of hatred and deadliness. 'Vengeance is mine,' saith the Lord. We must remain on the defensive. I still have faith that God will put a stop to this sad affair before blood has been spilled."

In view of McSween's attitude, the Kid had apprehensions that the battle might lengthen into a siege. After darkness had fallen, he brought indoors two barrels of rain-water standing in the sheltered court. These would provide the little garrison with enough water for drinking and cooking purposes for a number of days.

McSween's faith was strengthened and renewed when the fighting ceased for the night without loss of life on either side. It seemed to him a Heaven-given sign that his prayers had been heard. He returned thanks to God on his knees and went to bed beside his Bible. . . .

Among the rocks on the steep hill that rose above the Montaña and Patron houses crawled Lucio Montoya and Charlie Crawford, crack riflemen of the Murphy faction. They settled into position side by side behind two huge boulders. Below them in the early morning sunlight lay the silent town, its long, winding street blocked and striped with the shadows of houses, trees, and fence-posts.

"Not a soul in sight," observed Crawford. "Town looks like nobody lived in it."

"All the people scared to come out," replied Montoya.

A quarter of a mile away they could see the McSween house, its adobe stucco chipped and scarred by bullets. Smoke began to ascend from its chimney.

"McSween's cooking breakfast."

"*Si, compadre.*"

"We're in a good spot. Ought to be able to pick off some of them Chavez fellers from here."

"*Mira, amigo !*" Montoya's voice rose scarcely above a whisper.

Martin Chavez emerged from the Patron house and

started to walk across the short space that separated it from the Montaña dwelling.

Montoya and Crawford snapped their rifles into position. Two bullets knocked up the ground at Chavez's feet.

"Darn poor shootin', I call that," said Crawford.

"Purty far," replied Montoya philosophically.

"Well, pard, let's wake 'em up."

They began to fire steadily. For hours they kept it up. Through the windows and doors of the two houses that sheltered Chavez's men crashed the bullets of the concealed marksmen.

Fernando Herrera of Chavez's command was famed among his people for his skill with a rifle. For a long time he scrutinized the hillside through a pair of field glasses. At every shot, Crawford and Montoya for an instant showed head and shoulders at exactly the same spot from behind their boulders.

Through a crack in the back door of the Montaña house Herrera drew a bead with his long-range buffalo rifle upon the spot at which Crawford would appear. He waited for a moment with his finger on the trigger. Crawford's rifle worked into position from behind the rock. His right shoulder appeared. His head came into view as he sighted along the barrel. Whang! Herrera's bullet went singing upward across the intervening space of nine hundred yards—afterward measured. It struck the hammer of Crawford's gun, veered at a slight angle, and ploughed through his body, breaking his back. Crawford's yell echoed up and down the cañon. He catapulted into the air, tumbled off a ledge, and came rolling and plunging down to the bottom of the hill. He fetched up on a level space at the edge of a field of standing corn which shielded him from sight of his enemies. There, wounded to the death, he lay in the broiling sun all day. He was dead when a searching party found him at night.

Montoya was Herrera's next problem, and he solved it in the same way. Herrera trained his rifle through the crack in the door on the spot at which he calculated Montoya would appear. He had not long to wait. Possibly Montoya was a little excited over the wounding of his comrade, possibly a little eager to avenge the injury. He was a little less cautious than had been his wont. When next he made ready to fire, he exposed half his body in a half-kneeling position, an elbow resting on one knee to steady his aim. Again Herrera's rifle cracked, again his bullet buzzed like an angry bumblebee across the wide gap of air, and Montoya collapsed behind his boulder with a shattered leg. There he, too, lay for the remainder of the day, groaning in agony, the hot sun beating upon him.

Crawford's death yell sounded with piercing shrillness in the McSween home.

"One less Murphy man," commented the Kid with a note of satisfaction. "They sure got that fellow."

But the cry of agony filled McSween's soul with awe and foreboding. Had his prayers been in vain? Would God withhold the miracle?

"I do not like that," he said. "Let us hope the poor man has not been killed. A God of love will not turn a deaf ear to my supplications. Out of the darkness He will speak and bring peace."

"Here's a rifle, Mr. McSween," said the Kid, thrusting a gun toward him. "Straight shooting will do more good than prayer."

But McSween raised his hand with a gesture of abhorrence.

"Never!" he exclaimed. "I will not be tempted into such ungodliness."

Colonel N. A. M. Dudley, commandant, sat in his office at Fort Stanton, busy with the day's routine. Through the window he saw a woman, bedraggled and plainly labouring under great excitement, hurrying toward him across the parade ground. In a moment she burst into the room like an apparition, pale, wild of eye, her clothing torn.

"For God's sake, bring your soldiers to Lincoln." Her voice was almost a scream. "The clans are fighting. This is the third day. They will fight till the last man is killed. Dead are lying in the street. The women and children will be murdered. The town will be destroyed. The people are afraid. They are cooped up in their homes. I am Mrs. Juanita Mills. I could not stand it any longer. I slipped out of town before dawn and have hurried on foot across the hills—nine miles. I have come to beg you to save us—the mothers, the babies, our homes. Only the troops can stop this madness. There is still time. But hurry. For God's sake, hurry."

The morning silence was shattered by the bugles. "Boots and Saddles" set the echoes flying among the hills. There was instant bustle of preparation. Scurrying officers shouted commands. Troopers in broken streaks began to converge toward the stables. Two squadrons of Negro cavalry, with two gatling guns and Colonel Dudley in command, were soon moving at double-quick on the road to Lincoln.

Murphy lookouts on watch at the upper windows of the Murphy store caught sight of a cloud of dust rising to the west in the direction of the Double Crossing of the

Bonito.   Puzzled as to what it might portend, they summoned Sheriff Peppin.   A strong body of horsemen was approaching.   But who were they?   The Murphy leaders were expecting no reinforcements.   If the riders under that cloud of dust were McSween partisans, the Murphy faction would better lose no time in taking to the hills. Their cause was lost.

"Fetch me my field glasses," Peppin called to one of his under-strappers.

The Murphy sheriff took a quick squint through the glasses.   His weather-beaten face broke in the parchment-like wrinkles of a smile.   The riddle was solved.

"Soldiers!   Colonel Dudley is bringing in his old army buffalo troopers.   I don't know what he aims to do. But it's all right, boys.   He's our friend."

Soon the long, blue-uniformed column, rounding a bend in the road, came marching into Lincoln, sabres clanking, carbines unslung, Colonel Dudley and his officers riding ahead.   Two gatling guns rolled smoothly along between the squadrons, awe-inspiring weapons in that day, mysterious in their lethal capability, efficient in slithering death.   A train of four-mule wagons loaded with tenting and camp equipment brought up the rear.

As the cavalcade clattered past the Murphy store, cheers came with muffled faintness from the abysmal depths of the old building, those who lifted joyous voices not daring to show themselves at the windows for fear a random McSween volley might cut short their enthusiasm. Colonel Dudley halted his command in front of the McSween home, a few days before the smartest house in town, decrepit-looking now, grown venerable overnight from the batterings of battle.   He sent an aide inside to summon McSween.

While the black troopers lounged at ease in their saddles, Murphy men came pouring into the road from their store and hotel fortresses and crowded about the McSween home. There was no danger now. They were under the ægis of the army. No McSween partisan was so desperate as to dare to flout the majesty of Uncle Sam by a pot-shot at Murphy foes. Nor were the beleaguered guardians of the McSween stronghold backward in curiosity. They, too, swarmed into the road and stood silent in front of the building, awaiting developments, their rifles resting in the crook of their arms, their restless eyes keeping suspicious watch upon their enemies.

Obedient to Colonel Dudley's summons, McSween stepped out the door of his home, halted at the throat-latch of the colonel's charger, and stood facing the stern-visaged soldier sitting rigidly erect in his saddle.

"Mister McSween," said Colonel Dudley in stentorian tones. . . .

But Jimmy Dolan did not wait to hear the import of the message Colonel Dudley was about to deliver to "Mister McSween." In the excitement aroused by the halting of the cavalry squadrons in front of the McSween home, Jimmy Dolan recognized an opportunity. He slipped unnoticed through the crowd along the line of troops toward the Murphy hotel, picking up Old Man Pearce, Charlie Hall, and that harum-scarum old ruffian and blackguard, Andy Boyle, on his way.

"It's our chance, boys," he said in cautious undertones. "Quick now. Come with me."

For a few brief moments the four conspirators rummaged about the hotel and its purlieus. Then they plunged down an embankment behind the hostelry and, hidden from view from the road, went at a run across the bottoms of the Bonito. Up the embankment they scrambled in the rear of the McSween barn and so came at last into the McSween backyard. In one hand Dolan carried a can of kerosene and in the other a tin cup. Andy Boyle brought a wash basket filled with shavings and chips. Old Man Pearce and Charlie Hall bore armloads of kindling and faggots of pitch pine.

The column of troops was standing at ease in the road fifty feet away. Billy the Kid and his fighting men, Mrs. McSween, Mrs. Shield, Mrs. Ealy, every member of the McSween garrison, were at the front of the house. McSween still stood at the throat-latch of the colonel's charger. The back of the house was deserted. In the rapt silence of the moment, Colonel Dudley's every word rang clear to the four men at their secret business in McSween's backyard.

"Mr. McSween," said Colonel Dudley in stentorian tones, "this fighting must end at once."

"I am powerless to end it," replied McSween.

"You must cease firing," ordered Colonel Dudley.

"Pile on your kindling, Pearce," said Jimmy Dolan. "That's the stuff. Now your pitch pine, Hall. That's good."

"I will be glad to cease firing," responded McSween, "if the Murphy faction ceases also. The Murphy side started this battle. We are besieged—besieged in my own home. We are fighting for our lives. End the attack upon us and you will end the battle."

"Stand back a little, boys," said Jimmy Dolan. "Give me a chance to souse on the coal oil."

Over the mass of shavings, kindling, and pitch pine piled high against McSween's back door Dolan slashed the kerosene. Filling his tin cup, he dashed quantities over door and lintels from top to bottom. On the sills of the windows he spread shavings and saturated them with oil. Over the window shutters and every piece of woodwork he threw cupfuls of the inflammable liquid until his can was empty.

"I have given you my orders, Mr. McSween." Colonel Dudley's voice had in it the ring of finality. "See that they are obeyed. Stop your fighting or suffer the consequences."

The colonel turned to his bugler with a sharp command.

"Now, strike your matches and touch her off," said Jimmy Dolan.

The staccato notes of the bugle sounded in the street. "Forward!" sang the trumpet. There was a rattle of arms as the troopers straightened to attention and dressed their ranks. The column got slowly under way.

The oil-drenched pile exploded into a mass of fire that shot up to the roof. As Dolan and his companions sprang down the embankment into the bottom-lands, a thin veil of blue-white fire was rippling and shimmering over door and window shutters. Fiery little tongues were curling eagerly about the woodwork as if relishing appetizing food. Slender red streamers that flashed to the shingles of the roof waved and fluttered like pennons of victory.

Clatter of accoutrements, pounding of hoofs, creaking of gun carriages, grew faint in the distance, fainter still, and ceased. Whitish smoke, soft, billowy, rose from the roof of the McSween home and drifted in a lurid mist into the empty street.

No sooner had the cavalry column got in motion than McSween and his group of home-defenders hurried back inside the house.

"Old Dudley made it plain as daylight that we must

stop shooting," sneered Billy the Kid. "But I notice he
didn't tell the Murphy gang to cease firing. Why not?
They were standing all around him."

Mrs. McSween sniffed the air suspiciously.

"I smell smoke," she cried. "What can be burning?"

She hurried into the next room. The acrid smell of fire
was more distinct. As she passed through the door into
the room beyond, a blue shadowy snake of smoke wriggled
slowly toward her in midair.

"Fire!"

The men rushed after her. As they darted into the
back room they stopped short, hardly able to breathe.
Through the thick swirls they saw the door and the shutters of the windows crumbling in charred fragments beneath the flames. As they stood there in momentary daze
a section of the roof came crashing down in blazing ruin
upon the floor. In an instant the situation of the little
garrison had rushed to desperate crisis. The house that
had been their refuge and fortress had been transformed
into a death trap.

Beleaguered by the deadly rifles of their foes, they
now had a more dangerous enemy to fight. There might
yet be time to save the building. They rushed to the two
barrels of rain water. Pitiful supply it was with which
to battle a conflagration. In pails and kettles and dish-
pans, they carried water to dash upon the flames. The
hopelessness of their task was soon apparent. The back
room was now a fiery furnace. The walls were bellying
outward with the heat; the partition was tottering.
Flames were leaping and crackling along the roof. Black
smoke was boiling into the sky.

The McSween residence was of one story, built of adobe
brick about three sides of a court that was open at the

rear.   It contained twelve rooms, four in the main portion which fronted on the street, four in the west wing, four in the east wing.   Dolan and his destroying angels had kindled the fire at the rear of the west wing.   A wind from the east was blowing the flames and sparks away from the other part of the house.   If the wind held, the destruction of the entire building could be compassed only when the flames had passed from back to front of the west wing, across the front, and from front to back of the east wing.

After the fire had reached the interior through the collapse of portions of the roof, its progress was rapid. McSween's men ceased to fight it, seeing the futility of their efforts, and turned their attention to saving the furniture, hustling it from one room to another in advance of the flames.

Mrs. McSween's piano in the front room on the west side of the house was in the direct path of destruction. Famous instrument—the only piano in all eastern New Mexico—whose music had cheered all Lincoln; to whose melodies the boys and girls of the town had danced in the street; whose wagon-borne journey across mountains and plains had been a royal progress; and whose arrival had marked a red-letter day in Lincoln's calendar.

"Save my piano," wailed Mrs. McSween.   "Let the fire rob me of everything else, but save my precious piano."

The men took hold with a will and in the crisis Billy the Kid won new laurels as a piano-mover.   From room to room across the front of the building they lifted and dragged the instrument laboriously, and landed it in the front room on the east side, far from the flames.

"There!" cried Mrs. McSween joyously.   "It's safe— safe, at least, for the time being."

In her passing flash of happiness, she sat at the instrument and let her fingers wander among the keys. Snatches of old tunes took form beneath her touch like fugitive ghosts. Before she knew it she was playing "Home, Sweet Home." She sang a bar or two softly—"There's no place like home." The music seemed the voice of her tragedy. Her home was burning. In a little while, with all its associations of love and happiness, it would be a mere heap of ashes and blackened timbers. As the last note trembled into silence, she bowed her head upon the piano and her tears dropped upon the keys.

There was a crash at the west side of the house. Portions of the red-hot adobe walls had fallen outward leaving two great gaps. Through the gaps the Murphy men rained bullets. . . . McSween read a chapter in the Bible and offered up a prayer. . . . Billy the Kid and his little band, half-blinded by whirls of smoke, pumped their Winchesters. . . . A fragment of the roof caved in, narrowly missing the Kid. He stepped to one side with a smile. A Murphy bullet knocked a cigarette from between his lips. "Now that's too bad," he said cheerfully. "I'll have to roll another."

"Colonel Dudley is our only hope, boys," said Mrs. McSween at last. "That's almost no hope at all. I have no faith in him. But he is the only one who can save us now. The cowards of the Murphy crowd are watching and waiting to murder us all. Soon there will be no walls left to hide us. Then we must die unless help comes. Colonel Dudley can rescue us if he will—if he will. I'm going to his camp and ask him—beg him on my knees— to save us."

She caught up her bonnet and put it on—adjusted it neatly on her head, saw that it was on straight.

"You must not go, my dear," said McSween. "The

Murphy men will kill you as soon as you step out the door."

"I'm going!"

She flung open the door and walked out. A cloud of smoke swooped down around her. Out of it she passed into the sunlight. Rifles began to crack from windows in the Murphy store. Bullets struck all about her. She paid no heed. She did not turn her head. A rifle ball struck so close it scattered dust over her skirt. She paused for a moment, stooped and brushed off the dust. Then she marched on down the road.

Colonel Dudley had gone into camp on open ground in the east end of town opposite San Juan Church, and having trained his gatling guns on the Montaña and Patron houses, sent for Martin Chavez in command of the McSween force garrisoning these two buildings.

"You see those guns?" Colonel Dudley said, pointing to the two pieces whose shining barrels bore upon the houses from directly across the road.

"*Si, señor,* I see," responded Chavez.

"If they should accidentally go off, they might blow those two houses down and kill your men."

"But, possibly, I do not understan'. You bring your soldiers for protec' life and property, no?"

"Exactly. That's what I'm here for. If your men fire another shot, the accident I spoke of may happen at any moment."

Chavez gave a shrug.

"It is best that you withdraw from Lincoln," Colonel Dudley continued. "I will grant you safe conduct out of town. But be sure you do not return or linger in the outskirts. If you take any further part in the fighting, I will send a troop of cavalry after you."

Chavez and his men thereupon mounted their horses which had been kept in the stables of the Ellis house and rode out of town, Colonel Dudley keeping them covered all the while with his gatling guns. The retreat of Chavez left McSween and the ten men with him to fight out the battle alone. Mrs. McSween was the only woman left in her home. Mrs. Shields and Mrs. Ealy had already taken advantage of the screen of troops halted in front of the residence to seek safety with friends in another part of town.

When, several hours after Chavez's departure Mrs. McSween made her way to Colonel Dudley's tent, she found him sitting with Sheriff Peppin and John Kinney, of the Murphy faction.

"Well," said Colonel Dudley, looking at her coldly. "What is it you want?"

"You are aware, Colonel Dudley," said Mrs. McSween, "that my home is burning down?"

"I have seen some smoke," replied Colonel Dudley indifferently.

"While you were giving your orders to my husband, Murphy men set my house on fire."

"I would require proof of that."

"There is no doubt about it. But I did not come to argue with you. It is too late now to save my home. I have come to beg you to save our lives. You hear the volleys the Murphy men are pouring into my blazing home. Unless you stop this attack upon us, my husband and the ten men with him will be killed."

"I have no authority to interfere," replied Colonel Dudley.

"Then," said Mrs. McSween, gasping in amazement, "why have you brought your troops into Lincoln?"

"I am here," returned the colonel sharply, "to assume charge only in case the situation escapes from the control of the civil authorities."

"'Civil authorities!'" echoed Mrs. McSween. "Who, pray, are these 'civil authorities'?"

"Sheriff Peppin here and the deputies under him."

"Sheriff Peppin is a Murphy partisan," Mrs. McSween flung back. "He is directing the attack upon us."

"Your men refused to surrender when called upon."

"If they had surrendered, they would have been massacred."

"I do not think so."

"The purpose of these 'civil authorities,' as you call them, is to murder us all. If the present situation does not warrant your interference, I can conceive of no situation which would. Force these lawless and conscienceless 'civil authorities' to stop their efforts to murder us. Let my home burn to the ground, but send your troops to save the lives of Mr. McSween and his men. Arrest them if necessary and give them protection as your prisoners."

"I am in command of United States troops," Colonel Dudley answered. "This is a civil matter——"

"It is barbarous!" cried Mrs. McSween.

"—and Sheriff Peppin seems to have the situation in hand. I will not interfere. I have no authority."

"So this is what it means to appeal to a soldier in the uniform of my country," shouted Mrs. McSween, now white with passion. "If my country's flag that flies in front of your tent cannot protect us, then God help us."

She returned to her home and groped back through the smoke into the flame-bright interior. The west wing and front of the house were gutted, blackened ruins. The fire was sweeping back over the east wing, the last remaining portion.

"Dudley refuses to interfere," she announced hopelessly.

Silence fell upon the doomed men, broken only by the crackling of the fire and the crash of charred timbers. For a long time Mrs. McSween paced the floor, wringing her hands.

"Dudley must interfere," she said at last as if to herself. "We are lost unless he does. Only the soldiers can save us. I am going back to fight it out with him."

She picked her way through the blazing embers out into the road once more. A roar of laughter came from Colonel Dudley's tent as she entered the camp. Evidently someone had told the soldier a good joke. Colonel Dudley was still with Sheriff Peppin and John Kinney. He seemed disconcerted as Mrs. McSween stepped into his tent. A bottle and glasses were on his table.

"You here again?"

"I have come again to beg you on my knees to save my husband's life and the lives of the men with him. Have you no mercy?"

"I have told you I have no authority to interfere."

Fury boiled in Mrs. McSween's soul at these words that closed the door of hope against her.

"Colonel Dudley," she screamed, "that is not true. You have the authority but you will not use it. I know, and we all know, what you are here for. You are here not to protect life and property but to help the Murphy faction. You have driven out of town Chavez and his men who might have helped us. You have left the Murphy side in control. They are not 'civil authorities' and you know it. They intend to murder us and you will stand by and see them do it."

Colonel Dudley grew purple with rage. "Get out of my tent," he stormed.

"I will not go," Mrs. McSween hurled back, "until you send your soldiers with me to save my husband's life."

"Orderly," called Colonel Dudley to a trooper on guard in front of his tent, "put this woman out of the encampment."

The orderly caught Mrs. McSween by the arm and led her into the road. There she halted.

"I will not budge another step," she said stubbornly, "until I have one last word with Colonel Dudley."

The orderly argued, protested, threatened, but Mrs. McSween stood firm. He hurried back to Colonel Dudley's tent and reported. But the colonel remained inside. Mrs. McSween determined upon a ruse. She began to shriek at the top of her lungs. The cañon echoed with her screams. Fearing some calamity had befallen her, Colonel Dudley came bounding from his tent to see what the matter was. Before he could plunge back, Mrs. McSween had her opportunity for a woman's last word.

"Colonel Dudley," she shrilled, "I am going back to see my home burned over my head and my husband murdered; but as long as I live, I will not leave a stone unturned to fasten on you the guilt of this great crime."

The day was now far spent. Shadows of evening were falling across the cañon. The McSween home was almost destroyed. Of its twelve rooms, only three remained. Mrs. McSween's announcement that all hope of aid was gone threw into despondency all members of the band except Billy the Kid, who for so many weary hours in the doomed house had been fighting fire and foes. As desperate in his optimism as in his crimes, the Kid received the news with an indifferent shrug.   The one chance in a million that remained to him kept him cheerfully hopeful. He wasted no words in bewailing his fate in being cooped in this two-by-four hell.   Confident in his own resources and courage, he was willing to play the game out to the end and, if luck went against him, accept the result like a good gambler.

Mrs. McSween's eyes rested sadly on her piano.   Flame reflections were leaping and dancing in its polished depths. It was fated to destruction.   A few hours more and it would be a wreck buried under flaming débris.

She threw herself upon the stool at the keyboard.   She still had hope—hope in Billy the Kid and his fighting men.   They were battling desperately in their last ditch. A war-song might inspire them to still more heroic courage. It might turn defeat into victory.   With one last brave swan-song before the ultimate silence, the piano might yet save the day.   At once she plunged into the stirring bars of "The Star-Spangled Banner."   Facing death, the men felt the lift and thrill of the old battle hymn.   "O say, can you see . . .   what so proudly we hailed at the twilight's last gleaming . . .   broad stripes and bright stars through the perilous fight . . .   so gallantly streaming. . . ."   The Kid whistled the tune. Tom O'Folliard beat time with his six-shooter.   Far through the noise of battle and the swish of flames, the music sounded in half the homes in Lincoln.   It rang against the cañon walls like a challenge.   It carried its message of courage and defiance to the enemy whose bullets thumped like an obbligato against the tottering walls and plunged with sibilant uproar among the smoking embers . . .   "does the Star-Spangled Banner still wave o'er the land" . . . The music died in the crash of a flaming fragment of the roof.

"You'd better hunt safety now, Mrs. McSween," said Billy the Kid. "Go to the house of some friend while there's still time. We'll do the best we can. We may get out of this yet. After dark, we'll make a break for it."

"Yes," agreed McSween. "While there is still time. Escape for the others will be less difficult if there is no woman here."

"I will not go," the brave woman proclaimed stoutly.

"It is best, my dear," answered McSween.

He folded her in his arms and kissed her good-bye.

"Let me stay and die with you," she pleaded.

McSween shook his head solemnly. "No, you must go."

Mrs. McSween turned away. Her husband drew her back for one last embrace.

"God watch over and protect you," he breathed.

Broken-hearted and blinded by tears, Mrs. McSween stumbled out of the blazing ruins of her home, through the dense smoke into the road flaming with the sunset to find safety and shelter at last with her sister and Mrs. Ealy.

Night fell. Two rooms were left. The Kid and his men still clung to their crumbling defenses. The fire marched steadily forward. One room remained—the kitchen. It was ten o'clock. With the roof blazing over their heads, the Kid and his men prepared for a dash for safety. The Kid gave his directions calmly. Certain men must go first; certain others must follow in order.

The Murphy men had closed in under cover of the darkness. They crouched behind the McSween stable and beneath the shelter of the adobe wall that shut off the stable lot from the backyard. They sensed the approaching crisis. Their rifles commanded the kitchen door at a distance of not more than ten yards.

"All right, boys, let's go," cried the Kid. "We've still got one chance in a million."

He threw open the back door. While the flames turned night into day, Harvey Morris and Francisco Semora rushed out to fall dead before a blaze of rifles from the adobe wall. Vincente Romero was the next to try and the next to die.

McSween was sitting in a corner, his Bible open on his lap, his lips moving in prayer. The tragedy closing in about him had left him in a state between lethargy and religious ecstasy. He realized that all hope was gone. Fear did not touch him. He felt only the despair and disappointment of a martyr whose faith had been in vain, whose prayers had not been answered. The Kid laid a hand upon his shoulder and shook him out of his reverie.

"Come on, governor," said the Kid with a flash of his gay courage, "it's your turn next. You've got to make a run for it."

McSween rose slowly to his feet.

"Take this gun." The Kid tried to shove a six-shooter into his hand. With a sweep of his long arm, McSween brushed the weapon aside. He had remained unarmed throughout the fighting. He would die as he had lived, with no stain upon his soul.

"Hit the trail, old man," shouted the Kid. "Go through that door like a streak of greased lightning. Head for the back fence. Roll over it in the dark. Keep going for the Bonito. And you'll see Mrs. McSween in the morning. Good luck."

As if unhearing, McSween drew himself to the full of

his imposing height and, with his glazed eyes, swept the broken, flaming walls of what had been his home.

"My home, my wife!" he muttered. "God of my fathers, hast Thou forsaken me?"

Before him was the open door. He strode toward it. For an instant he paused upon the threshold, his Bible clutched to his breast as he gazed upon his ruined dooryard and the three corpses sprawled about it. Quietly, head up, he walked out into the red glare of the flames.

"Here I am," he called in a hollow voice. "I am McSween."

A streak of fire leaped from the blackness beyond the adobe wall. A dozen rifles blazed almost simultaneously. Tiny puffs of dust leaped out from McSween's coat. He half-turned, stumbled forward, and fell dead upon his Bible, true to his faith to the last, his hands innocent of man's blood.

"I got him," shouted Bob Beckwith, waving his smoking rifle high above his head. "I got McSween."

A demoniac chorus of yells went up to the sky. The men behind the adobe wall went wild with boisterous joy. They fired a half-dozen wanton shots at McSween's body. Several bullets thudded into the corpse, causing it to jerk as with a spasm. Others splattered earth over the dead face. Then there was silence. The ambushed watchers waited for fresh victims.

Out of the door, one after the other, plunged Tom O'Folliard, Jim French, Doc Skurlock, José Chavez y Chavez, Ignacio Gonzalez, and Ighenio Salazar. Salazar was cut down, dangerously wounded; he lay limp and motionless, feigning death. Gonzalez's arm was shattered by a bullet, but he continued his flight. As by a miracle, all but Salazar ran the gauntlet of bullets, tumbled over the back wall, and escaped. They were joined in their stampede for the hills by Charlie Bowdre, George Coe, and Hendry Brown, who ran from the McSween store at the same time.

The Kid was the last to leave. He hitched his belt a little tighter, pulled his hat down more firmly on his head. He looked with sharp scrutiny at his two six-shooters, one in either hand. He cocked them. He shot a glance through the open door into the ruddy splendour. His quick eye calculated the positions of the five men lying motionless, all dead except Salazar, shamming death. He determined his course among them; he must be careful not to trip over a corpse. Between him and the back wall of the yard was a space of thirty feet. Across it, death would be snapping at his heels at every step. But if he had to die, he would die fighting.

There was ominous silence off at the side along the adobe wall. His lurking, unseen foes were waiting for him, their rifles ready, their fingers on the trigger. All about him was the devouring sibilance of the fire. Flames were bursting through the walls and ceiling of the room, darting, twisting, crawling like brilliant serpents greedily alive. He braced himself for the start. Half the roof crashed in behind him. Smoke and a myriad fiery sparks leaped after him as he darted out the door, his guns blazing.

A yell of triumph went up from his enemies. This was the man they wanted. "Here comes the Kid!" They rose behind the wall. They threw their rifles to a level on the flying figure. "Get him, boys!" "Kill him!" A salvo of twenty guns welcomed him into that crimson square of death.

The Kid's trigger fingers worked with machine-gun rapidity.   Fire poured from the muzzles of his forty-fours in continuous streaks.   Bob Beckwith, slayer of McSween, fell dead across the wall, his rifle clattering on the ground, head and arms dangling downward limply.   John McKinney of Las Cruces was struck in the mouth, the bullet carrying away half the gallantly up-turned moustache of the handsome youth.   Another ball cut a deep notch in Old Man Pearce's ear, whispering the nearness of death.   One man killed, two branded for life—this was the Kid's score as he hurtled toward the sheltering darkness, never for an instant hesitating, never slackening his pellmell speed.

Pumping their Winchesters, churning shots from their double-action revolvers, his foes fired more than fifty shots at him as he rushed across the space of thirty feet. Bullets sang about his ears, ripped shreds from his blue flannel shirt, bored holes through his white steeple sombrero, enveloped him in an invisible frame of hissing lead. Every bullet was aimed at his heart and every one was winged with deadly hatred.   But not a bullet touched his body.   On he ran like a darting, elusive shadow as if under mystic protection.   He cleared the back wall at a leap.   He bounded out of the flare of the conflagration. Darkness swallowed him at a gulp.   Splashing across the Bonito, he gained the safety of the hills.

The firing ceased.   Five men had been killed within five minutes and lay within a space of five square feet in the McSween backyard.   The Murphy men swarmed in.   Old Andy Boyle, thinking he detected signs of life in Salazar, kicked him in the ribs, caught him by the cartridge-belt and shook him up and down against the ground, pressed the muzzle of a rifle at last against his heart.

"No use wasting good lead on that greaser," said John Kinney as Boyle was about to press the trigger; "he's dead."

So Boyle did not fire.

Jimmy Dolan touched with the tip of his boot a dead man lying near the kitchen door. He turned him over.

"Here's McSween!" he shouted.

The others crowded round. They laughed, they hurrahed, they shook hands. Old Man Pearce produced a whisky flask.

"Have one on me, boys," he yelled.

The bottle went round and everybody took a swig.

"What's this?" Dolan poked with his rifle at something lying beside the corpse. He stooped over and looked more closely.

"The Bible!"

There was a roar of laughter.

"Where's his gun?"

"Don't appear to have none. Died with his Bible in his hand."

"Now ain't that a hell of a note?"

"His Bible in his hand!"

Again they roared with laughter.

So died McSween, enigma and paradox of the Lincoln County war; a man of the Christ-complex owning the allegiance of murderers and desperadoes; an apostle of peace and the leader of a fighting faction in a deadly feud; intellectual, yet a child in his understanding of men and life; filled with human kindness, yet innocently fomenting war and drawing upon himself the bitterness of lethal hatreds; a futile shadow among relentless realities; a pathetic marionette caught in a whirlwind and swept to destruction; a Sir Galahad of the vendetta, moving with serene, unclouded soul toward inevitable tragedy and finding at last the peace of the Holy Grail in death.

It was a famous victory, worthy of festal celebration. George Washington and Sebron Bates, ancient Negroes, who from time out of memory had made music at the fandangos of the town and countryside, were fetched from their homes. Perched like black imps on the adobe wall with violin and guitar, the old darkies struck up merry tunes while the victors danced, drinking whisky and roaring out songs. All Lincoln crowded around to watch the bacchanalian carousal. The backyard with its sprawling dead men lay red in the glare of the flames; the blackness of the night shut it in like the walls of a cave. "Swing your partners!" The tipsy revellers caught each other about the waist and whooped and yelled in a furious, farcical quadrille. "Ladies to the centre!" In and out among the corpses they careened and reeled. "Hands all round!" They cavorted in burlesque pigeon-wings with boisterous buffoonery and horse play, their uncouth antics silhouetted in weird, tremendous shadows that flickered over the ghastly field of death and plunged off into the darkness. It was a primordial orgy of blood-crazed savages commemorating a warpath triumph with a scalp dance.

It was long past midnight when the devil's saturnalia ended and the drunken rioters dispersed to their homes, filling the night with oaths and ribaldry. The fire died out; only wisps of wan smoke curled among the blackened ruins. Among the corpses, a form, that throughout the death-masque had lain stretched motionless upon the ground, stirred as if in resurrection, rose upon hands and knees, began to crawl with stealthy movement toward the rear wall. It was Salazar. Upon the murderous crew he had palmed off a heroic subterfuge that had saved his life. Shot through, sorely wounded, he managed to scramble over the wall. In the darkness, he staggered away to safety.

CHAPTER XI

LOOKING out across Bonito Valley a few miles west of Lincoln, a quaint adobe farmhouse stands to-day on a shelf of land at the foot of tall hills from whose slopes the winds bring the fragrance of piñon. Fields of wheat, oats, and alfalfa spread to the little river which here loiters in lazy loops and still pools. Cattle and sheep graze in the pastures. Orchards hang heavy with apples, pears, plums, and peaches. Within a few yards of the farmhouse door, a brimming asequia sings a song of peace.

This is the home of Ighenio Salazar who by miracle is alive to-day to tell of the bold ruse that saved his life in the great adventure in Lincoln nearly a half century ago. A cheery, gravely courteous man, he is well past three-score and ten, with iron-gray hair and moustache, and tall, broad-shouldered frame that suggests the power that must have been his in his younger years.

"Billy the Kid," said Salazar, "was the bravest fellow I ever knew. All through the three-days' battle he was as cool and cheerful as if he were playing a game instead of fighting for his life. When it began to look as if we should all be killed, the other men stood about silent, with long faces, hopeless. But not the Kid. He was light-hearted, gay, smiling all the time. 'You look *muy contento,*' Chavez y Chavez said to him with a sort of resentment. 'Well, why not?' answered the Kid. 'No use getting excited.'

"A little while before we made a dash for our lives, the Kid rolled a cigarette. I watched him. It seemed just then as if he had about a minute and a half to live. But when he poured the tobacco from his pouch into the cigarette paper he did not spill a flake. His hand was as steady as steel. A blazing chunk of roof fell on the table beside him, barely missing his head. 'Much obliged,' he said; and he bent over and lighted his cigarette from the flame. Then he looked at me and grinned as if he thought that was a good joke. He didn't roll that cigarette because he was nervous but because he wanted a good smoke. You could tell by the way he inhaled the smoke and let it roll out of his mouth that he was getting real pleasure out of it. If you had seen Billy the Kid roll that cigarette and smoke it, señor, you would have known at once that he was a brave man."

Salazar spoke in the language of his fathers, which was Spanish, rapidly, with fire, and dramatic emphasis. He pointed his story with picturesque gestures and more than once arose to illustrate his narrative by convincing pantomime. The old man has a histrionic flair, which is one of the reasons he escaped alive out of the murderous holocaust.

"When it came my turn to dart out the door of the McSween house," he went on, "the Murphy men were firing at a distance of ten yards. Why we were not all killed, I never could understand. I had not run a dozen steps when I was struck by three rifle bullets—in the hand, the left shoulder, and the left side, the bullet in my side passing entirely through my body. I stumbled, twisted over in the air, and fell on my back among the dead bodies of McSween, Romero, Semora, and Harvey Morris.

"I lay there unconscious for a while. When I came to

my senses, the fight was over and the Murphy men were laughing and drinking whisky among the corpses. It came to me in a flash that my only chance was to play dead, and a pretty slim chance it was. I relaxed all my muscles and sprawled on the ground as limp as a rag. Those fellows had sharp eyes, and how I managed to fool them I don't know. It was a wonder that the twitch of an eyelid or the tremor of a muscle did not betray me. I have always thought I must have been under the protection of guardian angels.

"When old Andy Boyle kicked me to see if I was dead, I thought to myself, 'It's all over now, Ighenio. Goodbye.' And let me tell you that old hombre's kicks were not love-taps. He planted his heavy boots in my wounded side with fearful force. That old man could kick like a mule. And every kick was torture. If he had kicked me only once more I think I must have groaned or yelled, the pain was so terrible. It took all the nerve I had to lie still and keep my eyes shut when I felt the muzzle of his rifle pressed down against my heart and knew that old murderer's finger was about to pull the trigger. I had hated Old Man Pearce, but, from my heart, I gave him a benediction when I heard him tell Boyle that I was dead and not to waste a bullet on me.

"I lay there motionless for three hours and you must remember that all that time I was suffering agony, which made my play-acting in the rôle of a dead man difficult. I knew that men's eyes remain open after death but I thought it best to keep mine closed. That would at least save me the danger of blinking. But at times I opened my eyes the least little bit and through narrow slits between my eyelids saw the Murphy men waltzing around and kicking up their heels as if they had gone crazy with joy. The tunes the two old Negroes played on their violin and guitar were as lively and merry as ever set the feet of girls dancing at a fandango, but to me they sounded like funeral dirges. And I thought the music would never stop. I wondered how much longer I could hold out. The pain seemed to be killing me, and I felt I had to move, change position, for relief. But I realized that the slightest movement would change me from a counterfeit dead man into a real one, and I lay still.

"When the crowd finally got tired of their fun and went away whooping and singing and laughing and left me lying there sick, weak from three wounds, in agony, and half dead, I was the happiest man in the world.

"I crawled away stealthily, making no noise, and got down by the river. There I fainted. When I revived, I stumbled on past the old stone tower, intending to go to the Montaña house, but I stopped when I saw the camp of the soldiers, and fell over in another faint. I was growing very weak from loss of blood. I reached the house of Francisco Romero y Valencia and pounded on the door, but Romero was afraid to let me in. I staggered a little way farther to Ike Ellis's place, but Ben Ellis, who answered my knock, wouldn't open the door either. Across a field I saw a light in José Otero's house where my sister-in-law, Nicolecita Pacheco, was staying. When I got there, Otero opened the door a little way and when he saw me, he was scared and slammed it in my face. 'I am Ighenio Salazar,' I said, 'and I am dying; let me in.' Still Otero wouldn't open the door again. But my sister-in-law had recognized my voice and she caught Otero around the neck and hurled him to the floor and opened the door herself.

"I stood by a little fire in the fireplace and warmed

myself, for the summer nights in the mountains are cold. My shirt was black and stiff with blood all over, and when my sister-in-law saw it she began to cry. For the third time I swooned and fell to the floor. Otero cut my shirt off my body with a butcher knife and put me to bed.

"Next morning, Terecita Felibosca drove over to Fort Stanton and brought Dr. Richard Wells, the post surgeon. While he was dressing my wounds, John Kinney, one of the worst fellows on the Murphy side, walked in with three other men. They had tracked me by my blood. Kinney said, 'I shot you last night and I've come to finish the job.' Doctor Wells told him not to talk like that. But Kinney said Billy the Kid had killed Bob Beckwith and he was going to have revenge on me for Beckwith's death. His swagger and big talk didn't scare Doctor Wells. 'If you kill this man,' he said, 'I'll see you hanged for it.' And he took Kinney by the arm and led him to the door and put him and the other three men outside. Doctor Wells was a brave man. He saved my life.

"In a day or two, Francisco Pacheco took me secretly to Las Tablas and then, after a short rest, to Fort Sumner, where I was confined to my bed nearly six months before I recovered."

Bob Beckwith is generally credited with having killed McSween, though a post-mortem examination revealed that six bullets had entered the faction leader's body. Most of these bullets, however, it was believed, had been fired after McSween was dead. Two minutes after Beckwith sent up his yell of exultation, he himself was killed by a bullet from Billy the Kid.

Six dead men were the net results of the three-days' battle that ended the Lincoln County war—Crawford, killed back of the Montaña house, and five slain in the

McSween holocaust.   Romero, Semora, and Crawford were buried by their relatives in Lincoln.   Beckwith was taken for interment to his old home at Seven Rivers, and beside his grave Bob Ollinger, his friend, swore to avenge his death in the blood of the Kid.

McSween and Morris were laid to rest beside Tunstall back of the McSween store.   The little plot of ground where the three men lie is bare to-day even of grass, and their unmarked graves are cluttered over with ashes, tin cans, and indiscriminate rubbish.

CHAPTER XII

HATREDS die hard, and peace came slowly. The peace that began tentatively to settle over Lincoln was like a hair-trigger, innocuous in itself but needing only the slightest pressure of a finger to render it deadly.

Murphy was not alive to enjoy the triumph of his faction. He died in Santa Fé shortly before the battle which ended McSween's life and hope of power at one blow. It was perhaps as well so. The war had ruined Murphy. His properties had been mortgaged to pay his fighting men. His creditors closed out his cattle ranch, his merchandising business, and his hotel, and the Big Store became the courthouse. Lord of the Mountains in his time, rich, wielding immense power, he died practically penniless.

But the war had also wrecked the financial fortunes of McSween. He left little to his widow but a heritage of hate. The vendetta, in fact, had swept over all Lincoln County like a pestilence, leaving ruin and desolation in its wake. Families had been impoverished, farms had remained untilled, business had come to a standstill. General bankruptcy was the price paid for rapine and murder. With Murphy and McSween both dead, their factions gradually disintegrated. War must be financed and there was no longer any money to keep it going.

General Lew Wallace came to New Mexico as governor

in August, 1878, determined to carry out President Hayes's orders and end the feud.

"When I reached Santa Fé," he wrote, "I found the law was practically a nullity and had no way of asserting itself. The insurrection seemed to be confined to one county which strangely enough was called Lincoln. I received statements of judges that they dared not hold court in certain districts. The United States Marshal told me he had a large number of warrants which he dared not serve and he could not find deputies rash enough to attempt service when they knew their lives would pay the penalty. The military commander at Fort Stanton sent me a list of murders that had been committed in that part of the country. I forwarded these combined statements to President Hayes."

Governor Wallace, in his investigation of the Lincoln County situation, acquainted himself with both sides of the story through conferences with Murphy and McSween men who met him in the capital. Mrs. McSween, through her lawyer, George Chapman of Las Vegas, prepared a number of affidavits which she forwarded to the governor, giving the details of the burning of her home, the murder of her husband, and Colonel Dudley's actions while in Lincoln with his troops. Sheriff Peppin and other Murphy leaders also sent affidavits. Both John Chisum and U. S. Commissioner Angel lcalled on Governor Wallace and endeavoured to give him a clear understanding of the vendetta, its causes, battles, and present status. However, with conflicting statements before him, clear understanding of so complex a problem was difficult.

Governor Wallace had grave doubts from the first as to his ability to end the feud. But that was the specific problem given to him to solve by President Hayes, and

he set himself to the task. His first step was to issue a
proclamation of amnesty to all who had taken part in the
war, except those under indictment for crime, on the understanding that they lay down their arms.   This action
was, to some extent, effective. There was practically
no more fighting nor, for that matter, had there been
since the big battle in Lincoln; but nothing the governor
could do could terminate the bitter hatreds the war had
kindled or prevent the deadly spirit of the feud from
smouldering dangerously for years.

Billy the Kid ignored the governor's proclamation.
Since the death of McSween, there was no faction leader
to claim his allegiance, but he had hatreds of his own and
a score of vengeance still to pay off. He had, moreover,
acquired the habit of outlawry. He doubtless had no
desire for any other mode of life but he believed, also, that
his enemies would kill him if he returned to peaceful
pursuits. He continued in arms, and since there was no
longer any McSween-faction exchequer upon which to
draw, he lived by gambling and the wholesale rustling
of livestock. The men who remained with him were
Charlie Bowdre, Tom O'Folliard, Jim French, John
Middleton, Hendry Brown, Fred Wayte, and Doc
Skurlock. They made their rendezvous for a while in
the mountains near Fort Stanton.

Governor Wallace determined to have a personal
interview with Billy the Kid and use his powers of persua-
sion to induce him to leave off fighting and lawlessness
and settle down to useful citizenship. With this purpose
in mind, he drove across country from Santa Fé by way
of Fort Stanton to Lincoln.

As Governor Wallace sat with General Hatch, Juan
Patron, and a group of army officers on the porch of the

Ellis House, a lone horseman appeared riding slowly toward them through Lincoln street.

"Here comes the Kid," remarked Juan Patron.

Governor Wallace was moved to quick interest. He viewed the picturesque figure of the young outlaw with fixed attention. The Kid carried a rifle across his saddle-bows, and if the governor's eyes had been keen enough, they might have noted that the gun was cocked. The Kid had ridden into Lincoln from the west by the Fort Stanton road and came on at a running walk past the Murphy store, headquarters of his enemies, without so much as turning his head to glance at a group of men lounging there who eyed him with cold hatred. Having hitched his horse in front of the Ellis House, he walked briskly up the path to the porch, his rifle in his hand, his six-shooter at his belt. Governor Wallace rose.

"So you are Billy the Kid," said the governor to the outlaw.

"I am," said the outlaw to the governor.

The two men shook hands. In appearance they were as much alike as a drawing room and a corral. Veteran of the Mexican and Civil wars, author, statesman, and diplomat, Governor Wallace had an air of scholarly distinction which his pince-nez glasses served to emphasize. His face was intellectual, his hair, moustache, and imperial, iron-gray. Over against this figure of the polished gentleman was the sunburned youth with lean, hard face, shrewd, cold eyes, a red bandanna knotted around his neck, and tricked out in spruce new cowboy trappings.

It was a meeting, not so much of two men, as of two worlds. They clasped hands across a gulf of ages. One was a product of culture and refinement; the other of a rough frontier; one finished, the other primitive; one

constructive, the other obstructive; one a representative
of the progressive present, the other of a dying past;
one a type that would soon be dominant; the other a type
that would soon be extinct. The governor was an intellect; the Kid a trigger finger.

The Kid did not recognize the gulf. He showed no
sign of embarrassment. He seemed as much at ease as
if he had been accustomed to meeting governors every
day. The trigger fingers of humanity take small account
of social distinctions. A bullet will make as short work
of a king as of a pauper. If there was any embarrassment, it was on the governor's side. He showed the
slight embarrassment of surprise.

"You don't look at all as I had pictured you in my
mind," said the governor.

"No?" The Kid smiled. "I left my horns and forked
tail back at camp."

"Not that." The governor raised a deprecating palm.
"But I had heard stories about you. If a man of whom
I have heard or read interests me, I always visualize
him." It was the novelist talking. "I formed a vivid
mental image of you. I was quite sure you had beetling
brows, black hair, and black, piercing eyes."

"And looked like a dead tough hombre," added the
Kid with a laugh.

"Well, yes. But here you are a clean-cut, good-looking
boy. You don't look bad."

The Kid declined to argue the point.

"How old are you?"

"Nineteen."

"I am—let me see—just thirty-two years older than
you. Old enough to be your father. So, Billy, I am going
to talk to you like a father."

The Kid nodded.

I have issued a proclamation of amnesty to all who have taken part in the feud, and I want you to share in it. President Hayes has sent me to New Mexico to establish peace. He has faith that I will do it. I am going to try to justify his confidence. Now, Billy, I have come all the way to Lincoln for the special purpose of persuading you to stop all this fighting and settle down."

"Settle down? I couldn't if I tried."

"Why not?"

"My enemies wouldn't let me."

"I think they would. If you proved to your enemies that you wanted to become a useful citizen, I believe they would leave you alone."

"Not in this country."

"Go to some other country, then, and start over again."

"No. This is my country and I'm staying here."

The Kid said it as Rob Roy might have said, "My foot is on my native heath and my name's McGregor."

"Stay, then. But turn over a new leaf."

"You don't know this country, Governor. Look up the street. Do you see that bunch of men standing at Murphy's store?"

"Yes."

"Know who they are?"

"No."

"They're Murphy men. There's Jimmy Dolan, 'Dad' Peppin, Andy Boyle, Old Man Pearce. Well, if I walked up the street without my guns, they'd kill me so quick I wouldn't know what happened."

"You just rode past them," replied the governor. "They made no move to kill you."

"The reason," said the Kid, "is right here in my lap."

He patted his rifle. "Here's another pretty good reason."
He rested his hand on the ivory handle of his six-shooter.
"They knew if they made a move, I'd get two or three of
them even if they got me. They didn't want to take a
chance. But just let 'em catch me without my shootin'
irons——" A shrug completed his sentence.

"I'm inclined to think you exaggerate the situation."

"I know what I'm talking about. I've gone too far
to turn back. I've done too much fighting. I've killed
too many men."

"But what of your future?"

"I wouldn't gamble much money on my future. I may
live a year or two; I may die in the next five minutes."

"You mean you expect to be killed?"

The Kid looked surprised at the question.

"Certainly. They'll get me sooner or later."

"But," urged the governor, "if you change your way
of living, you may change your way of dying. If you
live by the six-shooter, you will probably die by the six-
shooter. But there is still a chance for you. You are
still in your youth. Life should still be sweet to you.
Cease to be an enemy yourself and you will soon find
yourself without enemies. I want to see peace again in
these mountains. You can help me bring it about. I
want you to surrender——"

"Me surrender?"

"Yes, and stand trial on whatever charges may be
brought against you. If you are acquitted——"

"No jury would acquit me of anything."

"—that will wipe the slate clean. If you are convicted, I give you my promise now that I will pardon you
and set you free."

"I wouldn't have a chance in any court in New Mexico."

"I repeat that I will pardon you if the verdict goes against you. But I want you first to stand trial like a man."

The Kid thought for a moment in silence. Abstractedly, he lifted his rifle and blew a fleck of dust off the magazine.

"No, Governor," he said, "I can't do it. No use. It's too late. I've got to go on as I am, and when the time comes, die with my boots on."

Neither spoke for a moment.

"I'm sorry, Billy," said the governor. "You are wrong in your attitude. But if I can't persuade you to change it, that would seem to end the matter."

They rose and shook hands.

"Good-bye, Governor," said the Kid.

"Good-bye, my boy," said the governor.

Governor Wallace watched the Kid as he rode off along the cañon road until he disappeared.

"If that boy would take my advice," he said, turning to his companions with a note of sadness in his voice, "I believe he has in him the making of a fine man."

Two years later, Billy, in the shadow of the gallows, recalled the governor's promise of a pardon. But the pardon did not come and his friendship turned to hate.

"The Lincoln County reign of terror is not over," wrote Mrs. Susan E. Wallace, the governor's wife, in a letter from Fort Stanton, "and we hold our lives at the mercy of desperadoes and outlaws, chief among them Billy the Kid, whose boast is that he has killed a man for every year of his life. Once he was captured and escaped and now he swears, when he has killed the sheriff and the judge who passed sentence upon him and Governor Wallace, he will surrender and be hanged.

"'I mean to ride into the plaza at Santa Fé, hitch my horse in front of the palace, and put a bullet through Lew Wallace.'

"These are his words.   One of my friends warned me to close the shutters at evening, so the bright light of the student lamp might not make such a shining mark of the governor writing until late upon 'Ben Hur.'"

Mrs. Wallace's picture of the author sitting by the open window of the palace working upon his book late into the night under the light of the lamp with the vague menace of Billy the Kid's six-shooter out in the darkness of Santa Fé's silent streets is singularly interesting and adds a touch of romance to the history of the novel whose fame was soon to fill the world.   What if the Kid had made good his threat and his bullet had come out of the night to stay the hand of the writer?   Where, then, would have been "Ben Hur," and how much pleasure would have been denied to millions of men and women in the reading of it?

Mrs. McSween was not a woman to sit and weep over her misfortunes.   She had the courage of her hatreds and faith in a God of vengeance.   The refusal of Colonel Dudley to interfere when he could have done so rankled in her soul and, carrying out the threat she had hurled at that officer, she now left no stone unturned to shoulder upon him the responsibility for the crime that had widowed her and left her homeless.   In elaborate affidavits, she laid her case not only before Governor Wallace but before the authorities at Washington.   The governor, it is said, favoured prosecution, but the attorney-general of the territory decided that the courts had no jurisdiction.

When it seemed that some official action was inevitable, Colonel Dudley himself demanded an investigation. Under warrant of the War Department, a military court was convened and sat for six weeks at Fort Stanton. As a result of the hearing, Colonel Dudley was exonerated. His defense was that he had no authority to interfere in the battle because Sheriff Peppin was on the ground and in command of the situation. The court decided that his position was technically sound. It may have been so; at least it was technically plausible. But the fact remains that while Colonel Dudley was splitting hairs over the technical question of his authority, the McSween home went up in flames and five men were slaughtered within two hundred yards of his camp where he had two well-armed squadrons of cavalry and two pieces of artillery. In arriving at its verdict, the court seems to have lost sight of the human tragedy in weighing the niceties of military law.

Billy the Kid added to his list of killings on August 5th during a horse-stealing raid on the Mescalero Apache reservation. Joe Bernstein, Indian agency clerk, saw the outlaws rounding up some horses not far from Blazer's sawmill, scene of the "Buckshot" Roberts fight. Supposing them to be cowboys labouring under a mistaken idea of ownership, he rode out to them. "Hey," he shouted, "what are you fellows about? Don't drive those horses off. They belong on this range." His blunder cost him his life. Without stopping to argue the matter, Billy the Kid shot him. "The horses didn't belong to him," the Kid explained afterward, "and it takes a bullet to teach some people to keep their noses out of other men's business. He was only a Jew, anyway."

Jimmy Dolan, Billy Matthews, Bill Campbell, and Jesse Evans foregathered in Stockton's bar. It was a chilly day late in February, 1879. The unpropitious weather depressed their spirits. Moreover, it had been deadly dull in Lincoln for a long time. The good old days when a man was killed every morning for breakfast seemed gone for ever. So these fighting men passed the bottle and braced their drooping spirits. When they sauntered out into the street they saw the world as through a glass, rosily. Their hearts were full of good cheer and friendliness when they spied Billy the Kid, Charlie Bowdre, and Tom O'Folliard lounging in front of the Ellis House.

"Come on," said Dolan, "let's make up with those fellows. The war's over. Might as well click glasses and call all bets off. It's time for another drink anyway."

They careened up to their ancient enemies.

"Hello, Billy," said Jesse Evans with hilarious good humour. "How's my old pal?"

The Kid eyed him with hard suspicion.

Evans stuck out his hand.

"Put her there, Billy," he said.

The Kid hesitated.

"Come on, Billy, shake hands," urged Evans. "We're all going to bury the hatchet and be friends."

Tough old Bill Campbell cut in with an amiable remark. Billy Matthews, who had shot the Kid and whom the Kid had once attempted to kill, admitted he was willing to call everything square.

"Come on over to Patron's and let's all have a friendly glass," said Dolan.

So to Juan Patron's bar they went, and drowned old enmities and ratified a pact of peace in rounds of drink.

It so fell out that Lawyer George Chapman arrived in Lincoln late that afternoon. After supper with Mrs.

McSween, he went to his sleeping quarters in the McSween store to start a fire and warm up the place.

"I'll be back in half an hour," he told Mrs. McSween.

In the meantime, the newly made friends had continued to celebrate their informal treaty of peace in generous potations. It was a grand and glorious thing for old enemies to get together at last on a basis of friendship, and they decided to make the occasion a joyous and memorable one. Hiring the two old Negro musicians, George Washington and Sebron Bates, they went the rounds of all the saloons in town, making merry with music and roistering good fellowship. But the best of friends must part and Billy the Kid, Bowdre, and O'Folliard finally went back to the Ellis House and got to bed while Jesse Evans, as full of friendliness as of liquor, tumbled in for the night at the Wortley Hotel, leaving Dolan, Campbell, and Matthews to continue their carousal.

On his way back to Mrs. McSween's home, Chapman ran into these three boozy revellers in front of San Juan Church.

"Here's that McSween lawyer," said Dolan, "trying to stir up trouble when we've sworn peace. Now's our chance to show him what's what."

He halted Chapman as the lawyer was brushing past.

"You seem to be a pretty big man," Dolan said.

"Perhaps," agreed Chapman.

"How tall do they grow where you come from?"

"They grow gentlemen where I come from."

"Well, I declare," answered Campbell. "Now, I reckon a gentleman like you ought to be a mighty good dancer. Suppose you start in and show us how nice you can dance. Hit her up. And since we ain't got no fiddle along with us now, I'll just play a little music for you with my six-shooter."

"I'll dance for no ruffians," Chapman replied hotly.

Mrs. McSween, sitting in her parlour perhaps fifty feet away, heard two shots.

"They've killed Chapman," she cried instinctively, springing from her chair.

"Oh, no," said a woman friend who was with her. "They're only shooting off their pistols in fun."

"I know they've murdered Chapman," repeated Mrs. McSween.

She ran to the window and peered out but it was too dark for her to see into the street.

A Mexican rushed in.

"There is a man lying dead in the road," he said excitedly.

"It's Chapman," cried Mrs. McSween.

But no one dared go out to see who it was.

Early next morning, Miguel Luna, then a little boy, was sent by his mother to the Montaña store to buy some groceries. In the half-light of dawn he saw something lying at the side of the road and smoke was rising from it. He thought it was a bundle of rags that someone had set afire. He went a little closer. He was horrified to see a dead man, his clothes burned half off and still smouldering and emitting little curls of smoke. He ran back in fright to his mother.

That afternoon Chapman's body was lowered into a grave behind the old McSween store beside the resting place of McSween, Tunstall, and Morris. The six-shooter that killed him had been held so close that the leap of flame from its barrel had set fire to some legal papers which he carried in the breast pocket of his coat.

Dolan, Campbell, and Matthews were tried for the murder at Socorro. Dolan testified that he had fired in the air. He and Matthews were acquitted. Campbell was convicted. Placed in jail temporarily at Fort Stanton, he escaped and was never heard of again in that country. He was a Texan and a desperate man. His real name was said to be Ed Richardson.

Most of the men who fought in the Lincoln County war have been sleeping peacefully in their graves for years. Riley was in business in Las Cruces for a time and then moved to Colorado, where he died in prosperous circumstances. John Copeland, the McSween sheriff, died in 1902. "Dad" Peppin, the Murphy sheriff, continued to live in Lincoln until his death in 1905. William Brady, Sheriff Brady's eldest son, was living on a ranch in Bonito Cañon in 1924. Bob Brady, another son, was jailer at Lincoln for several years. Josefina Brady, who married Florencio Chavez, died in Lincoln a few years ago. Billy Matthews moved to Roswell, where he was postmaster in 1904.

Dolan bought the old McSween store from Tom Larue and ran it for five years, living in a residence he built across the street which is now the Bonito Inn. He also purchased the old Tunstall ranch on the Rio Feliz and continued in the cattle business. The tragic associations of these two places, once owned by men whom he had hounded out of life, weighed nothing with him. Dolan was of iron stuff and not afraid of ghosts. After his marriage to a daughter of the Fritz family, he moved to Las Cruces, where he became registrar of the Land Office. He died in Roswell and was buried in the little family cemetery on the Fritz ranch.

After the big battle Mrs. McSween lived four years in Lincoln in a new residence she built opposite San Juan Church, almost on the spot where she had had her memorable interviews with Colonel Dudley. Two years after McSween's death, she married George L. Barber, a lawyer. When John Chisum turned over to her two hundred red heifers in payment of a debt he had owed to McSween for legal services, she moved to Three Rivers, where she established a cattle ranch and became known as "the Cattle Queen of New Mexico." Before leaving Lincoln, which had been the background of so many tragic experiences, she sold the old McSween store to Tom Larue. Having disposed of her cattle ranch in 1917 to Albert B. Fall, United States Senator and Secretary of the Interior under President Harding, she moved to White Oaks.

White Oaks lies in a beautiful little cup of a valley in the Jicarilla Mountains twelve miles from Carrizozo, a railroad town on the plains. As you drive toward it, you catch your first view of the town from a rise in the cañon road. You are surprised at its impressive appearance. White Oaks, you think, must be a busy, bustling place. You see at a distance long rows of brick and stone business buildings lining the main street and, dotted over a wide area, handsome residences in tree-shaded yards. You splash across a creek in a deep arroyo and turn into the main street. If you were surprised at first at what you thought a vision of prosperity, you are amazed now to find only silence. All the stores are dark and deserted, except one in which a gray-bearded merchant smokes his pipe and waits for trade that rarely comes. Rows of big plate-glass windows, gray with dust and cobwebs, blink out upon the dreary emptiness of the weed-grown street. The sidewalks are caved in. Paint has peeled from the half-obliterated and weather-stained business signs which still tell dimly that here was a saloon, here a dance hall. Most of the residences are vacant and falling into ruin. Vagrant cows straggle through gaps in broken fences and crop the herbage of once well-tended lawns. White Oaks is a ghost town. When it was a booming gold camp in the late '70's, its streets were crowded, its merchants waxed rich, saloons, dance halls, and gambling houses were in full blast day and night, drinks were paid for in raw gold weighed in little scales on the bar, and gamesters bet buckskin bags full of gold dust on a card at faro. But the veins of gold on Baxter peak pinched out, the people left for other parts to seek their fortunes, and the town's glories suddenly departed. In the days of the gold stampede, White Oaks had more than two thousand inhabitants; now it has fifty.

Mrs. Barber is a fragile wisp of a woman in the twilight of life with traces of the comeliness and charm that made her famous as a frontier beauty and no little of the energy and courage that enabled her to weather the tragedies and sorrows of her pioneer days. The havoc and bloodshed of the feud are fresh in her mind and its old hatreds still vivid.

"Once settled at Three Rivers," she said, "I felt like a soul that had lived in torment and had escaped from hell to Heaven. After Lincoln, I cannot tell what happiness it was to gallop over the hills on my own ranch and breathe in the clean, pure air. I knew peace and contentment again for the first time in years.

"John Chisum himself assisted in driving my herd of heifers from the Pecos to my new home. The cattle were a godsend. They enabled me to build a new prosperity after the war had robbed me of nearly everything I had.

'You have a fine business mind,' John Chisum said to me.
'I would be glad to have you manage one of my own ranches.
You are going to make a wonderful success in cattle. 'So
he encouraged me and I lived up to his prophecy.

"I managed my ranch myself. I did all the buying of
supplies and provisions, watched expenses closely, kept
books, put my affairs on a strictly business basis. I rode
with my cowboys, directed round-ups, calving, branding,
cutting out beeves, and did all my own marketing. I
suppose the merchants and cattle buyers with whom I
dealt fancied that, as I was a woman, they could pull
the wool over my eyes; but I quickly undeceived them and
they found that I drove shrewd bargains.

"As my business expanded, I built a beautiful home
back from the river in the foothills of the White Mountains. I set out more than four thousand apple, pear,
peach, and plum trees which in time bore splendid crops
of luscious fruit. I increased my land holdings and my
ranch extended three miles along the river, and it filled me
with joy to see my herds grazing on a thousand hills.
My cattle numbered eight thousand head when I finally
sold out. Whenever I dropped into Albuquerque or
Santa Fé for a visit, the public prints referred to me as
'the Cattle Queen of New Mexico.' As far as I know, I
owned more cattle than any woman in the Southwest.
I came to White Oaks because it is so peaceful here. My
life has been so strenuous, I have seen so much fighting
and killing, that in my old age, I want peace."

So in the deep peace of the mountain valley, Mrs.
Barber awaits the final summons—a ghost woman in a
ghost town, the curtain slowly falling on the bitter drama
of her life, left alone with her memories that are crowded
with dead men and desolate with graves.

CHAPTER XIII

A STRANGER FROM THE PANHANDLE

DOWN from the mesa lands, by the Texas road, three weather-beaten men rode into old Fort Sumner on a February day in 1878. Across their pommels rested long buffalo rifles; frying-pans and certain other cooking utensils clanked from their cantles; and their lean shaggy ponies looked as if they were not on speaking terms with oats or curry combs.

There was some mention of grub among them as soon as they had picketed their ponies by the Pecos River. Wherefore they searched their pockets carefully and fished up one dollar and thirty-five cents in nickels and dimes. They strolled into town where appetizing odours from a restaurant saluted their nostrils.

"Ham and eggs!"

The rich, greasy aroma of the cooking was like attar of roses to these famished souls. They were about to stampede into the place when a sign in the window caught their eyes:

MEALS FIFTY CENTS

They sighted at the sign from all angles. But the fatal words remained coldly immutable. They counted their nickels and dimes again. But no miracle happened. They laughed in one another's face with good-humoured hopelessness and invested their finances in a piece of side

meat, some flour, and canned tomatoes. Going back to
their horses they cooked their own meal on a camp fire.

"I've travelled far enough," said one of the hungry
triumvirs. "This town looks good to me and I'm going
to settle here."

Fort Sumner did not impress the other two so favour-
ably and they climbed into their saddles and again took
up the trail westward. The one who was left behind sat
cross-legged on the ground and watched them disappear
in the distance. Then he got to his feet, stretched himself, and started out to look for a job. He needed one.
He was without a penny in the world.

He found Pete Maxwell, richest man in that part of
New Mexico and owner of great herds of cattle and sheep,
standing on the porch of his home.

Maxwell looked him over with a dubious smile. The
visitor looked less like a cowboy than a scarecrow that
had decided to quit its vigil in a cornfield and try a more
exciting occupation. He was gaunt and bronzed and
stood six feet four and a half inches in height. His
clothes were frayed and unkempt and, because he had been
unable to buy a pair of pants long enough for him, he had
pieced out the ones he wore with leggings of buffalo hide,
the hair on the outside. But this long-legged, scarecrow
man, standing there in the road leaning on his rifle, had a
merry twinkle in his eye and an ingratiating note in his
drawling voice.

"I may not look exactly like a puncher just now,"
he went on suavely with an infectious smile, "but I'm an
old hand with cows. I can do anything there is to be
done around a herd of cattle; I can throw a rope as good
as any man and ride anything that ever looked through a
bridle."

"Well," said Maxwell, "go out and see my foreman and tell him I said to put you to work. You'll find his camp about five miles up the river."

"All right."

The man turned to leave.

"By the way," said Maxwell, "what might be your name?"

"Pat Garrett," replied the stranger.

So the man who was to win national fame as the sheriff of Lincoln County, establish law and order west of the Pecos, ring down the final curtain on the drama of Billy the Kid, and become the friend of President Theodore Roosevelt and many other great men of the nation, made his undistinguished entrance upon the stage of New Mexican history.

You might suspect from his name that Pat Garrett was an Irishman direct from the "auld sod," but he was a Southern man with many generations of American breeding behind him and connected with some of the best families in the South. Patrick Floyd Garrett was born June 5, 1850, in Alabama. When he was six years old, his parents moved to Louisiana, where his father became a large slave holder and the owner of two plantations embracing three thousand acres. The Civil War swept away the fortune of the family, and his father and mother died soon after the long struggle between North and South closed at Appomattox. Left without means, Garrett, as a boy of eighteen, struck West in 1869.

He dropped a semicolon into his Western peregrination when he went to work on a cattle ranch in Dallas County, Texas. A bold, roving, adventurous spirit, he fell into the life of a cowboy as if it were his native element and in the next few years punched cattle all over southwestern

Texas. He put on cowboy habits with his first pair of chapareras and was accustomed, in these care-free days of his youth, to ride into the nearest town on pay-days with his roistering companions and spend his wages in drinking, gambling, and riotous fun, which was the way of the breed. He joined a trail outfit starting out from Eagle Lake for the railroad markets in Kansas in 1875, but went only as far north as Denison, where he quit the drive and joined a party of buffalo hunters bound on an expedition into the Texas Panhandle.

From the fall of 1875 until the end of January, 1878, he earned his livelihood as a professional buffalo hunter in the Panhandle and on the Staked Plains. The buffalo were still fairly plentiful in that part of the country when he began his career as a hunter; when he ended it, they had almost disappeared. The vocation was lucrative in 1875; in 1878 it was only precariously profitable. Garrett shared in the last days of a slaughter that is memorable in the history of the continent.

In January, 1878, having received the money for his last buffalo hunt and having lost it, it is said, at cards in Tascosa, Garrett with two companions headed toward the setting sun to seek his further fortunes. With empty pockets and light hearts the three adventurers travelled with only such equipment as they could carry on their ponies and lived on the game that fell to their rifles. When, after the long, hard winter's ride across the track-less wilderness, Garrett finally arrived at Fort Sumner, it is small wonder that he should have determined forth-with to locate in the crude little frontier settlement that must have seemed like Heaven to his weary soul.

For six months Garrett punched cattle for Pete Maxwell, living up to the encomiums he had passed upon himself when he got the job and proving his skill in every phase of cowboy craft. He and Maxwell had a disagreement finally, and Maxwell discharged him. Garrett had enough money to open a small restaurant, which he operated until Beaver Smith took him into partnership in a general merchandise store and saloon. He was by this time an established citizen and an integral part of the life of the place. During a residence of more than two years in Fort Sumner, he married twice. Juanita Martinez, his first wife, died a few weeks after the wedding. His second wife, Apolinaria Gutierrez, another Fort Sumner girl, whom he married in 1880, bore him five children and still lives, as his widow, in Las Cruces.

Fort Sumner was at that time an abandoned army post. Among the military establishments of the Southwest, it had distinction as the scene of the Government's first experiment in educating the Indians to ways of peace and self-supporting thrift in a concentration colony. From the days of the first Spaniards, the Navajos in the northwestern part of New Mexico and the Mescalero Apaches in the southeast had swept out of their mountain fastnesses to harry the settlements in innumerable raids and wars. Campaigns against them had brought only short-lived peace. Left unguarded to their own counsels in their wild homelands, they were ready in a short time for other outbreaks.

To end these constant depredations, the Government rounded up almost the entire tribe of Mescalero Apaches in the early '60's and settled them under the guns of Fort Sumner at Bosque Redondo on the Pecos River. Kit Carson a little later crushed the Navajos in his famous campaign of 1864 in the Cañon de Chelly country and transplanted several thousand of these warlike natives to the Fort Sumner colony.   A band of Utes, captured in Colorado, swelled the Indian population of Bosque Redondo to nearly ten thousand.

Kit Carson, then a brigadier general, was appointed superintendent of the settlement.   He had lived among the Indians, understood them, and had the welfare of the race at heart.   Guarded by troops, the Indians were kept at farming and constructive labours.   Fifteen hundred acres were planted to grain and vegetables.   An irrigating ditch seven miles long was constructed to water their farms.   For a time, the colony was contented and prosperous and New Mexico's Indian problem seemed on the verge of solution.   But there came a year of crop failure, supplies ran short, the aboriginal agriculturists were threatened with starvation, and trouble developed between Navajos and Apaches, who had been immemorial enemies.   As a result, the Indians were sent back to their old homes, and the Government's experiment at transforming warrior tribes into peaceful farmers ended in disaster.

Fort Sumner stood on the north bank of the Pecos where the river makes a wide turn to the southeast.   After its abandonment as a military post, settlers moved into its buildings, and it became a town that remained an army post with the army left out.   In Garrett's day, Pete Maxwell lived with his mother, Mrs. Luz Maxwell, and his sister, Paulita Maxwell, and the family servants, in a great two-story house that had been officers' quarters and faced the spacious parade ground to the east.   To the north and south were rows of adobe houses that had been the barracks of the soldiers and were now the homes of Mexican and white families.   Stores and saloons backed against the river suggested that the wide, unpaved space in front of them was the main street. To the northeast stood the old military hospital, used now as a place of habitation and as a dance hall. Near it an excavation, left when earth had been taken to make adobe bricks for building purposes, had been filled with water and formed a little lake with grassy, flower-sprinkled shores. At the northern edge of town was a peach orchard, planted by the Indians and covering many acres. In the warm spring days, the orchard in full billowy bloom was like heavy, low-lying pink smoke from a fragrant censer, and in the summer it was a source of pies and cobblers for every housewife who cared to gather the ripened fruit.

But the glory of Fort Sumner was a broad, smooth avenue four miles long leading northward to the little Mexican village of Punta de la Glorietta and lined its entire length with twin rows of giant cottonwoods, thirty feet apart, that testified to the constructive labours of Indians under the urge of soldier bayonets. Shady and cool on the hottest days, this noble thoroughfare had on one side the bronze-red Pecos swishing noisily down from its mountain sources and on the other the fields and orchards of Mexican farmers. Mocking birds still sing in the towering branches of the survivors of these old trees that have seen pass beneath them, as along a king's highway, the pageantry of the frontier past—pioneers, Indians, soldiers of the old army, descendants of Spanish conquerors, Kit Carson, Billy the Kid and his outlaws, Pat Garrett and his man-hunters, John Chisum the cattle king, and the multitude of forgotten men who played their part in building civilization in the Southwest.

Billy the Kid made Fort Sumner his headquarters from the fall of 1878 until his death. Of the men who had followed him during the Lincoln County war, Charlie

Bowdre, Tom O'Folliard, Doc Skurlock, Fred Wayte,
Jim French, John Middleton, and Hendry Brown remained
with him.   Bowdre sold out his ranch on the Ruidosa
and set up housekeeping with his Mexican wife in rooms
in the old hospital in Fort Sumner.   O'Folliard lived with
him.   Others who joined the Kid's band here were Tom
Cooper, Dave Rudabaugh, Billy Wilson, Tom Pickett,
and Tom Webb—all cattle rustlers, Rudabaugh having
recently broken jail at Las Vegas after killing the jailer.

There was no vendetta now to give to the Kid's activi-
ties even a spurious legitimacy in the minds of the people.
From now on, he was an outlaw pure and simple and his
Fort Sumner years marked the heyday of his career.
He was not a robber of the Frank and Jesse James sort;
he looted no banks, held up no travellers on the highway.
He confined himself exclusively to stealing livestock, and
his operations covered half New Mexico.   He rounded
up cattle on the Canadian River and in the Texas Panhandle and sold them in the southern part of the territory;
or he stole beeves in the south and marketed them in Las
Vegas and the northern settlements.   He was well known
everywhere, and those who bought from him were under
no illusions regarding the transactions.   So easy was it
for him to dispose of his stolen stock that he had regularly
established marketing connections.   Pat Coughlin, known
as the "King of Tularosa," who had grown rich on government contracts as Murphy had before him, was one of his
most important customers and had an agreement with
him to take at a fair price all the cattle he could rustle.
The Kid did a thriving business with His Majesty of
Tularosa until the arrest and conviction of Coughlin
broke off the alliance.

The Kid made outlawry pay.   It was a hard life but it

was the kind of life he loved and easy money was the reward of its hardships. When he had filled his pockets by the sale of other men's steers, he returned to Fort Sumner to rest and invite his soul and spend his money with a free hand at bars, gambling tables, and fandangos among companions as reckless as himself. A short life but a merry one summed up his philosophy, and when his funds ran low, he was off on another raid; living in the present, snapping his fingers at the future, like the buccaneers of old Caribbean days who, having squandered in the boozing-kens of Port Royal or Tortuga the gold looted from treasure galleons, financed another carouse by sacking Porto Bello or Maracaibo. He was, after his fashion, a Sir Henry Morgan of the purple sage, his flagship a bronco pony, the cattle ranges his Spanish Main.

Joe Grant was saved from oblivion by a bullet from Billy the Kid's six-shooter in January, 1880. Grant was from Texas, posed as a bad man, and pretended to want to join the Kid's gang. Nothing more is known about him and he would have been utterly forgotten long ago if he had not achieved the ultimate distinction of being killed by a famous desperado. Grant was in the braggadocio phase of intoxication in José Valdez's saloon when the Kid and some companions entered.

"Say, Kid," blustered the Texan, "I'll bet you I kill a man to-day before you do."

The Kid smiled off the challenge. Grant noisily urged him to accept it.

"If you think I don't mean it, I'll bet you twenty-five dollars and put up the cash."

He shoved a roll of bills across the bar into Valdez's hands, and to humour the drunken fellow the Kid covered the money.

With some Chisum cowboys the Kid came into the saloon again in the evening, having in the meantime forgotten about Grant and his wager. Valdez held whispered confidence with him at the end of the bar.

"Better be on your guard, Billy," he said, "Grant's full of whisky and ugly. He took a couple of shots out of the back door at nothing this afternoon and muttered something about getting you. He might want to kill you for the glory of it or the reward."

The Kid walked up to Grant in friendly wise.

"That's a pretty ivory-handled gun you've got, Grant," he said. "Let me have a look at it."

Suiting the action to the word, he coolly lifted Grant's six-shooter from its holster and examined it with a show of admiration. He noted empty cartridges in two chambers. Before handing the gun back he revolved the cylinder so that in the first two attempts to fire it the hammer would fall on the empty shells. The crowd had a drink or two. Edging around a corner of the bar and facing the Kid, Grant jerked out his revolver.

"I'll win my bet with you right now," he roared and, levelling the weapon full at the Kid's face, pulled the trigger, the hammer clicking harmlessly. Before the look of surprise faded from his drunken face, the Kid killed him with a bullet through his throat which cut his windpipe and shattered his backbone. The Kid laughed quietly as he dropped his six-shooter back into the scabbard.

"That's a good joke on Grant," he said. "And as I win the bet, Valdez, you might as well pass over that fifty dollars."

They will tell you in New Mexico that the Kid broke with John Chisum in these later years and, in his thefts, did not spare the herds of the cattle king. There is some doubt as to whether the Kid stole Chisum's cattle, though it seems probable he did. Certainly he quarrelled with Chisum and threatened his life, but on the surface at least this quarrel was patched up. There is one story that in appreciation of the Kid's services in the Lincoln County war, Chisum gave him permission to help himself to Chisum steers whenever he needed money. There is another that the Kid look this liberty without Chisum's permission on the grounds that Chisum owed him for his services in the vendetta and had not paid him. Mrs. Sallie Roberts admits that a little unpleasantness arose between Chisum and the Kid but denies that it ended their friendship. She attributes this unpleasantness to busybodies who had carried malicious tales to the Kid that Chisum had been talking about him in uncomplimentary vein.

"Billy met Uncle John in Fort Sumner," said Mrs. Roberts, "and accused him of talking about him and drew his gun. If Uncle John had lost his head he might have been killed, but he remained perfectly cool. Before making any answer, he calmly tamped some tobacco in his pipe, lighted it, and blew a mouthful of smoke into the air.

"'Don't believe everything you hear, Billy,' he said quietly. 'I have always been your friend and expect to remain your friend.'

"He soon calmed Billy down and they had a drink together, shook hands, and parted just as good friends as ever. If Uncle John paid Billy any money on that occasion, I never heard of it. I will say, too, that we never thought Billy stole any of our cattle, and it would be difficult to make me believe that he did. He had been a

good friend of ours for several years, and, once a friend,
it was hard to change him."

Frank Coe gives another version of the story.

"The Kid," said Coe, "figured Chisum owed him five
hundred dollars. He said Chisum had promised to pay
him for fighting on the McSween-Chisum side during the
feud and had not kept his promise. He had tried to find
Chisum and collect the debt but Chisum had always
dodged him. They met finally in Fort Sumner.

"'Hello, Chisum,' said Billy. 'I've been looking for
you to collect that money you owe me.'

"Chisum smiled that dry smile of his that saved his life
more than once.

"'And I have been looking for you to pay it to you,
Billy,' he said.

"The Kid remarked that right then was a good time to
pay it and Chisum wrote him a check for the five hundred
dollars.

"'Don't you fail to let this check go through,' said Billy
as he stuffed it in his pocket. 'If you stop it, I'll kill you
if it's the last thing I ever do.'

"'Don't worry,' replied Chisum. 'You can cash it any
time you like. I'll honour it.'

"That's all there was to it," added Coe, "except that
Chisum honoured the check."

Billy the Kid lost three members of his band in 1880
at Tascosa on the Canadian River in the Texas Panhandle,
where he was camped for several weeks disposing of a
herd of horses stolen in the Bonito Cañon, many of them
from Charles Fritz, into whose family Jimmy Dolan,
Murphy's old partner, had married. Hendry Brown,
Fred Wayte, and John Middleton, all of whom had taken
part with the Kid in a number of desperate affrays,

decided to forsake outlaw life and tried to persuade the
Kid to join them and adopt ways of peace. Brown and
Wayte went to the latter's old home in the Indian Territory where Wayte settled down and eventually, it is said,
served as a member of the Oklahoma legislature. Brown
travelled on into Kansas, where he became marshal of
Caldwell, an old cattle-trail town. While an officer of
the law, he remained at heart an outlaw, and always he
heard a still small voice calling him back to the old, wild
life. With three companions, he rode into Medicine
Lodge, Kansas, one day, with his marshal's star still on
his breast, and held up the bank, killing Wiley Payne, the
president, and George Jeppert, the cashier. A posse of
citizens pursued the robbers, killed two in flight, and
hanged Brown and the other bandit to the limb of a
cottonwood tree. John Middleton changed his name,
went into business in a Kansas town and, it is said, lived
the remainder of his life as a law-abiding and prosperous
citizen.

Meanwhile, with the Kid in Fort Sumner at frequent
intervals, he and Pat Garrett warmed to each other and
became, if not bosom cronies, at least intimate friends;
which, in the light of subsequent events, might suggest
to a cynical philosopher a few quaint reflections on friendships in this world.

CHAPTER XIV

A BELLE OF OLD FORT SUMNER

BILLY THE KID was a youth of many light affairs, but he loved but one woman. This at least is what the Southwest has believed for nearly fifty years. His love for her was his soul's one clear drop of poetry. On his way to hell, it gave him his one vision of Heaven. Concerning the identity of his sweetheart, there has been much speculation. She lived in old Fort Sumner—that much is certain. When, later on in his story, Billy the Kid escaped from Lincoln, it is generally conceded he could have got quickly into old Mexico where he would have been safe from pursuit. Life and liberty beckoned him across the Rio Grande. But the love in his boy's heart longed for his sweetheart and he headed straight for Fort Sumner. For the one woman of his dreams he risked his life in his life's most desperate chance. For love of her he died.

Mrs. Paulita Jaramillo of New Fort Sumner, who in her youth was Paulita Maxwell, daughter of one of New Mexico's famous families, throws much interesting light on this old sweetheart romance. She and Billy the Kid were friends, and the friendship of this good, pure girl was a gracious influence in his life. Time has dealt gently with Mrs. Jaramillo. No one would be so ungallant as to inquire how old she is, but it may be whispered that in 1881, when Billy the Kid met death in her home, she was a blooming girl of eighteen. Streaks of gray have only begun to show in her coal-black hair; when she smiles, the suspicion of a dimple still shows in the olive smoothness of her cheeks, and there is a sparkle in her black eyes that age has had no power to dim.   It is easy to fancy her as the dashing beauty she is said to have been when she was the belle of old Fort Sumner.

Mrs. Jaramillo unites the blood of Spanish hidalgos and American pioneers.   Lucien B. Maxwell, her father, was a friend and companion of Kit Carson, and at one time was reckoned the richest man in the Southwest.   He was a native of Illinois and settled in New Mexico when the country was still a part of old Mexico.   He married Señorita Luz Beaubien of noble ancestry, tracing back to the aristocracies of France and Spain.   She was the daughter of Charles Hipolyte Trotier, Sieur de Beaubien, a Canadian, who embarked in the commerce of the Santa Fé trail and settled in New Mexico in 1823.   Her mother had been Señorita Paula Labata, descended from a family that came to the New World soon after the conquest of Mexico by Hernando Cortez and arrived in New Mexico in the wake of Oñate's pioneers.   So Mrs. Jaramillo has, as her intimate background, the proudest family traditions in all that part of the country.

With Don Guadalupe Miranda, the Sieur de Beaubien obtained, as a reward for pioneer services, from the government of old Mexico a grant of land of vast extent in the northern part of the province of New Mexico, famous in later years as the Maxwell Grant.   Miranda sold out his interest to Beaubien and, upon the latter's death in 1864, Maxwell purchased all the land from Beaubien's heirs and became sole owner of a tract larger than three states the size of Rhode Island and embracing more than a million acres.   The land comprised in the original

Maxwell Grant is to-day dotted with towns, timber claims, mines, farms, and ranches, and at an extremely modest estimate is worth fifty million dollars.

Maxwell built a palatial home at Cimarron, where for years he lived in a style of baronial magnificence. Here he dispensed lavish hospitality, and the guests who came and went in endless procession included traders of the Santa Fé trail which passed his door, cattle kings, governors, merchants, army officers, and men distinguished in public life and international affairs in Europe and America. His cellars were stocked with liquors, champagnes, and costly vintages, and his table was laid each day for two dozen guests who ate their food from dishes of solid silver and drank their wines from chalices of solid gold.

Owner of great herds of sheep and cattle, this feudal lord of the old frontier finally sold his vast estate to Jerome B. Chaffee, David H. Moffat, and Wilson Waddington for the reputed sum of $750,000 and lived to see the purchasers sell out to an English syndicate for $1,350,000, almost twice what they had paid him. Maxwell founded the First National Bank of Santa Fé, which he sold in 1871 to Stephen B. Elkins, Thomas Catron, and others. He lost a quarter of a million dollars which he invested in a corporation for the construction of the Texas Pacific Railway. Other investments proved unfortunate. Generous, improvident, picturesque, this magnificent old pioneer retired to Fort Sumner, where he died comparatively poor in 1875.

Mrs. Jaramillo passed her childhood in frontier luxury on her father's estate at Cimarron. Her mother died in 1881. The other Maxwell children were Pedro, Odila, Amilia, Virginia, and Sophia. Pedro, known throughout New Mexico as Pete Maxwell, lived, until his death, at

Fort Sumner, and in his later years was the richest sheep man in the Pecos Valley. Amilia and Odila became the successive wives of Don Manuel Abreu. Virginia married Captain Alexander Chase of the U. S. Army, and with her husband is buried at the Presidio at San Francisco. Sophia married Telesfor Jaramillo, a brother of José Jaramillo, to whom Paulita Maxwell was married in January, 1882. Of these children, only Mrs. Paulita Jaramillo and Mrs. Odila Abreu are left alive (1924).

Where the ancient cottonwood avenue that was the glory of old Fort Sumner ends four miles to the north, stands new Fort Sumner to-day on the Belen Cut-off of the Santa Fé Railway. Don't confuse old Fort Sumner with new Fort Sumner. They are fifty years distant from each other, though by linear measurement only four miles. One is the past, the other the present; one poetry, the other prose. New Fort Sumner is without tradition, romance, or picturesqueness. It seems asleep, but its slumber is not idyllic like that of Lincoln nor haunted by ghosts like that of White Oaks. It has the dreariness of stagnation. The raw town sprawls over its sandhills by the Pecos in sun-drenched ugliness. Here the road of dreams that leads out of the past and is shaded by trees rooted in romance, crashes head-on against the iron highway of a modern transportation system.

You find Mrs. Paulita Jaramillo in her own little cottage in the outskirts of the town. If the day is pleasant, she will perhaps be sitting in a rocking chair on her porch, working an embroidery or crocheting a mantilla.

"An old story that identifies me as Billy the Kid's sweetheart," says Mrs. Jaramillo with an indulgent smile, "has been going the rounds for many years. Perhaps it honours me; perhaps not; it depends on how you feel

about it. But I was not Billy the Kid's sweetheart.
I liked him very much—oh, yes—but I did not love him.
He was a nice boy, at least to me, courteous, gallant,
always respectful. I used to meet him at dances; he
was, of course, often at our home. But he and I had no
thought of marriage.

"There was a story that Billy and I had laid our plans
to elope to old Mexico and had fixed the date for the night
just after that on which he was killed.   There was another
tale that we proposed to elope riding double on one horse.
Neither story was true and the one about eloping on one
horse was a joke. Pete Maxwell, my brother, had more
horses than he knew what to do with, and if Billy and I
had wanted to set off for the Rio Grande by the light of
the moon, you may depend upon it we would at least
have had separate mounts. I did not need to put my
arms around any man's waist to keep from falling off a
horse. Not I. I was, if you please, brought up in the
saddle and plumed myself on my horsemanship.

"Billy the Kid, after his escape at Lincoln, came to
Fort Sumner, it is true, to see a woman he was in love with.
But it was not I. Pat Garrett ought to have known who
she was because he was connected with her, and not very
distantly, by marriage. The night the Kid was killed,
Garrett asked Pete Maxwell why the Kid was in Fort
Sumner. Pete shook his head and said he didn't know.
But he merely wanted to save Garrett embarrassment.
He knew and I knew. I was standing beside Pete's
chair at the time and I would have answered Garrett's
question if Pete, by a look, had not warned me to keep my
mouth shut.

"But if I had loved the Kid and he had loved me, I
will say that I would not have hesitated to marry him and

follow him through danger, poverty, or hardship to the ends of the earth in spite of anything he had ever done or what the world might have been pleased to think of me. That is the way of Spanish girls when they are in love."

With an air of frankness, Mrs. Jaramillo tells you the name of the woman who, she declares, was the sweetheart whose fascination drew Billy the Kid to his death. Mrs. Jaramillo's answer to the conundrum that has intrigued the Southwest for almost half a century has, even at this late day, a certain piquant interest; but it is charitable, and perhaps wise, not to rake this ancient bit of gossip out of the ashes of the past. The woman Mrs. Jaramillo names has been dead many years.

"Billy the Kid, I may tell you, fascinated many women," Mrs. Jaramillo continues. "His record as a heart-breaker was quite as formidable, you might say, as his record as a man-killer. Like a sailor, he had a sweetheart in every port of call. In every *placeta* in the Pecos some little señorita was proud to be known as his *querida*. Three girls at least in Fort Sumner were mad about him. One is now a respected matron of Las Vegas. Another, who died long ago, had a daughter who lived to be eight years old and whose striking resemblance to the famous outlaw filled her mother's heart with pride. The third was his inamorata when he was killed.

"Fort Sumner was a gay little place. The weekly dance was an event, and pretty girls from Santa Rosa, Puerto de Luna, Anton Chico, and from towns and ranches fifty miles away, drove in to attend it. Billy the Kid cut quite a gallant figure at these affairs. He was not handsome but he had a certain sort of boyish good looks. He was always smiling and good-natured and very polite and danced remarkably well, and the little Mexican beauties made eyes at him from behind their fans and used all their coquetries to capture him and were very vain of his attentions.

"We had quite a bevy of pretty girls in Fort Sumner. Abrana Garcia, Nasaria Yerbe, and Celsa Gutierrez had a Spanish type of beauty that you associate with castanets and latticed balconies and ancient courtyards filled with the perfume of oleander. They were very graceful dancers, too, and with these three, I think, Billy the Kid danced oftenest. Manuela Bowdre, Charlie Bowdre's wife, was a dark, glowing, slender little creature of high spirits. Poor girl, it broke her heart when Charlie Bowdre was killed by Pat Garrett and his man-hunters. But time mends broken hearts and Manuela married Lafe Holcomb, a cow-puncher, and was living over in the Capitans when I last heard of her. Juanita Martinez, Garrett's first wife, and Apolinaria Gutierrez, his second, were sparkling young women, who had the charm of gaiety and light-heartedness and were always surrounded by admirers at our dances. Juanita was the sister of Don Juan José Martinez, who still lives in new Fort Sumner. Everyone loved her and mourned for her when an unkind fate changed her bridal gown into a shroud three weeks after her wedding. Garrett was more fortunate in his second love affair. Soon after his marriage to Apolinaria Gutierrez, he moved to Roswell and I saw little more of him or his wife, but I always understood they were very happy together.

"You doubtless suspect our Fort Sumner dances were not very fashionable affairs. Well, perhaps not; but they were great fun. The girls were not burdened with wealth and did not get themselves up in expensive and elaborate toilets. But in their simple gowns, made by themselves for the most part, with perhaps a red rose in their black hair or a bunch of blossoms at their waist, they were alluring enough to set any man's heart going pit-a-pat. Nor were they unskilled in the subtle graces and diplomacy of the coquette. They knew how to use their black eyes to good advantage, and they were adept in the old-fashioned Spanish art—gone now from the Southwest—of making their fans talk when their tongues were silent. I will venture it would be hard to find at modern balls and cotillions more spirited or graceful dancers than our Fort Sumner girls. No orchestra concealed behind palm fronds played for us, but we had very good music; generally six pieces—violins, guitars, clarinets, and sometimes a tambe or Indian drum.

"It might surprise you to know that our dances were extremely decorous. Everybody attended them, old and young. We girls of Fort Sumner were not accustomed to dueñas, but with our mothers and grandmothers looking on at our merriment, we were quite well chaperoned. There was no drunkenness, no rowdyism. Our men would not have tolerated anything of the kind for an instant. The men did not wear evening clothes, but they lived up to the old West's traditions of chivalry. I suppose you are amazed that an outlaw and desperado like Billy the Kid should have been a favoured cavalier at our dances. But in the code of those days, any man who was courteous to a woman was considered a gentleman, and no questions asked; and, as there was little law in the country, an outlaw who measured up to this simple standard was as welcome at Fort Sumner's social affairs as anybody else."

You are naturally curious to know how this beautiful and cultured daughter of the House of Maxwell chanced to meet the Southwest's most desperate man-slayer.

"I have a perfectly clear picture of Billy the Kid the first time I ever saw him," says Mrs. Jaramillo. "He was eighteen years old and I was fifteen and back home for a vacation from St. Mary's convent school in Trinidad. It was the Kid's first visit to Fort Sumner. He had ridden over from Lincoln with several of his men, among whom was José Chavez y Chavez. This Chavez y Chavez was a bad fellow; he later served a long term in the penitentiary; he was only recently released and now lives near Las Vegas. Telesfor Jaramillo, who was afterward my brother-in-law, was drunk and met Chavez on the street back of our house. Chavez wanted to shake hands with Telesfor and said, 'You and I are cousins.' That may have been true; I don't know; but Telesfor, being drunk, repudiated the relationship. He drew himself up and refused to shake hands. 'No thief is a cousin of mine,' he said. That made Chavez very mad and he drew his gun. 'I'll kill you for that,' he said.

"My mother saw it all and ran out and caught Telesfor by the arm and tried to drag him away. 'Don't shoot him,' she said to Chavez, 'he's drunk. Wait till he's sober and settle it.' But Chavez refused to be quieted. 'I don't care whether he's drunk or sober,' he said. 'He can't insult me.'

"Just then we saw a young man walking rapidly across the road toward us and someone in the little crowd that had gathered said, 'Here comes Billy the Kid.' I became very much frightened when I heard that name. I had heard many stories of Billy the Kid and his desperate exploits in the Lincoln County war and I said to myself, 'Now we will all be murdered.'

"The Kid had a hard little smile on his face when he came up to us and I was surprised that he looked so boyish and not a bit dangerous.

"'Don't let this man kill my friend,' my mother begged of him.

"The Kid touched his sombrero to my mother. 'Don't be afraid, señora,' he said, 'I'll straighten this out.'

"He said something in Spanish to Chavez, who at once put his six-shooter back in its holster, and the Kid took him by the arm and they walked away.

"Telesfor in the meantime was weaving about unsteadily, and we took him into the house. He had had a very narrow escape, which he didn't seem to realize, being very drunk. But mother and I always thought that he never would have lived to be my brother-in-law if it had not been for Billy the Kid that day."

Don Manuel Abreu, who lives on a ranch within view of the site of old Fort Sumner, tells a piquant little tale about Mrs. Jaramillo.

"Not long after Billy the Kid's death," says Don Manuel, "Pete Maxwell, Paulita, and myself were sitting one night in the living room at the Maxwell home in old Fort Sumner. It was growing late. The town and house were silent. Suddenly we heard a strange noise like softly padding footsteps. It gave us all a thrill. The Kid had been killed in an adjoining bedroom. The sound was ghostly. It ceased. It began again. Just like someone walking softly in stockinged feet.

"'What is that?' Paulita's voice was touched with suppressed excitement.

"'Can it be,' I asked, 'that the Kid has come back from the dead?'

"'Every night since his death,' observed Pete, 'I've heard queer noises about the old house.'

"'Pooh!' Paulita shrugged her shoulders.

"'But, Paulita,' I urged, 'they say the spirits of murdered men often return to haunt the place where they were killed.'

"'Absurd,' she replied.   'I have no patience with people who believe in ghosts.'

"'Have you heard nothing at night of late?' asked Pete.

"'Nothing.'

"'Listen!'   The sound like padding footsteps started up again.

"'Billy the Kid's ghost,' breathed Pete, and made the sign of the cross.

"'I'm not afraid,' said Paulita.   'I'll go see what that is.'

"'Better not go,' I advised her.

"She threw open the door and boldly stepped out on the porch.   In a moment she came back laughing.

"'The ghost of Billy the Kid, eh?' she flung at us contemptuously.   'It was nothing but a stray jackrabbit hopping along the porch.'

"Paulita's discovery relieved the situation that had become oppressively spooky.

"'So, Paulita,' said Pete at length, 'you're not afraid of ghosts?'

"'Not a bit.'

"'And you don't believe the Kid's spirit can come back?'

"'Of course not.'

"'Yet you would be afraid to pass his grave at night.'

"'I'd not be afraid.'

"'Oh, yes, you would.'

"'I tell you I should not.'

"Pete puffed at his pipe a moment in silence.

"'You talk very brave, little sister,' he said.   'I dare you to go out to his grave now.   It is only a little way. What do you say?   Will you go?'

"'Don't be silly, Pedro. Why should I do anything so crazy?'

"'But you say you are so brave. Give us some proof of your courage.'

"Paulita shook her head.

"'It would be foolish of me.'

"Pete looked at me with a smile.

"'She's afraid, Manuel,' he said. 'She hasn't the nerve to go.'

"'Well,' I answered, 'I don't blame her. I wouldn't go myself.'

"'There is no reason for such an imbecile performance,' asserted Paulita.

"'I tell you what I'll do.' Pete pulled out his watch and looked at it. 'It now lacks a few minutes of midnight. I'll give you ten dollars if you go out to Billy the Kid's grave right now.'

"'You're only fooling,' replied Paulita. 'You wouldn't pay me the money.'

"'Here,' said Pete, 'I'll put it up in Manuel's hands.'

"He drew a roll of money from his pocket and passed me a ten-dollar bill. I waved it airily.

"'The money is yours if you win it, Paulita,' I declared.

"'I'll go,' she said.

"'But,' inquired Pete, 'how will I know you have been at the grave?'

"'Why, you'll have to take my word for it, I suppose.'

"'Bring me back something to prove it.'

"'What?'

"'Oh, a weed, a wildflower, a pebble—anything. I will want proof.'

"Paulita marched out the door, through the gate, and on across the old parade ground. Pete and I stood on the porch and watched her fade out of sight in the moonlight.

"'She'll come running back scared to death in a minute,' remarked Pete.

"'I'm not so sure,' I replied.

"We waited a long time.

"'She'll never go through with it,' argued Pete. 'She's a brave girl but she hasn't the nerve to go all alone to Billy the Kid's grave at midnight.'

"'That's the hour when ghosts are said to walk.'

"'She'll pick up a pebble somewhere to fool me and offer it as her proof and claim my ten dollars. You'll see.'

"Pete chuckled.

"She was gone so long we began to grow uneasy. Then at last we heard footsteps. Directly we made out her dim figure in the moonlight coming back.

"'She seems to be carrying something,' said Pete.

"'Yes. What can it be?'

"'The Lord knows.'

"Laughing merrily, Paulita stepped on the porch and shoved some strange-looking object into Pete's arms.

"'Here's your proof,' she said. 'Now give me my ten dollars.'

"Pete carried the object into the lighted parlour to see what proof she had brought. And what do you suppose it was?"

Don Manuel Abreu shook with laughter.

"It was," says he, "the little wooden cross that had stood at the head of Billy the Kid's grave. No possible mistake about it, either. There was his name painted on it."

When Don Manuel's sprightly anecdote is repeated to her, Mrs. Jaramillo smiles with a slightly embarrassed air.

"Yes," she says, "I did that.   But," she adds hastily, "I sent a servant out to the cemetery next morning and had the cross put back in place."

Mrs. Jaramillo, you discover, has a quaint gift for poking fun, and that immemorial quality of mankind known in this modern day as "four-flush" is a favourite butt of her ridicule.

"Barney Mason, Pat Garrett's brother-in-law, lived in Fort Sumner for many years," she says, "and wanted people to think he was much braver than he was.   But despite his boastfulness and his pose as a bad man, Fort Sumner always took his courage with a few grains of salt. When Billy the Kid and his followers were at the height of their success, Barney pretended to be a great friend of theirs; he gave them information, warned them of danger, and could not do enough for them.   But when Pat Garrett was made sheriff and the forces of law began to close in on the Kid, Barney had a change of heart.   He accepted a deputyship under his brother-in-law and became as great an enemy of the Kid as he formerly had been a friend. This embittered the Kid, and he sent word to Barney that he was going to kill him on sight.   Secretly the Kid's threat scared Barney half to death, but he put up a brave show.   'The Kid can't scare me,' he boasted.   'I'll teach him a thing or two if we ever meet.'

"But every time the Kid rode in, Barney rode out.   He never got within a mile of the Kid if he could help it. One day when Barney was driving to town from Santa Rosa with his wife beside him on the wagon seat, he saw the Kid coming toward him on horseback along the road. The situation looked ticklish for Barney; the country was open range and not a tree or rock to hide behind, and a desperado who had sworn to kill him about to pass him within a few feet and face to face.   In this crisis Barney did some quick thinking.   While the Kid was still far off, Barney jerked her black mantilla off his wife and draped it about his own shoulders and clapped her sun-bonnet on his own head.   Then he snuggled down into his seat, made himself look as small as possible, and clucked up his horses into a brisk trot.   With his face concealed beneath the sunbonnet, he drove past the Kid and was greatly relieved when he arrived in Fort Sumner to find himself still alive.   Then he went strutting about town, telling how he had met the Kid on the road and had opened fire on him and the Kid had taken to his heels and had been lucky to escape behind a hill.   'I told you what I'd do to that fellow if we ever met,' boasted Barney.

"And along toward evening, the Kid came jogging into Fort Sumner and, as usual, the panic-stricken Barney got on his horse and ran away and hid himself in the hills. Everybody, of course, wanted to hear from the Kid all about his narrow escape from death at Barney Mason's hands.   When the Kid heard the story Barney had been telling, he bent double with laughter.

"'I recognized him the minute I saw him,' he said. 'His mantilla and sunbonnet didn't fool me.   I would have killed him if his wife hadn't been with him.   I didn't want to drop him over dead in his wife's arms.   His wife was all that saved him.   But with his mantilla and his nice pink sunbonnet, wouldn't he have made a pretty corpse?'"

The only photograph Billy the Kid ever had taken was in possession of the Maxwell family for many years.

"It was taken by a travelling photographer who came through Fort Sumner in 1880," says Mrs. Jaramillo. "Billy posed for it standing in the street near old Beaver

Smith's saloon. I never liked the picture. I don't think it does Billy justice. It makes him look rough and uncouth. The expression of his face was really boyish and very pleasant. He may have worn such clothes as appear in the picture out on the range, but in Fort Sumner he was careful of his personal appearance and dressed neatly and in good taste.

"We had an old servant living with us who went by the name of Deluvina Maxwell. My father had bought her as a child for fifty dollars from a wandering band of Navajo Indians and she had been in our family ever since. Billy the Kid was Deluvina's idol; she worshipped him; to her mind, there never was such a wonderful boy in all the world. When Billy was locked up in the Fort Sumner calaboose after his capture at Arroyo Tivan, Deluvina went to visit him. It was a cold winter's day and, as the little jail was unheated, Deluvina came home and got a heavy scarf she had knitted and took it to her hero. In return for this kindness, the Kid gave her his only photograph which he had carried around in his pocket. He could have given Deluvina nothing she would have prized more.

"My mother kept the picture in a cedar chest for years, and finally my sister, Odila, gave it to John Legg, a Fort Sumner saloon keeper and friend of the family. Legg was shot and killed and Charlie Foor, as executor of his estate, came into possession of the picture. When Foor's house was burned down, the original was destroyed but fortunately many copies of it had been made. A wash drawing made from this photograph hangs in the Governor's Palace at Santa Fé.

"Deluvina is still living at the ranch of my sister, Mrs. Abreu. She is very old and very fat and very superstitious.   She, for one, will not pass, after dark, the little cemetery where the Kid lies buried.   She declares stoutly that she has seen the ghost of a murdered Negro soldier there.   But she says she has never seen the ghost of Billy the Kid.   'Oh, no,' she insists, 'the spirit of that poor child sleeps in peace.'"

Mrs. Jaramillo is not a great admirer of Pat Garrett and, as Garrett killed Billy the Kid, perhaps this is not to be wondered at.

"I remember the first day Pat Garrett ever set foot in Fort Sumner," Mrs. Jaramillo goes on.   "I was a small girl with dresses at my shoe-tops and when he came to our house and asked for a job as a cowboy, I stood behind my brother, Pete Maxwell, and stared at him in open-eyed wonder.   He had the longest legs I had ever seen and he looked so comical and had such a droll way of talking that after he was gone, Pete and I had a good laugh about him. I came to know him well; and after he had gone into business with old Beaver Smith, he used to spend many an evening in our home, spinning yarns about his adventures hunting buffalo in the Panhandle.   He was an easy-going, agreeable man, a good story-teller, and full of dry humour. He was fond of a social glass, and was a great hand to play poker and monte, and everybody liked him.

"Pat Garrett was as close a friend as Billy the Kid had in Fort Sumner and was on friendly terms with every member of the Kid's gang.   When we saw Pat and Billy together we used to call them 'the long and the short of it.'   Pat towered over Billy and would have made two of him.   He ate and drank and played cards with the Kid, went to dances with him and gallivanted around with the same Mexican girls.   I have seen them both on their knees around a horse blanket stretched on the ground in the

main street gambling their heads off against a monte game.
If Pat went broke, he borrowed from Billy, and if Billy
went broke, he borrowed from Pat.   Sometimes they had
friendly shooting contests.   Both were wonderful shots.
It was a toss-up between them when it came to the rifle,
but Billy was the better shot with a revolver.   I remember
once Garrett emptied his pistol at a jackrabbit scampering
through the street and missed it every time and Billy
knocked it over with one bullet from his six-shooter.   Oh,
yes, Garrett and the Kid were as thick as two peas in a
pod.

"Nothing ever gave Fort Sumner such a shock of surprise as Garrett's selection by the cattle interests to be
sheriff of Lincoln County.   He was unknown, he had no
experience as a man-hunter, and no reputation as a fighter.
As far as anybody knew at that time, his only qualification
for the office was his intimate friendship with the Kid and
his men.   He was familiar with all their old trails, their
favourite haunts, their secret places of rendezvous and
refuge.   The one thing Garrett was called on to do as
sheriff was to hunt down these old friends and kill them
or put them in the penitentiary, and he did it methodically
and in cold blood.   I do not say this with malice; it is
simply a fact.   There is no law against a man's turning
against his old friends or hunting them to their deaths.
But it was against the unwritten code of the frontier; and
many men would rather have been killed themselves than
undertake such a job.   I will say for Garrett that he was
absolutely frank about what he proposed to do.   When he
became sheriff, Billy the Kid knew exactly what it meant.
From that time on, it was war to the death between them.

"I knew both men well and, in my opinion, Garrett was
just as cold and hard a character as the Kid.   The great

difference between them was that Garrett had the law on his side and the Kid was outside the law.   I will add this—and there are many men in New Mexico who will tell you the same thing—Pat Garrett was afraid of the Kid and of his own free will would no more have dared to meet him alone than he would have dared to enter a den of lions. Garrett finally killed the Kid, but the Kid was shot in the dark and did not have a chance on earth for his life.   It was not cowardly in Garrett.   He killed him in the only way the Kid could have been killed.   But if the Kid had had an inkling of the danger he was in, Garrett probably would have been the one to die."

CHAPTER XV

THE West was in the golden period of its development in 1880. Days of the covered wagon were gone. The Oregon and Santa Fé trails were memories. Colonists were swarming westward over trails of steel. Towns, churches, schools were springing up all over the old ranges of the buffalo. The prairies were being turned into farms. Kansas, Nebraska, and Dakota had become rich agricultural states. Settlers were pouring into Texas, Colorado, Wyoming, Montana, and on into Utah, Idaho, California, and the states of the Pacific Northwest. Land was cheap; much of it was free; prosperity and a farm home awaited all who cared to come and work. The West was calling poor men, rich men, investors, labourers, with a voice of welcome. It was the continent's last wonderful land of opportunity—bonanza land—and boom days were upon all the country west of the Missouri.

But with the human tides sweeping westward, New Mexico was neglected. The vast, vague land beyond the Pecos was as little known to the people of the East as Timbuctoo to-day. It was regarded as a region of lawlessness, desperadoes, and sudden death. The Lincoln County war and the subsequent reign of terror Billy the Kid had set up had given the territory an evil reputation. Yet the Santa Fé railroad had crossed the Ratons. Vast areas of rich soil awaited the settler. Opportune fields for livestock breeders lay in the boundless, unfenced pastures. Irrigation projects promised wealth to investors. It was a country of many-sided opportunity lying practically uncultivated. If New Mexico was to build for the future and take advantage of the immense westward movement of home-seekers it was vitally necessary that it first clean house. If this potentially rich territory was to share in the prosperity of the new day that was dawning in the West, the desperado must be exterminated and lawlessness suppressed.

John Chisum had the future of New Mexico at heart and recognized the crisis. If law and order were to be established, a war was necessary. Chisum launched that war. It was a war primarily against lawlessness. Incidentally it was a war against Billy the Kid as the head and front of lawless forces. The extinction of the outlaw was imperative. The new era demanded it. The call of statehood was the desperado's trump of doom.

Pat Garrett had moved to Roswell. John Chisum, J. C. Lea, and other cattlemen, casting about for a man they deemed qualified to conduct the war against lawlessness, selected him. They urged him to run for sheriff of Lincoln County. They promised his election. In making him the offer they laid their cards on the table. The position was to carry one positive obligation—the extermination of Billy the Kid. Garrett had been a friend of Billy the Kid. So had Chisum. That made no difference. This was to be a fight for New Mexico. Sentimental considerations must be waved aside. Friendships must be forgotten. The work called for a man of shrewdness, courage, determination, and force of character. Garrett was that kind of man. He accepted the proposition, was nominated and elected.

With Sheriff Garrett in the saddle, the toils began to tighten about the Kid. All the forces of law were marshalled to the aid of the new sheriff. The United States Government sent Azariah F. Wild, a Secret Service operative, into Lincoln County. Frank Stewart, with a posse of man-trailers in the employ of a cattleman's association of Texas, was out on the hunt for the outlaw. John W. Poe, in the service of cattle interests in the Panhandle and the Canadian River country, was on the trail.

The Kid was growing wary. With Billy Wilson, Dave Rudabaugh, Charlie Bowdre, and Tom O'Folliard he spent his twenty-first birthday in White Oaks; but he did not celebrate the occasion hilariously in saloons and dance halls. He kept under cover, and a few swigs out of a bottle among clandestine friends were his only commemoration of the event. As he and his band rode out of town next day, the Kid remarked Deputy Sheriff Jim Woodland standing on the main street in front of the Pioneer saloon. Riding along a hillside, the Kid dropped a bullet close to the deputy's feet by way of hail and farewell. "It was only a friendly shot," he explained to O'Folliard, who protested that Woodland had been an old friend in Texas and they had come to New Mexico together. Misinterpreting the Kid's winged message of friendliness, Woodland, with Jim Carlyle and J. N. Bell, also deputies, sent a six-shooter volley after the Kid which was not friendly but happened to be futile.

White Oaks thereupon agreed officially that the Kid's impudence merited drastic punishment and a posse was organized to pursue him. With Deputy Sheriff Will Hudgens in command, the posse consisted of Johnny Hudgens, brother of the leader, J. N. Bell, Jim Carlyle, Jim Watts, John Mosby, Jim Brent, J. P. Langston, Ed

Bonnell, W. G. Dorsey, J. P. Baker, and Charles Kelly, all White Oaks men, Will Hudgens being a saloon keeper as well as deputy sheriff.

Early in the morning, with heavy snow on the ground and bitterly cold, they came upon the Kid's camp at Coyote Springs. The outlaws, eating breakfast about a camp fire, leaped on their horses and dashed away under a fusillade of bullets. The Kid's horse was shot dead. On foot and hard-pressed, he escaped into the high hills. His overcoat and gloves were found in camp, and Carlyle appropriated the gloves. After following the rustlers for several miles, the posse gave over the pursuit and returned to White Oaks.

Word came on November 27th that the Kid and his men had rounded up at Jim Greathouse's ranch and roadhouse forty miles from town on the trail to Anton Chico. Again the posse took up the hunt, and dawn found them lying in ambush around the Greathouse building. John Steck, the Greathouse cook, emerging to gather firewood, was captured and gave the posse definite assurance that the Kid and his followers were inside. Will Hudgens sent in a note by Steck demanding the Kid's surrender. Greathouse himself brought back the Kid's reply. It read simply: "Go to hell."

Deputy Carlyle suggested that he himself go in and have a talk with the Kid, whom he had met often at White Oaks bars and with whom he had been on terms of cautious friendliness. Leader Hudgens refused to permit such foolhardiness. Then up spoke Greathouse. "The Kid won't hurt him," said he. "I'll agree to be your hostage. If the Kid kills Carlyle, you can kill me."

Hudgens accepted this proposition, still with vague doubts. Carlyle, he thought, might be able to make clear to the Kid the hopelessness of his situation and persuade him to surrender without bloodshed. The Kid was to be given to understand, Hudgens impressed upon his emissary, that Carlyle must return to the posse by two o'clock in the afternoon. If he failed to return, Hudgens was to assume that the Kid intended to kill him, and Greathouse's life was to pay the penalty. So, laying aside his six-shooter and rifle, Carlyle walked into the house.

He found the Kid and his men in the barroom in the front part of the building. The Kid received him with indifferent friendliness, told him that gang outside never would take him alive and invited him to have a drink. Espying his gloves sticking from Carlyle's pocket, the Kid snatched them out. "What are you doing with my gloves?" he asked. Carlyle attempted to explain. "I suppose you've got my overcoat, too," said the Kid. No, somebody else had that. The Kid looked a little ugly. "I thought you were a friend of mine," he said, "and here you are hunting me and trying to kill me." Carlyle argued that he was there to try to save the Kid's life by inducing him to give up. For a moment the Kid glowered resentfully.

"I'll just kill you while I've got a good chance!" he said at length, and drew his six-shooter. "Go on and drink your drink. It's the last you'll ever take on earth."

Carlyle turned off his whisky and the outlaws drank with him. The Kid set down his glass, smiled, and slipped his gun back in its scabbard.

"I was just joking, Jimmy," he said pleasantly. "I wouldn't kill you."

Carlyle found that talking surrender was useless; he suggested that he go back to his own men. But the Kid would not let him go. Two o'clock came, marking the expiration of the time limit of his mission. One of the posse outside foolishly shot off his rifle. Carlyle jumped to the conclusion that Greathouse had been killed and his own death would follow. He made a sudden dive through a window, crashing through glass and framework. The Kid jerked his revolver, and while Carlyle was in midair, sent a bullet through him. Badly wounded, Carlyle struck the ground on his hands and knees and began to crawl away. The Kid's second shot stretched him out dead in the snow.

At once the posse opened a bombardment of the house with their rifles. For hours they kept it up, and during the excitement Greathouse escaped. Shortly after dark, half-frozen, with fingers so numb from the cold they could hardly pull a trigger, without blankets for the night and not daring to kindle a fire, the posse gave up the adventure and went back to White Oaks. An hour or so later, the Kid and his band, with six-shooters blazing in the empty darkness, dashed out the door, thinking themselves still hemmed in by hidden foes. Discovering the enemy gone, they made their way to Anton Chico. Here, having refreshed themselves and obtained new mounts, they rode away to Fort Sumner.

Greathouse showed good wisdom in flight. Carlyle's death inflamed the possemen, who, regarding Greathouse in a measure responsible, would have murdered him doubtless in retaliation. The next day the posse returned and burned the Greathouse place to the ground. Greathouse did not venture back. He was later killed while asleep by Joel Fowler, a drunken desperado, who was lynched by a mob in Socorro for another and equally cowardly murder.

Christmas Eve in old Fort Sumner. Good cheer and happiness in the air. Latchstrings hanging out. Warmhearted hospitality in every home. Healths pledged in cheerful bumpers in old Beaver Smith's saloon. A great amphora of egg-nog standing invitingly on José Valdez's bar. Women with happy faces slipping through the streets with furtive bundles tucked beneath *rebozos*. Deluvina Maxwell, the Navajo servant, roasting the family turkey in the Maxwell kitchen. Christmas trees hung with gifts and lighted with wax tapers to be seen through the windows. Happy little ones tucked in beds to dream of Santa Claus. Snow on the ground; the Pecos frozen over; a clear sky spangled with stars.

There was to be a great ball in Fort Sumner on Christmas night. All the gay young fellows and the pretty girls of the upper Pecos Valley were to attend. Paulita Maxwell had had a costly gown made for the occasion by a fashionable modiste in Las Vegas. Billy the Kid and his merry men were to ride in and give the affair its last touch of dashing gaiety. The gallant young outlaw, so the village gossip ran, had sent word that he would surely be present. And, his message added, he would come in from the north by the Texas road and arrive in Fort Sumner late on Christmas Eve.

Barney Mason, having a sly and eager ear for village gossip, spurred hard across bleak, wintry wastes to carry these tidings to Sheriff Pat Garrett at Roswell ninety miles away. To Garrett the welcome news was like a direct message from Billy the Kid inviting him to keep an appointment and setting the trysting place. Hastily gathering together fifteen men seasoned in fighting and upon whose courage he could rely, he set out for Fort Sumner and, by hard riding, reached it on Christmas Eve.

After nightfall, he slipped unnoticed into town and, having put up his horses in Pete Maxwell's barn, went into comfortable ambush in the old military hospital at the edge of the village on the Texas road and settled down to await the coming of his quarry.

So on this night when all the world was happy, a bare room in the old hospital was filled with heavily armed men. A fire of pitch-pine knots roared in the chimney, irradiating the chamber with ruddy light. Smoke from pipes and cigarettes hung in the air in strata and lazily drifting whorls. The men, the majority Mexicans, stalked about restlessly or sat cross-legged on the floor along the walls, their rifles across their laps. There was desultory talk.

Sheriff Garrett, Barney Mason, Tom Emory, and Bob Williams played poker on a blanket on the floor. Frank Stewart, the cattle detective from Texas, Lee Hall, Louis Bozeman, and Juan Roibal stood watching the game. Jim East took his ease stretched out on a blanket and whiffed at a meditative pipe. Lon Chambers mounted guard in the road outside.

"What time is it?" drawled East.

"Quarter to twelve," replied Lee Hall, pulling out his old silver timepiece.

"Old Santa Claus in his reindeer sleigh has snow to travel on to-night and he ought to be in Fort Sumner pretty soon," reflected East. "Only a quarter of an hour till Christmas. Wish I was with the folks back in Tascosa."

"Two cards," said Garrett at his poker game on the blanket.

"One to me," chimed Emory.

There was a jingle of silver coins as the men tossed their bets into the pot.

"I'll call," said Emory. "What you got?"

"Three kings," replied Garrett.

"Beats aces up."

Garrett was raking in his winnings when Chambers burst in at the door.

"All right, boys," he called. "The Kid's coming."

The four poker players left their cards scattered on the blanket. A thrill of excitement ran through the crowd. Each man gave his rifle a hasty examination and hitched his six-shooter a little to the front. They rushed out of the door into the white clear night. A little distance out the road, hidden by a corner of the building, they could hear the thud of horses' hoofs approaching at a gallop.

"Five of them," whispered East, peeking around the corner.

They waited for the horsemen to come nearer. The hoofbeats sounded just beyond the building. The men crowded out into the road, rifles cocked and ready. Less than fifteen yards away the five outlaws were bearing down upon them. One rode a little way in front.

"Throw up your hands!"

It was Garrett's voice and he had his rifle at his shoulder. The foremost horseman whipped out his six-shooter. Before he could fire, Garrett sent a bullet through his body close to the heart. The rifles of the possemen began to crack. The four other riders wheeled their horses and raced away in the darkness under a rain of bullets.

The man whom Garrett had shot, still sitting upright in his saddle, his horse suddenly reined to a walk, rode in among the possemen.

"Get those hands up quick or I'll kill you," cried Garrett.

"Don't shoot any more," answered the man. "I'm as good as dead already."

He began to waver. As Garrett and Barney Mason stepped to his horse's side, he fell over and slipped down into their arms. It was Tom O'Folliard.

They laid him in the snow. He had lost consciousness and they thought him dead. Suddenly he revived and began to scream curses on Garrett's head.

"I'll put a dead man's curse on you," he shouted. "You've killed me but you'll die like a dog yourself some day, and I hope you burn in hell."

Barney Mason bent over him.

"No use making a fuss, Tom," said he. "Be game. Take your medicine like a man."

They carried him inside and laid him on a blanket in a corner. There, as he writhed in agony, he raved and swore and called down maledictions on Garrett. His voice gradually grew weaker. Weaker still. He was plainly dying. He could not last much longer.

Garrett, Emory, Mason, and Williams went back to their card game.

"I'm betting two dollars on my hand," remarked Mason.

"That's a lot of money, Barney," returned Garrett, "but I'll just see what you've got."

He tossed some coins to the centre of the blanket.

The curses from the corner ceased. The dying man went into a spasm. His limbs twitched and straightened. He made a convulsive effort to sit up.

"God damn Pat Garrett," he muttered, and fell back dead.

"Jacks and eights," said Barney Mason.

"The dead man's hand," answered Garrett. "It wins."

For several hours, on the authority of Jim East and

Barney Mason, the poker game continued while O'Folliard lay dead on his blanket in the corner.

The four outlaws who had been with O'Folliard when he was shot were Billy Wilson, Tom Pickett, Dave Rudabaugh, and Charlie Bowdre.   Billy the Kid had separated from them a few miles from town for some prudent reason of his own and was riding alone along the cottonwood avenue when he heard the firing.   He swung about on the back trail and rejoined his companions in their mad dash to escape which ended at Wilcox's ranch ten miles north of Fort Sumner.   Here the outlaws passed the night in warm beds, and after breakfast next day struck northward, disappearing like gray ghosts in a blinding blizzard. Dave Rudabaugh's horse had been shot by Garrett's men and fell over dead a mile from town, where it subsequently was found, Rudabaugh mounting behind Wilson to continue his flight.

It would have been useless for Garrett to take up the pursuit of the outlaws next morning.   Before dawn, a driving snowstorm had set in and extinguished the trail as one blows out a candle.   The posse remained in Fort Sumner and buried O'Folliard in the little cemetery east of town.   It was a strange little funeral, without bead or book or ceremony, fit period to the futile, wild career of the youth who had followed blindly and faithfully the fortunes of Billy the Kid.   Only a handful of men stood about the grave as the rough pine box containing all that was left of Tom O'Folliard was lowered into the earth; among them, Pat Garrett, who had killed him, tall and grim in the slithering, wind-blown snow.

When the storm ceased after nightfall, Pecos Valley lay buried a foot deep in feathery whiteness; the skies cleared as if the clouds had been swept away by a broom: a windless calm followed the blizzard, and it fell bitterly cold. Rancher Wilcox rode in with the information that the outlaws had headed in the direction of Stinking Spring, otherwise known as Tivan Arroyo, where there was an old abandoned stone house once used by sheep herders, in which he surmised they probably would take shelter. With this clue, Garrett and his posse set out from Fort Sumner at midnight, following a blind trail through the endless drifts and the white silence.

The first glimmer of dawn was in the east when they arrived at Stinking Spring. Before them, the little gray stone hut took form in the blue obscurity, the snow drifted about it, three horses shivering with drooping heads in front, tethered by ropes to the *viga* poles of the flat roof. The house had no windows and only one door; within was profound stillness. Leaving his horses concealed in a draw in charge of Frank Stewart and several Mexicans, Garrett posted sentinels around the house. Then with Jim East, Lee Hall, and Tom Emory, he stole silently through an arroyo and halted under shelter of its embankment within thirty feet of the door.

The glow of approaching sunrise was red on the snow when the silent watchers in the arroyo heard sleepy voices and the slight stir of awakening life inside the hut. Out the door stepped Charlie Bowdre, in his hand a canvas nose-bag half-filled with oats for his pony.

"We've got you covered, Charlie. Throw up your hands," called Garrett.

Bowdre, with the automatic gesture of old custom, snatched his six-shooter from its holster. The movement was fatal. A bullet from Garrett's rifle crashed through his chest. He swayed and staggered convulsively in the snow as if in half-delirious dance. Another ball from Lee

Hall's gun struck him in the shoulder, almost knocking him down. He turned and blundered back into the
house.

Here was a man who had been Billy the Kid's comrade
for years, dared death with him, gone with him through
innumerable dangers. It might be fancied the Kid
caught his sorely wounded bosom friend in his arms, laid
him gently down, made his last moments on earth as comfortable as possible. But the strange psychology of the
young desperado had been fashioned in a mould of ice.
There was no hope for his old-time companion in arms
whose life was fast ebbing. Dying, he appealed to the
Kid merely as an opportunity—an opportunity for vengeance. The voice of the Kid came with cold clearness to
the ambushed men in the ditch.

"They've got you, Charlie," said the Kid. "You're
about done for. Go out and see if you can't kill one of
those fellows before you die."

The door opened meagrely. Bowdre staggered out,
helped by a slight push from the Kid's hand. The rising
sun shone full in his face. With unsteady, zigzag steps,
he walked toward his hidden foe, his six-shooter clutched
in his hand dangling helplessly at his side, his eyes staring
blankly, his face of ashen pallor. Garrett and his comrades knew he was dying on his feet and did not fire. Fal-
tering and weaving, Bowdre reached the brink of the arroyo. "I wish—I wish——" he murmured. What did
the poor devil wish? No one will ever know. He pitched
dead into the arroyo, into Pat Garrett's arms.

In addition to the three horses tethered to the *viga* poles,
the outlaws had two horses inside the house. The horses
offered the one vague hope of escape. Resting their rifles
on the bank of the arroyo and drawing careful beads,

Garrett and East cut the ropes of two of the ponies with bullets and the frightened animals galloped away. Garrett killed the third horse, which fell in such a position that its body blocked the doorway. It was a piece of strategy that rendered the two horses inside useless to the outlaws. No chance now for the Kid to ride out of the door and make a wolf-dart for freedom.

Garrett opened a parley; across the thirty feet intervening between besiegers and besieged it was possible to carry on a conversation with distinctness.

"You'd better surrender, Billy," called Garrett. "You haven't a chance to escape. You won't have any more chance to-night than you have to-day. If you fellows try to make a dash, we'll kill you as fast as you come out the door."

"Go to hell, Pat," sang out Billy cheerfully. "You haven't got me yet. I'll show you a trick or two by and bye."

Garrett heard the outlaws picking with their knives at the mortar between the stones on the far side of the house with evident design to open a hole, through which escape after nightfall might be attempted. He sent East and Emory around the house to guard against such an eventuality.

Never before had the Kid been in more desperate plight; nor in one more poignantly uncomfortable. The one chance in a million seemed lacking. The door, which offered the one avenue of escape, opened on sure death. He and his men had had nothing to eat since breakfast the day before. Hungry and numb with cold, they sat miserably in their bleak prison and debated contingencies.

"It looks bad," Billy the Kid was heard to remark. "But you never can tell. We may get a chance yet.

No use surrendering. They'll hang us if we do. I'd rather die by a bullet than the rope."

"Garrett will kill every man who shows up outside the door," argued Tom Pickett. "He's killed O'Folliard and he's killed Charlie Bowdre and he'll kill us. We'd better give up."

Late in the afternoon, Garrett sent over to Brazel's ranch house not far away for food and coffee for his men. A wagon brought back bacon, eggs, coffee, and utensils in which to cook them. He kindled a little fire in the bottom of the arroyo and prepared a hot meal. The appetizing savours of the cooking penetrated to the four dispirited men cooped up in their stone jail.

"Hey, Pat," the Kid shouted, with what humour remained in him, "send us over a pot of coffee."

"Come on out and get some, Billy, but come with your hands up," called back Garrett. "Hot coffee goes mighty good this cold weather."

The end came quickly now and the smell of that campfire coffee may have been the deciding factor. The sun was setting when Garrett spied something white fluttering above the roof. It proved to be a handkerchief fastened to a rifle barrel and poked up out of the chimney.

"We'll surrender, Pat," the Kid called, "if you give us your word you won't shoot into us as we come out."

Garrett gave his promise and the Kid and his three companions filed out the door, hands up, into the crimson sunset.

Despite Garrett's promise, Barney Mason, "that traitor," as East calls him, remembering Billy's threats against him and his threats against Billy, levelled his rifle at the Kid's breast; but East and Hall covered him with their guns instantly and prevented the assassination.

With Bowdre's body rolled in a blanket in a wagon, Garrett took his four prisoners to Brazel's ranch house, where they spent the night; and so to Fort Sumner next day. Jim East and Louis Bozeman carried Bowdre's body into his home. When Manuela Bowdre saw her husband dead, she went into a hysteria of weeping. With the madness upon her, she seized a branding-iron and bent it over East's head, his hat alone saving him from a cracked skull. The two men dropped the corpse on the floor at the feet of the grief-crazed woman and hurried out the door.

"I always regretted the death of Charlie Bowdre," wrote East in after years. "He was a brave man and true to his friends to the last."

This tribute of a warrior to a vanquished foe is worth remembering. Bowdre was an outlaw and a member of a cut-throat band. But what nobler qualities can any man possess than courage and loyalty to his friends "to the last?"

They buried Bowdre beside O'Folliard. There were two graves in a row now in the little cemetery. Before many moons waxed and waned there was to be a third. Sheriff Pat Garrett's campaign for law and order was progressing notably.

CHAPTER XVI

THE DANGLING SHADOW

SHERIFF GARRETT planned to take his four prisoners on horseback across country to Las Vegas,
forty miles by the Santa Rosa road, and then on
by rail to Santa Fé. Before starting he bought them a
drink in Beaver Smith's saloon as a warm bracer for the
hard, cold journey. Now that Billy the Kid was his
prisoner, there was no show of resentment or enmity on
the part of either. As far as appearances went, a spirit of
cordial camaraderie prevailed between them. They addressed each other as "Billy" and "Pat" and seemed as
friendly as they once had been in their days of intimate
association in Fort Sumner. They talked of old times,
discussed old friends, recalled old incidents.

"Remember, Billy, the time you knocked over the jackrabbit with your six-shooter when I had missed it six
times?"

"Yes, I remember. That was a joke on you, Pat."

"I'm better with a rifle. Ought to be. Had enough
practice killing buffalo for a living in the Panhandle."

"I'm better with the six-shooter. Ought to be. Had
plenty of practice with it. At tin cans and men."

So they fraternized in pleasant talk. Except that the
Kid wore handcuffs and Garrett was never without rifle
and six-shooter, you might have thought them comrades
with only affection for each other. But if the occasion
had warranted, either would have killed the other between

anecdotes. Laughter and death were accepted as mere details of the day's routine by these men who carried their lives in their hands and never knew what moment would be their last. When it was requisite to kill, they killed; when there was no immediate necessity for murder, they observed the ordinary amenities.

Deputy Sheriff Jim East, a distinctly human sort of man, as kindly as brave, had found especial favour with the Kid and the Kid presented him with his Winchester rifle as a keepsake. "But," says East, "old Beaver Smith made such a roar about an account he said Billy owed him that, at the Kid's request, I let the old reprobate have the gun. I am sorry now I did not keep it."

Accompanied by Deputies East and Emory, Sheriff Garrett with his prisoners rode across the hills to Las Vegas, Billy the Kid wearing about his throat the heavy scarf the Indian woman, Deluvina Maxwell, had given him. Las Vegas was a danger point. Only a few months before Rudabaugh had killed the jailer there and broken to freedom. But it was the only convenient point at which the railroad could be reached. When Garrett arrived, the Santa Fé train, which made up at Las Vegas, was standing in the depot yards almost ready to pull out. As the spot was in the outskirts, the sheriff got his prisoners into a coach without attracting much attention. But somehow the news of his arrival was quickly bruited through the town, and in a little while citizens, still nursing their wrath against the slayer of the jailer, were swarming to the train from all directions. In vain Garrett jerked at the bell-cord to signal the engineer to start. The mob had anticipated him by dragging the engineer from the locomotive cab. This bit of strategy accomplished, it surged hooting and yelling about the coach in which the prisoners were held.

"Where's Rudabaugh?" shouted the blood-mad citizens. "String him up to a telegraph pole."

"Hang Billy the Kid, too."

"Make a clean sweep and lynch 'em all."

While the crowd stormed outside, Garrett turned to Billy the Kid, who sat in his seat without sign of perturbation looking out a window with half-smiling, curious interest.

"Billy," he said, "it looks ugly. If they rush the door, I'm going to take off your handcuffs and give you a six-shooter and I'll expect you to help stand them off."

"All right, Pat," returned the Kid cheerfully. "You and I can lick 'em all. I'll guarantee to kill a man with every bullet."

Garrett's appeal to the outlaw in this desperate crisis showed clearly the estimate he placed upon Billy the Kid as a fighting man.

Leaving East and Emory to guard the prisoners, Garrett stepped out on the platform alone and faced the howling, swirling mob. He raised his hand for silence.

"Take my advice, men," he said. "Don't break the law yourselves. Play the part of good citizens. Go back to your homes. The law will take care of these men. As an officer of the law, I am here to protect them and I'm going to do it. You can't take any of these men away from me, and if you try, some of you are going to be killed."

The mob greeted the speech with curses and crushed forward. Several clutched at the platform rails, swung upon the car steps, but fell back when they looked into the muzzle of Garrett's revolver. Suddenly the train be-

gan to move.   Deputy Sheriff Tom Malloy of Las Vegas
had jumped into the engine cab and thrown the throttle
wide open.   With a rattle and click of wheels on rails, the
train gathered quick headway and went skimming out of
town, leaving the baffled mob cursing, yelling, shaking
impotent fists.

Billy the Kid and the three other prisoners finally were
landed in the jail at Santa Fé, the penitentiary now there
not having yet been built.   Placed on trial for the murder
of the Las Vegas jailer, Rudabaugh was sentenced to be
hanged.   Sent back to Las Vegas, he broke jail a second
time and never was heard of again in that country nor is
it known to this day what became of him.   Pickett and
Wilson, after serving a jail sentence in Santa Fé, were set
at liberty and returned to peaceful pursuits.   Billy the
Kid was taken to Mesilla in March for trial.

Mesilla was not unfamiliar to the young outlaw.   In
the little town, predominantly Mexican, on the west bank
of the Rio Grande opposite Las Cruces, he had been bap-
tized for all time in quaint cowboy nomenclature as Billy
the Kid.   Here, too, he had adventured pleasantly in
younger days with Jesse Evans, Jim McDaniels, Billy
Morton, and Frank Baker, the latter two murdered by
him at Agua Negra.   But only a few gamblers and saloon
keepers had now any definite memories of the boy who
once had hung about the town bars and picked up a
precarious living at faro and monte.   Everybody knew
him by reputation, however, and everybody wanted to
see the famous man-killer who for years had terrorized
New Mexico.

The trial was a memorable event in Mesilla's history.
The town was crowded as it never had been before.
Country folk came in from miles around.   Wagons and

saddle horses stood in close ranks up and down the streets. Men and women elbowed their way along the usually empty sidewalks toward the old courthouse in the public square as if to a theatre in which the curtain was about to rise on a fascinating drama.

When the doors were thrown open, the courtroom was packed to the walls in a trice, and those who failed to gain entrance stood at the windows on boxes and barrels and peered over the heads of the more fortunate ones inside.

Judge Warren H. Bristol was on the bench. This was the magistrate whose life the Kid once had threatened and who had refused to hold court in Lincoln while the desperado in the rôle of frontier Robespierre drew up his proscription lists and directed his reign of terror.

A scuffle of feet sounded at the door. "Make way," cried a voice. A buzz of excited interest swept the courtroom. There was a craning of necks. All eyes were bent upon a slender youth who walked through the aisle to a chair in front of the tribune, guarded by Deputy Sheriffs Bob Ollinger and Dave Woods. The crowd gasped. Was it possible that this pale, smiling, neatly dressed lad was the notorious man-slayer? With his wavy brown hair and smooth, beardless face, he looked like a clean, unsophisticated, good-natured boy. If there was murder in his soul, there seemed none in his frank, friendly gray eyes. The daintiness of his feet in their half-boots of soft leather did not escape attention. His hands, as small and delicate as a woman's, seemed unequal to dealing death from heavy six-shooters. In comparison the two armed deputies looked lowering and brutal. It seemed a shame that this harmless-looking youth should be in the custody of such burly savages. Feminine eyes softened with pity.

"Have you a lawyer?"

It was Judge Bristol who asked the question, leaning forward with manner that was at once courteous and impersonal, and looking into the eyes of the youth who once had sworn to kill him. The Kid shook his head.

"No money with which to hire a lawyer?"

"No." The Kid's eyes tightened and his mouth hardened at the admission. This was an unexpected humiliation. He had had promises of financial assistance. But not a friend had dared come to his aid in his extremity. The famous outlaw stood before the court as a pauper.

Again with impassive, formal courtesy, Judge Bristol appointed Ira E. Leonard of Lincoln to conduct the defense. It was the Kid's first acquaintance with the machine-like precision of court procedure. He began to sense for the first time in his life the cold, inexorable power and momentum of the law.

The Kid was placed on trial for the murder of Agency Clerk Bernstein on the Mescalero reservation. There had been no eyewitnesses except members of the Kid's own band. These were dead now or driven out of the country. The evidence for the prosecution was inconsequential. The jury brought in a verdict of acquittal without leaving the box. The Kid took heart. He smiled broadly. His prospects were looking up.

He was tried immediately afterward for the murder of Sheriff Brady. There had been several eyewitnesses to this assassination. "Dad" Peppin, Billy Matthews, "Bonny" Baca took the stand. Peppin and Matthews had been Brady's companions; Baca had witnessed the murder from the old stone tower in Lincoln that the pioneers had built as protection against the Indians. One after the other they told clear, straightforward stories that fastened guilt irrefutably upon the Kid and that Attorney Leonard, for all his shrewdness as a cross-examiner, was unable to shake.

The speeches were made. That of the prosecuting attorney was packed with facts; that of the counsel for the defense, fervid with eloquence. Lawyer Leonard emphasized "the reasonable doubt." He sounded the sentimental note . . . "this poor persecuted boy" . . . "a conspiracy of hatred to railroad an innocent youth to the gallows" . . . "the dead mother who loved him tenderly" . . . "if he were your own son" . . . The jury retired.

The courtroom relaxed. The crowd gossiped, weighing the case with light comment, advancing guesses on the outcome. "He's innocent." "Ought to be hanged." "You never can tell." "The dear God himself does not know what a jury will do."

Loud raps sounded on the door from inside the jury room. A bailiff bustled out. The jurymen came back into court and filed into the box. An instant hush fell upon the crowd.

"Gentlemen," said the judge, "have you agreed upon a verdict?"

"We have."

"The clerk will read it."

The clerk took the folded paper from the foreman's hand. As he opened it and smoothed it out, the crackle of the sheet of foolscap could be heard to the farthest corner in the perfect stillness.

"We, the jury, find the defendant, William H. Bonney, guilty of murder in the manner and form charged in the indictment and we fix his punishment at death."

The Kid received the verdict stoically. It was hardly a

surprise. He had always said he would have no chance in any court in New Mexico. Well, he was right. But his trial struck him as a sort of farce. He had seen sportsmen refuse to shoot a jackrabbit sitting in the sagebrush. They must first kick him up, let him run, and then neatly bowl him over. That was like this court justice that had been dished out to him. The judge had been polite. He had given him a lawyer. He had let him think he had a chance. And then the verdict of death. In the rabbit's case, it was sportsmanship; in this case, it was justice. Humph!

"William Bonney, stand up."

The Kid stepped before the bar.

"Have you anything to say," asked the judge, "why sentence of death should not be passed upon you?"

"No," replied the Kid with conversational nonchalance, "and if I did have anything to say, it wouldn't do me any good."

"Your crime," said Judge Bristol in austere tones, "was atrocious. You have had a fair trial. Everything has been done to protect your interests. After weighing the evidence, the jury has found you guilty. It is now my duty to pass judgment upon you. It is the order of the court that you be taken to Lincoln and confined in jail until May the thirteenth and that on that day, between the hours of sunrise and noon, you be hanged on a gallows until you are dead, dead, dead. And may God have mercy on your soul."

The solemn words of doom fell upon the silence in the courtroom like clods upon a coffin in a grave. The Kid stood erect, staring at the judge with unblinking eyes. There was neither defiance nor bravado in his look. He listened to the judgment with a certain grave dignity.

Back to his cell in the little jail he marched between his guards. When the iron door had slammed upon him, Bob Ollinger, his ancient enemy, stood outside the bars and surveyed him with a sneer.

"So you got the rope, Kid?" he taunted. "Serves you right. They'll hang you like a dog. And I'll be standing right under the gallows. I want to see you kick."

An unpleasant character was this Bob Ollinger, with whom it is requisite, for a brief term, to get on terms of more intimate acquaintance. He played a definite part in the drama of Billy the Kid and left a certain fame in New Mexico, due, perhaps, more to his death than his life, though his life was not without colourful episode. A broad-shouldered, powerful man, well past forty, dour, inflammable, of quick energy, with red face and whitish-blue eyes. Of colossal egotism, he fancied himself a hero of melodrama and was for ever dramatizing himself with spectacular tricks. He posed as a desperado and delighted in the awe his pose inspired.

He was vain of his personal appearance, which, in fact, was picturesque. He wore his hair so long it fell upon his shoulders, imagining his flowing locks made him look like Wild Bill Hickok, though he in no wise resembled that famous frontiersman either in appearance or character. He loved to parade in public in a buck-skin hunting coat, fringed and elaborately decorated with designs in coloured beads and porcupine quills after the manner of the scouts and Indian fighters of an earlier day. He always carried a six-shooter hanging from his cartridge belt on one side and a long bowie knife on the other.

Thus gorgeously costumed and armed to the teeth, with his sombrero cocked on the side of his head, his pants tucked in his gaily embroidered boots, he was an eye-filling spectacle and looked as if he might have stepped out of the pages of the most lurid dime novel that ever thrilled the soul of boyhood. No chance tenderfoot ever set eyes upon him tricked out in his frontier bravery who did not immediately accept him as the beau ideal of the traditional bad man. When he visited such polite centres as Santa Fé and Las Vegas, he caused a furore. In the rôle of a daredevil of the plains, he swaggered about the streets, followed by crowds of small boys, and luxuriated in the sensation he created; lounging regally after meals in front of a restaurant and nonchalantly picking his teeth with his ten-inch blade for the benefit of an admiring populace.

It might be fancied that such grotesque play-acting was laughed at in that country of tragic realities and disillusion. But Ollinger took his melodrama seriously and laughter was safest behind his back. Though he revelled in his mock heroics, he was not all actor. He set himself a dangerous rôle in that hair-trigger land, but the worst part about it was that he lived up to it. His character was worse than his pose. Beneath his histrionism was the spirit of murder. He acted the part of desperado, but he lived it also without ever stepping out of character. There was some doubt as to his courage, but none as to his deadliness. He was unquestionably a killer. He placed no more value on human life than Billy the Kid, but he lacked that youthful desperado's cheerful willingness to risk his own. He was generally and cordially hated. Judged by his deeds, he was merciless, revengeful, treacherous, murderous, devoid of magnanimity or sense of fair play. Certain of his exploits might suggest a psychopathic taint which made blood as satisfying to him as drink to a drunkard. He was less a fighter than a murderer and the murders he committed stand out through the

perspective of the years in unrelieved blackness and bru-
tality. Most bad men have their apologists. Ollinger
has none. The Southwest to-day has only obloquy for his
memory.

He had killed three men, treacherously and brutally,
without danger to himself. While Ollinger was marshal at
Seven Rivers, Juan Chavez, who had known him for years
and always had been on friendly terms with him, offended
him in some small way. Nursing the grudge in secret,
Ollinger kept up a show of friendship. He met Chavez
on the street one day.

"Hello, Chavez," he said pleasantly.

Chavez extended his hand. Ollinger seized it with his
left hand and with his right drew a revolver and shot
Chavez to death.

Circumstances under which Ollinger was himself killed
years afterward seemed an echo of this old murder. A
voice called to him in friendly wise and death followed
hard upon the salutation. With this treachery standing
against him, Ollinger's death seemed to smack of atone-
ment and retribution. "With what measure ye mete, it
shall be measured to you again."

John Hill was another of Ollinger's victims. The details
of this crime of a half century ago seem to have passed out
of living memory. All that is known is that Hill was shot
without warning—some say in the back—and was given
no chance for his life.

Ollinger's third murder was equally heartless. There
lived in Seven Rivers a man named Bob Jones. Between
him and Ollinger bad blood existed. Jones was said to be
dangerous and Ollinger was said to be afraid of him.
Though the two men met on the streets every day Ollinger
had never deemed it wise to bring the quarrel to a crisis

and shoot it out in fair fight. A warrant was issued against Jones for some misdemeanour and placed in the hands of Deputy Sheriff Pierce. Ollinger volunteered to assist Pierce in making the arrest. Jones surrendered peaceably. While he was under arrest, unarmed and defenseless, Ollinger shot him—three times, it is said—killing him instantly. The crime was unprovoked and without extenuation. Ollinger's assistance in making the arrest was not needed. The charge against Jones was of minor consequence. Serving the warrant upon him was a mere formality without danger. But it gave Ollinger the opportunity his bloodthirsty soul desired, and he murdered the man he hated under a thin disguise of law.

When Ollinger first appeared in New Mexico he worked for John Chisum as a cowboy. He had a bad name even then. He lived at Seven Rivers for years and was identified with the Murphy faction during the Lincoln County war. He took part in several skirmishes in the vendetta. Some say he was in the three-days' battle in which McSween was killed. Some say he was not. As Billy the Kid fought on the opposite side, he was naturally Ollinger's enemy, but Ollinger's deadly hatred of the Kid dated from Bob Beckwith's death. Beckwith was Ollinger's closest friend. He killed McSween in the three-days' fight and Billy the Kid killed him a moment afterward.

Sheriff Pat Garrett had no illusions regarding Ollinger, and excused Ollinger's appointment as his deputy on the ground that deputies in that dangerous period were hard to find.

"I was out once with Ollinger on a hunt for a Mexican," said Garrett. "We ran on the Mexican hiding in a ditch. Ollinger began to manœuvre for a position from which to kill him. I managed to get the drop on the Mexican and took him prisoner. He was badly scared. He believed Ollinger would kill him and begged me to save his life.

"When I brought the Mexican out, Ollinger came running toward us, his six-shooter cocked in his hand and his long hair flying in the wind. I never saw such a devilish expression on any man's face. The Mexican jumped behind me but Ollinger circled around trying to get at him. 'Leave him alone, Bob,' I said to him sharply, but he paid no attention to me, continuing to dodge around in an effort to get in a shot. I finally threw my gun in his face and told him I would kill him, if he didn't behave. That brought him to his senses.

"Ollinger was a born murderer. He was the only man I ever knew who I believe was literally bloodthirsty. I never camped with him that I did not watch him closely. After I had acquired a little fame, I believe he would have killed me if possible for the reputation it would have given him. I was always careful never to give him a chance to shoot me in the back or when I was asleep. I don't know that he was exactly a coward; he may have had a certain sort of courage; but he was a devil and had murder in his heart."

Mrs. Susan E. Barber said: "After Ollinger was killed, I met his mother. I had never had any use for Ollinger; he was a ruffian and a brute and was more generally hated than any man in the country. But out of courtesy, I expressed my sympathy to his mother in what I supposed was her bereavement. I was greatly shocked when the old woman said to me, 'Bob was a murderer from his cradle and if there is a hell, I know he is there.' I never heard or read of any other mother using such terrible words about a son."

Emerson Hough, in drawing a comparison between

Ollinger and Billy the Kid, had this to say: "One was a genuine bad man and the other the genuine imitation of a bad man. They were really as far apart as the poles and they are so held in the tradition of that bloody country to-day. Throughout the West there are two kinds of wolves—the coyote and the gray wolf. Either will kill and both are lovers of blood. One is yellow at heart and the other is game all the way through. In outward appearances both are wolves and in appearance they sometimes grade toward each other so closely that it is hard to determine the species. The gray wolf is a warrior and is respected. The coyote is a sneak and a murderer and his name is a term of reproach throughout the West."

The day after the Kid had been sentenced, Deputy Ollinger and Woods set out on horseback with the prisoner through the mountains for Lincoln. Throughout the long journey, Ollinger never ceased to revile the Kid in tirades of scurrility and billingsgate.

"If you don't like the idea of cashing out through a trapdoor, Billy," he said, "why don't you try to escape? There's a good spot in the road ahead of us to make a break for it. Suppose you just fall off your horse and take to the woods. Then I'd have my chance to pot you like a rabbit. My only objection to the gallows for you is that it will rob me of the pleasure of murdering you."

Occasionally the Kid sent back a joking reply to his tormentor's sallies but usually he kept silent.

So at last they arrived in Lincoln. The Lincoln jail being insecure, the Kid was confined in an upper room in Murphy's old store. There, manacled hand and foot and under close guard, he awaited the hour set for his death upon the gallows.

CHAPTER XVII

A LITTLE GAME OF MONTE

DON'T you or Bell ever let the Kid see the colour of your back," said Sheriff Pat Garrett to Bob Ollinger. "Keep your faces to him and your eyes on him every minute. You never can tell what's in that boy's mind. He's got a mighty deceivin' smile. There's murder back of that smile of his."

Deputy Sheriff Bob Ollinger and Deputy Sheriff J. W. Bell of White Oaks were Billy the Kid's death watch during the days of his imprisonment in Lincoln.

"You don't have to worry about me, Pat," replied Ollinger. "I know the Kid and I'm never takin' no chances with him. I watch him like a hawk. I always got my six-shooter on and my double-barrelled shotgun loaded with buckshot in my hands. The Kid knows better than to try any monkey business with me. Just let him make one false move and I'll fill him full of lead. He knows that."

"That's the idea, Bob," said the sheriff.

"But Bell's different," went on Ollinger. "I'm more afraid of him than I am of the Kid. He's always layin' himself wide open. Plays cards with the Kid. I told him that ain't no way to do. But Bell says he feels sorry for the Kid and wants to cheer him up. The only way I'd like to cheer him up is with a load of buckshot. Bell gets to studyin' about the game. But the Kid ain't interested in cards; what he's interested in is gettin' his hand on that six-shooter Bell's got shoved down in his belt. I've warned Bell but he only laughs. Says there ain't no danger."

"Bell don't unlock the Kid's handcuffs, does he?"

"No, the Kid plays with his handcuffs on."

Sheriff Garrett pondered a moment.

"Well," he said, "I don't know as I see much harm in the Kid's playin' cards with Bell now and then to pass the time, if his shackles are left on. He can't do nothin' very desperate with his hands chained together."

"I don't like it," Ollinger declared. "There is danger. All the time the Kid's talkin' about this, that, and the other, he's lookin' over the top of his cards at Bell's revolver. He'll grab that gun some day if Bell don't look out."

"Bell must watch himself, of course."

"Bell's careless in other ways, too. He likes to read the newspapers. He ain't got no business readin' newspapers on guard. With the Kid sittin' six feet from him, Bell needs all the eyes he's got. Lemme tell you somethin'. Bell was readin' a newspaper one day. The Kid sittin' on his cot. Bell held the paper so close to his face he couldn't see the Kid at all. The Kid got up without makin' no noise whatsoever and sneaked a step or two toward Bell. He was standin' within three feet o' him without Bell knowin' it when I come in the door quietlike. The Kid looked mighty sheepish when all of a sudden he seen me standin' there in the door and went on over to the window and pretended to be lookin' out."

"That sounds bad. Bell ought to be more careful."

"And Bell told me himself of one or two suspicious moves the Kid's made. He said one time the Kid started to walk up and down the floor, makin' believe he was exercisin'. He kept edgin' closer to Bell every turn, and keepin' up a lot of talk to throw Bell off. But Bell happened to be on to his racket that time and just quietly laid down his hand on the butt of his gun. When he did that the Kid seen Bell was on to him and quit exercisin' mighty sudden. I can see that boy's tryin' to figure out some way he can get hold of Bell's six-shooter. And if he ever does, there'll be hell a-poppin'. The Kid's got everythin' to win and nothin' to lose. He might get killed tryin' to escape. But he's got to die on the gallows anyway. So what's the difference?"

"I'm glad you told me this," said Sheriff Garrett. "I'll caution Bell. The Kid don't look dangerous. He's as innocent-lookin' as a schoolboy. But he don't care no more about killin' a man than eatin' his breakfast. He's about as murderous a little hombre as ever stood in shoe leather. Bell's got to know he can't take any chances."

Billy the Kid's smile was almost as famous as his trigger finger. He smiled in victory, he smiled in defeat. His cool, daredevil smile was a part of him. He smiled still in the shadow of the gallows. With death closing in, his smile was as light-hearted and boyish as in his days of freedom. He cracked jokes and laughed at the jokes of others. His talk was light, casual, touched with humour. He seemed less a man about to die than a youth anticipating happy years.

In the whisky glass of life that he had drained, one drop remained and that drop was hope. He retained his gambler's faith in the break of the luck. The one chance in a million that had saved him before might save him again. The cards had run against him. He had lost. But the game was not yet quite over. He still had one white chip left. This lone white chip was his courage. If the cards broke his way on just one hand, he would bet his white chip as if it were a million dollars. That was the way he played the game. One drop in life's whisky glass, one white chip, one chance in a million. If he lost, he would shove his chair back from the table with a smile on his face and bid the boys good-night. But if he should win. . . .

The shadow of the gallows is imponderable, yet it has weight to crush the bravest souls. But upon his soul it seemed to lie as lightly as the shadow of a tree in the morning sun. Whatever else he may have been, this boy was no whimpering coward. Regard him, if you will, as cold-blooded, conscienceless, merciless, but credit him with courage, that one splendid quality which, since the world began, has been the same in sinner and saint, outlaw and martyr, thief and knightly crusader. The man who can smile while death waits just outside the door with a hangman's rope to strangle him is of the mould of heroes.

Night and day the Kid was kept bound hand and foot. The steel shackles on his wrists and ankles were never removed. He ate with them on, slept with them on. The chain that held his hands together was six inches long; that which bound his feet, twelve inches. If he took a drink of water or a smoke, he must lift cup or cigarette to his lips with both hands. If he walked the floor for exercise, his steps were perforce short and mincing. Imprisonment between four walls was hard on a youth whose life under the blue sky had been as free as the wind that comes and goes; but harder still were the shackles that changed him, whole-limbed and full of restless energy, into a helpless cripple.

Deputy Sheriffs Ollinger and Bell kept him under constant surveillance. During most of the day, both were on duty; one always, night and day. If he raised his manacled hands thoughtlessly, they watched the gesture with meticulous suspicion. If he tossed in his sleep, a pair of cold gray eyes quickened to keen alertness in the dim light of the midnight lamp.

These two men had been selected as his death watch because they were his enemies and might be depended upon to guard him with the vigilance of hatred until his death upon the gallows worked their revenge. Ollinger hated him because he had killed Bob Beckwith; Bell hated him because he had killed Jimmy Carlyle.

But the two deputies differed in character as night from day. Ollinger was a devil; Bell a man. Ollinger kept up his nagging torture. He gloated over the Kid's unhappy fate. He longed with the eagerness of consuming hatred for the day of the Kid's death.. The thought of seeing his enemy choking at a rope's end filled his soul with voluptuous thrills. With the Kid helpless in his power, he took delight in tormenting him, playing with his victim with the purring malice of a cat with a mouse. He harped upon the gallows; he dangled the hangman's noose constantly before the Kid's eyes.

"Good-morning, Kid," was his daily salutation. "One day less between you and the rope."

Though Ollinger's hatred grew more intense as the days went by, Bell's gradually diminished, until at last it merged into pity that was akin to friendship. Bell was a tall, grim-looking man with a livid knife-scar across his cheek, but at heart he was generous and kindly. The mercilessly cold-blooded murder of his friend Carlyle at the Greathouse ranch had inflamed Bell with bitterness against the Kid. But with the gallows looming to wipe out the score, Bell was filled with the sympathy of a magnanimous spirit. The pathos of the Kid's situation softened his heart and he felt only pity for the slim youth, pale from months of imprisonment, bound hand and foot like a mad beast, yet bearing up with cheerful fortitude and smiling bravely as death drew nearer hour by hour, day by day, with the slow momentum of inevitability.

The old Murphy store in which the Kid was held prisoner was the largest building in Lincoln. Of adobe brick, covered with smooth adobe stucco, it was two stories in height and stood on the south side of Lincoln's single street near the western limits of town. It had been Murphy's citadel as well as his place of business in the days of his prosperity, and its solidity and imposing proportions seemed to connote his importance and power. If earthly tidings could have reached the spirit land, it would doubtless have rejoiced the ghost of the old feud leader to learn that Billy the Kid, who had been his most inveterate enemy, and whose relentless hatred had done so much to bring his plots to naught, was at last captive in the old Murphy fortress and was soon to meet his doom in the shadow of its massive walls.

With Murphy's death and the passing of his power and fortune, the old building had been transformed into the courthouse and at periodical sessions of court was a scene of bustling activity, its rooms filled with lawyers and clerks and its corridors crowded with litigants from the remotest corners of Lincoln County. But in the long intervals between judicial sittings it gathered dust and cobwebs in its silent and deserted halls.

The Kid was quartered in the courtroom, a great, bare chamber sixty feet long by fifty wide that occupied the entire east side of the second story and was lighted by six windows, two in front overlooking the street, two at the back, and two in the east wall. At the rear of the chamber was the judge's bench on a low dais, the jury box at one side, and at the other the witness stand and a railed-off enclosure where the clerk and other court attachés had their desks. A door in the west wall gave upon a wide hall that ran through the centre of the building. At one end of this hall a door opened upon a roofed-over, second-story porch along the front of the building, reached from the street by stairways at either end. At the other end of the hall was a room known as the armoury, in which rifles, six-shooters, and munitions of war were stored for emergency use by sheriff's posses in that unsettled time. Just in front of the armoury, a stairway led down from the hall through a walled-in passage which, halfway down, turned at a sharp angle to the left toward a ground-floor door opening on a rear courtyard. Across the courtyard stood the little adobe jail, deemed too precarious for the confinement of such a desperate character as the Kid, and another small building which served as the jail kitchen and the sleeping quarters of Old Man Goss, the jail cook.

The Kid's sleeping cot was in the northeast corner of the courtroom with the cots of the two members of his death watch near by. His prison chamber was at least light and airy. The window in the east wall near the front is known to this day as Billy the Kid's window. Sitting in a chair before it he spent much of his time looking down upon the scenes of his many adventures. In plain view were the fire-blackened ruins of the old McSween home where McSween and three of his followers had gone down in death and where the Kid, fighting for his life against desperate odds, had slain Bob Beckwith, thereby gaining the undying hatred of the devilman who now watched with malevolent joy the Kid's last sands of life filtering away.   Beyond was the old McSween store now owned by Tom Larue; from the far end of it, the Kid and his men had lain in ambush and killed Sheriff Brady and George Hindman, the crime for which he was sentenced to die.   Just behind the store he could see the grave of Tunstall, the Englishman to whom he had given the loyalty of his youthful friendship and whose death he had avenged in full measure of blood.   Beyond, in its grove of trees, stood the Ellis House, where he had had his memorable interview with Governor Lew Wallace.   In bitterness of spirit, he recalled the governor's promise of a pardon, which might have saved him from his present desperate predicament but which never came.   So as he sat by the east window and puffed a cigarette, his mind lingered upon various experiences that had befallen him here in Lincoln, and in Lincoln's winding street of many tragedies his thronging memories jostled the ghosts of the men he had killed.

But there were other things in Lincoln street to interest him besides memories and ghosts.   From his box seat by the window he watched the homespun drama of village life.   It was his daily amusement.   Upon the comings and going in the street, humdrum commonplaces, trifling incidents, he passed his criticism and comment to the sympathetic Bell.   Mrs. Saturnino Baca, he noted, was wearing a new bonnet; purchased, doubtless, on her recent trip to Santa Fé.   Well, she looked *muy bonita*.   She was a handsome woman, anyway.   ...... Jimmy Dolan was in from the Fritz ranch.   Dolan was a lucky dog to marry so much money.   ...... "Dad" Peppin's pinto pony was lame in its off hind foot; probably needed shoeing.   ...... There was Nicolecita Pacheco.   First time he had

seen her in a month of Sundays.   She was carrying home
a leg of mutton in her market basket.   ...... José
Otero had caught a fine string of trout down in the Bonito.
He wished he was going to take dinner with José Otero.
Turned in cornmeal over a slow fire, these mountain trout
certainly made mighty good eating.   ......   Pat Garrett seemed to be having some sort of an argument with
a couple of Mexicans in front of the Wortley Hotel.
What could that old he-coon be arguing about?   Old Pat.
If shot so as not to spoil his beauty, he'd make a fine look-
ing corpse.   ......

Tilted back in his chair against the wall, Bob Ollinger
sat at ease.   With a casual gesture, he brushed a straggling
lock of his long lank hair over his shoulder and adjusted
his sombrero, tilting it slightly on the side of his head.

"April twenty-eighth, ain't it, Bell?"

"If it don't rain."

Bell was reading a newspaper by a front window.   The
Kid sat on his couch rolling himself a cigarette.   Ollinger
let his cold, whitish-blue eyes rest on the pale, slender
prisoner chained hand and foot.

"You're lookin' kind o' peaked, Kid."

"Four months in jail ain't good for the complexion."

"Eatin' your vittles regular?"

"Yes."

"What's the matter then?"

"I need a bucking pony under me."

"Well, buck up.   We'll give you a nice long ride at the
end of a rope.   Only fifteen days more to wait."

"I always figured I wasn't born to die that way," the
Kid remarked with slow deliberation.

"Looks like you figured wrong.   Garrett bought the
rope yesterday.   Good stout manila.   Ever see a hang-

man's knot? Got seven turns to it. The rope slips through it smooth as silk."

"Better tell 'em to put eight turns in it. Might be a slip-up in my case."

"Only slip-up there'll be is when that old rope slips up tight around your throat under your jawbone. Then the old trap'll swing down—bang! That's when you'll begin to dance. Plenty of good Lincoln County air for your dancing floor. Always heard you were a mighty fine dancer."

"That's no way to talk, Bob," cut in Bell. "Leave the Kid alone. No sense in aggravatin' him like that. He'll take his medicine like a man when the time comes. I'll bet on that."

"Like a man, eh?" answered Ollinger. "He'll die like a dog."

"To throw a steer," observed the Kid philosophically, "you've first got to get a rope over his foot. There ain't any noose around my neck yet."

"Feel up around your Adam's-apple May thirteenth and you'll find one there."

"A lot can happen between now and then."

"But nothin' that can help you any." Ollinger's brow wrinkled. He bent a savage look upon the Kid. "You hintin' at escapin'? You ain't got a chance on earth."

Ollinger had a double-barrelled shotgun lying across his lap. He broke it at the breach.

"Look here, Kid," he said. "See these two shells?"

"Going quail hunting?" Billy smiled.

"Each one of them shells is loaded with nine buckshot. Try to escape. I wish you would. I'd like to see you kickin' at a rope's end but, when I come to think about it, I believe I'd rather murder you myself. Go ahead and make your break and you'll get eighteen buckshot between your shoulder blades."

"Eighteen?" The Kid gave a little, sneering laugh. "That's too many to waste on a slim young fellow like me. But eighteen would be just a nice fit for a man of your size. It would be a joke if you happened to stop those eighteen buckshot yourself. Eh, Bob?"

Footsteps sounded in the hall. The door for a moment framed the impressive figure of Sheriff Pat Garrett, six feet four and a half inches tall, slightly stooped in the shoulders, dark clothes accentuating his slender frame that suggested careless strength, trousers tucked in a pair of high-heeled boots of soft leather, his face under his gray sombrero a mixture of iron sternness and good humour. With a cheery salutation he strode in. How was everything? Kid getting along all right? Old Man Goss sending in enough grub? *Bueno, hombres.* Only a few minutes to stay. Just wanted to see how things were going.

"I'm riding to White Oaks this morning, boys," he said to the deputies. "Got to see about the gallows. Get some timbers freighted over right away. Not much time left. Going to try to find a good carpenter, too."

"Hurry up with that gallows, Pat," remarked the Kid. "Ollinger can't sleep good till it's up."

"I'll be back to-morrow or next day," the sheriff added. "You boys be on your guard. Don't go to sleep on the job. Take no chances. I'm depending on you. My reputation's at stake."

"Rest your mind easy, Pat," replied Ollinger. "We'll answer for the Kid."

"So long, Billy."

"*Adios*, Pat."

A clatter of hoofs sounded in the street below the windows, passed into the distance, died out in dusty silence. Sheriff Garrett was off on the road to White Oaks.

Noon came.   It was the dinner hour in Lincoln.   Ollinger rose and stretched himself.

"I'll step over to the hotel and put on the feed-bag, Bell," he said.   "Won't be gone over an hour.   When I come back, you can go for grub."

He turned at the door and patted the shotgun held in the crook of his arm.

"Eighteen buckshot, Kid," he snarled.   "Don't forget what I said.   Make a break and you get 'em right between your shoulder blades."

On his way out of the building by the back stairs he stopped at the armoury and stood his shotgun against the wall just inside the door.

Standing at the east window, Billy the Kid watched him swagger down the road to Larue's store.   A cryptic, unpleasant little smile hung for a moment at the corner of the Kid's mouth.

The spring day was as warm as summer.   Orchards about town and the fruit trees in the yards were in full bloom.   Through the open window the Kid inhaled the faint fragrance of them.   His ears were filled with the drowsy droning of bees.   A robin was on her nest in a box-elder tree at the corner of the courthouse, her mate preening his wings on a neighbouring limb.   These robins were the Kid's pets.   He had seen them arrive from the South, had watched their courtship, their home-building, their start in domesticity.   Every day he had saved bread from the meal which Old Man Goss brought in to him and had scattered crumbs along his window sill for the birds; and the robins had eaten his good-will offerings, cocking their bright eyes at the shackled youth as if to say, "We're chums of yours." He wondered vaguely if the little couple would hatch out their nestlings before he dropped through the trapdoor of a gallows.

Across the street, his eyes noted a hen scratching fussily with a new brood of fuzzy chicks about her. A group of idlers lounged in the shady porch of the Wortley Hotel, smoking, gossiping languidly. Two Mexican boys were spinning tops down near Larue's store. He remembered when he was spinning tops back in Silver City not so many years ago; he was only twenty-one now. Nobody else was in sight. Lincoln was taking a siesta. The sun was pouring down its heat from a cloudless, indigo sky. The dusty road was a crooked ribbon of white; at its edges the shadows of houses and trees lay as if painted in solid black. He could hear plainly the murmur of the Bonito River through the noonday stillness. It was like a lullaby.

The Kid took a luxurious drag at his cigarette, tossed the butt out the window, and turned back into the room.

"Let's have a little game of monte, Bell," he drawled, "to pass the time. What do you say?"

"Might as well kill a little time that way, Kid, if it'll amuse you," answered Bell.

"Well, not much time left to kill."

On a large round table standing at the front of the room near the door were a deck of cards and a box of matches. The table was a relic of Murphy's prime. Many a roistering poker game for big stakes the old Lord of the Mountains and his knights of the round table had enjoyed about it, with the drinks coming fast from the bar below stairs. Almost every day the Kid and Bell had been accustomed to while away monotonous hours playing cards. Now it was a game of freeze-out poker with matches for chips;

again, seven-up or casino, and sometimes monte. When
the game was poker, seven-up, or casino, the Kid occupied
a chair at one side of the table and Bell a chair at the
other.   When it was monte and Bell dealing, the Kid bal-
anced himself on top of the table to be above the layout
in a position that made it easy for him to put down his
bets with his manacled hands.   Now Bell took a seat in
a chair at the table and Billy, as was his habit, perched
himself on the table-top, his shackled feet resting on the
seat of a chair.

"You bank, Bell," said the Kid.   "I'll buck the game."

The Kid shot one shrewd, furtive glance at Bell's six-
shooter.   Bell was wearing it to-day without a scabbard,
stuck down his pants leg on his right side betveen his
shirt and his belt.   As Bell sat down its muzzle rammed
into his flesh.   With a casual gesture, he adjusted it,
pushing the handle slightly farther back toward his hip.
Then, taking up the deck, he shuffled it with the ease of
old familiarity, riffling the cards like a faro dealer, giving
them deft cuts that made a slapping noise.

"Help yourself to chips out of the match box, Kid," he
said.   "Ten matches the limit on a card."

"*Bueno, muchacho.*"

Bell began to deal.   He pulled a few cards from the deck
and laid them face up on the table.   His monte layout
began to assume form.

"I'm out for blood this game," warned the Kid jovially.
"Coffee talks."

"Bet ten dollars on that deuce of diamonds."

The Kid piled ten matches on the card.   Bell went on
turning.   The bet lost and he raked in the matches with
a laugh.

"I'm a system player," chortled the Kid.

"System ain't workin' right to-day."

"It's pulled me out of many a hole. May do it again. Never can tell."

The Kid edged over a few inches farther toward the centre of the table—a few inches closer to Bell.

"I'll beat this deal yet," he said. "No game's lost, Bell, till the last card's played."

Again a cryptic little smile hovered for a moment at the corner of his mouth, which Bell didn't see, being busy dealing. And again the Kid hunched over slightly nearer the centre of the table—slightly nearer Bell.

Bell pulled out the jack of hearts and laid it on the table.

"Jack of hearts, eh?" laughed Billy. "That's my lucky card."

"Luck run in hearts?"

"In bullets mostly. But in hearts sometimes. Knock off the limit, Bell. Make it the ceiling. I'll bust the bank on this play or lose my last white chip."

Bell shook his head with a good-natured laugh.

"Ten matches are the limit."

"Once over in San Patricio," remarked Billy, "when I was dealing monte——"

He reached out his manacled hands to place his wager of ten matches when, seemingly by accident, he brushed the jack of hearts off on to the floor at Bell's left side.

"Didn't mean to do that, Bell," he apologized. "Hard to play with handcuffs on like this."

"That's all right, Kid. I'll get it."

Bell bent over to pick up the card. Holding the deck in his left hand, he reached for the card with his right.

To do so, he had to turn slightly away from the table. For a fraction of a second his head dipped below the level of the top, his eyes intent upon the card on the floor.

It was Billy the Kid's chance in a million for which he had been waiting for weeks with the deadly patience of a panther. As Bell stooped, the butt of his six-shooter projected within reach of the Kid's hand. Leaning across the table, the Kid snatched the weapon. When Bell raised his head, he was looking into the muzzle of his own gun. He rose to his feet, knocking over the chair. He staggered back a step, his face abruptly white, his eyes wide.

"What the hell, Kid!"

"Do as I tell you, Bell, and be mighty quick about it," ordered the Kid in crisp, sharp tones. "Don't make a false move. You're a dead man if you do. I don't want to kill you. I'm not going to kill you. You've been good to me. Turn and walk out the door. I'm going to lock you in the armoury."

Bell hesitated. The tables had been turned so quickly, he could not for a moment grasp the desperateness of the crisis.

"Quick," snapped the Kid. "No time to waste."

Bell faced about silently and marched out the door, the Kid hampered by his leg irons shuffling after him. He turned south in the hall. A sudden surge of anger, chagrin, hurt pride, swept through him. Why had he been such an easy dupe? Deaf to repeated warnings, he had been caught napping. He had fallen into a trap through which he should have seen with half an eye; a trap the Kid doubtless had been planning since their first card game together. This absurd situation was the upshot of his pity, his kindliness. He might have expected it. He had been a soft-hearted fool. What would Garrett think of him? What would that devil, Ollinger, say? Was there no way out of this? Desperate thoughts raced through his mind. Could he turn quickly and overpower the Kid? No. That seemed suicide. But if he could trick the Kid as the Kid had tricked him, he might yet save his reputation. Once out of the Kid's clutches, he would organize the citizens and recapture or kill him. He came to the head of the back stairs just beyond which was the armoury door. He shot a furtive glance over his shoulder. The Kid had fallen perhaps six feet behind him, making awkward progress, his ankle chains clattering.

There were not more than a dozen steps from the upper floor to the point where the stairway turned. Once behind the angle of the wall Bell would be safe. The stairs were his one forlorn hope. Swerving sharply, he plunged down them. In one flying leap, he made the bend. His outthrust hand struck the plastered wall; the heels of his cowboy boots cut splinters from the steps as he lunged for the shelter of the turn. One step more and the wall would shield him. . . . But behind him was the quickest, deadliest coördination of eye, mind, and muscle in the Southwest. At that instant, the Kid sprang to the head of the stairs. Almost before his hobbled feet struck the floor, his six-shooter coughed fire. The hall shook with a deafening report. The bullet struck Bell beneath the left shoulder blade, cut through his heart, and buried itself in the wall beyond. He pitched forward on his head, crumpled over in a somersault, rolled down the few remaining steps and lay lifeless at the bottom, his limp body half out the courtyard door.

The Kid paid no further attention to Bell. That much

of his problem was solved, and he dismissed it from his mind. He did not go down to the bend of the stairs to learn the result of his shot. He knew. There was no time to lose. His life hung upon a split second. What he did now he had not planned; but he did it as if he had thought it out in detail and carefully rehearsed it. He translated lightning-like thoughts into lightning-like action. Every move counted. Jamming Bell's six-shooter into his belt for emergencies, he stepped to the door of the armoury, flung it open, caught up Ollinger's shotgun leaning against the wall within arm's reach. Turning he sped through the hall with strange swiftness, with strange noiselessness, gauging his quick, staccato steps to the exact reach of his ankle chains. Like a flitting shadow, he curved into the courtroom, glided across the floor, and halted against the wall by the east window. From the moment Bell fell dead on the back stairs until now, the clock of eternity had ticked perhaps ten seconds.

Back of him at the other side of the room stood the round table, the cards scattered on it, the jack of hearts on the floor, Bell's overturned chair. Within the chamber was the stillness of death; without, the stillness of the sunlit noon. The Kid cocked the hammers of his shotgun. He peeked furtively out of the window into the road. For a moment he stood there against the wall, gun poised, face set, every muscle taut, like an ambushed panther about to spring.

A little distance down the road from the courthouse on the long shady porch of Larue's store Ollinger met Jimmy Dolan. He was glad to see Jimmy Dolan. He clapped him on the back.

"Don't know a man in Lincoln County I'd rather take

a drink with," he growled cordially. "Come on in, Jimmy, and have three fingers of red liquor with me."

"Well, Bob, don't care if I do."

They strolled into the bar. Larue set out the bottle and glasses.

"Garrett went over to White Oaks to-day to order the gallows," said Ollinger. "Kid's gettin' scared. Dropped some talk this mornin' about makin' some kind of break. Like to see him do it. Got my old shotgun loaded with eighteen buckshot. I'd like a chance to plaster him with both barrels right between the shoulder blades. Little devil. Killed Beckwith. But I'll get my revenge when the trap falls. I want to see him kick. Little devil. Hope he strangles."

"That's the stuff," echoed Jimmy Dolan.

They raised their glasses.

"Here's to the rope that chokes the life out of him," said Ollinger.

Ollinger strolled back to the hotel which stood just across the street from the courthouse. The liquor had warmed the cockles of his heart. Thoughts of the Kid dancing on air in a hangman's noose cheered him. It was, too, one grand spring day. The world was full of sunshine. It was good to be alive. He stepped on the hotel porch. Savoury odours of roast beef and potatoes saluted his nostrils. By jiminy! That smelled good. That was a dish to hit the spot. Roast beef and potatoes. . . .

A sudden crashing noise over in the courthouse startled him. Then silence. What was that? For a tense moment all his senses listened. He could hear nothing more. The world seemed suddenly soundless. There across the way stood the old courthouse, peaceful, silent, in the glare of the sun. But that crash sounded like a shot. What did it mean? Possibly the Kid had made his break and Bell had killed him. Or possibly. . . . He jerked out his six-shooter, and holding it cocked in his hand started across the road at a lumbering run, his long hair tossing about his shoulders.

He would pass along the east side of the courthouse and go in by the back door. That would be easier than climbing the steep steps of the second-story porch at the front. If anything were wrong, this would be safer. His eyes kept sweeping the building. Nothing stirred. Not a sound reached him. The open windows of the upper floor revealed only shadowy emptiness. Perhaps nothing had happened, after all. He slowed down to a walk. It occurred to him vaguely that the road was deep with dust. His boots would look like the devil. It was hot. Not a breath of air stirred. The box-elder tree at the corner of the courthouse was like a painted tree in a picture, its massed, dusty leaves motionless. He passed the little, irregular patch of noontide shade beneath the branches; took one step beyond into the sun again.

"Hello, Bob!"

The voice came to him out of the silence. He knew that voice. It was the Kid's. It was even, pleasant, friendly. There was a purring softness in it. For a fraction of a second he felt a sense of relief. Everything was all right. His suspicions were groundless. The Kid was probably sitting up there in his old familiar east window, taking it easy. Perhaps sprinkling crumbs along the sill for the robins. He looked up.

Almost directly above him was the Kid, leaning half out of the window, Ollinger's own shotgun loaded with eighteen buckshot pressed tightly against his shoulder.

Over the shining length of the double barrel gleamed the Kid's hard gray eyes and the Kid's cold white face. He was smiling.

Ollinger stopped dead in his tracks. It may have been the shock of surprise that stopped him. It may have been the paralysis of fear. It may have been the helpless realization that he was at the end of his journey of life—everything. His cocked six-shooter hung useless in his hand at his side. He stared up at the Kid with a startled, foolish, hopeless look. His eyes popped half out of their sockets. His mouth fell open. . . . The Kid pulled the trigger. All Lincoln heard the roar of the gun. A puff of blue, acrid smoke drifted off into the street. Nine buckshot struck Ollinger in the breast. The impact spun him half round. He lunged forward and measured his length on the ground, his arms outstretched, his cocked six-shooter still grasped in his hand.

The report of the shotgun brought the townspeople to their doors up and down the street. News of some sort of tragedy at the courthouse spread quickly. Billy the Kid had done something terrible again. "I told you so," ran from mouth to mouth. The desperado was loose; he might be planning other atrocities. Panic fell upon the town. Best for Lincoln to keep indoors. So the villagers, having rushed out, rushed in again, drew the bolts, and closed the shutters. Half-a-dozen men eating dinner in the Wortley Hotel crowded pell-mell out upon the porch. That was as far as their curiosity took them. Enthusiasm for investigation evaporated when they saw Ollinger stretched dead across the street. They remained on the porch as spectators, awaiting the next act in the play.

The front door in the second story of the courthouse opened. Out upon the porch high above the street stepped Billy the Kid.   He still wore his leg irons, but the handcuffs had disappeared from his wrists; he had slipped them off without great difficulty over his remarkably small hands.   The sheer bravado of his appearance was his gesture of drama.   It made him a fair target for death from a dozen places of concealment; but no hidden foe ventured a shot to avenge Ollinger and Bell.   With the porch as his stage, he stood for a moment leaning upon his shotgun like an actor awaiting the applause of his audience at the close of a big scene.

He moved a few paces to the east end of the porch. Standing at the head of the steps that led down to the street, he caught sight of Ollinger's body sprawled face downward beneath him.   The Kid's eyes rested on the spot between the shoulder blades.   His tormentor's threat flashed back upon him.   .   .   .   "Eighteen buckshot between your shoulder blades."   The Kid regretted he had only nine buckshot left.   Beneath the shoulder blades of the limp form lying there lay the heart that had hated him, that had beat high at the thought of seeing him kick at the end of a hangman's rope, that had exulted in the prospect of his dancing a death dance on air.   Here was his opportunity to add the completing detail to his revenge— the last, finishing touch of an artist in murders.   He raised the shotgun to his shoulders and took deliberate aim. Again all Lincoln heard the roar.   The dead man seemed to jump as the nine buckshot drove home between the shoulder blades.

The Kid raised the gun high above his head and with all the strength of his lithe arms flung it crashing down upon the corpse of the man he hated.

"Take that to hell with you, you cowardly yellow cur!" he snarled and, turning, hobbled back into the building.

The Kid's task was only half completed. His liberty was still precarious. He had yet to escape. He had reason to believe he was in greater danger than he was; he had no inkling of the state of mind of the townspeople. For all he knew they might be arming and organizing to surround and kill him. But the grave possibilities of his situation did not weigh upon him. His plan was definite and he set about working it out patiently, systematically, without excitement and without hurry. He went first to the armoury where he armed himself with two six-shooters and a Winchester rifle. With cool indifference to the lapse of time, he loaded the chambers of the revolvers and charged the magazine of the rifle with cartridges. He selected two cartridge-belts and filled the loops of one with revolver cartridges and the loops of the other with Winchester bullets. This was slow work. Then he went down the back stairs, stopping at the bend to examine for a moment critically the bloodstained hole in the wall bored by the bullet that had passed through Bell's heart. At the bottom of the stairway he stepped carefully over Bell's body, which lay in the door, and walked out into the courtyard at the rear of the building.

Old Man Goss, the cook, had locked himself in the jail kitchen. The Kid rapped at the door. Shaking with fear, the old man opened it.

"Don't be scared, Goss," said the Kid. "Any man who can cook ham and eggs like you is safe with me. Get an axe and chop the chain of these leg irons in two."

Goss brought an axe from the wood pile.

"Don't make any mis-strokes," cautioned Billy, swinging a six-shooter carelessly close to Goss's head.

With a few vigorous strokes, Goss broke the chains The Kid tied pieces of twine to the two shattered end.

and, pulling the chains taut up along his legs, fastened the strings to his belt. The movements of both hands and legs were now unencumbered.

Back of the courthouse was a two-acre pasture under fence. In it a black horse was cropping grass along the irrigating ditch near the foot of the south wall of the cañon.

"That Pat Garrett's pony?" asked the Kid.

"No, it's Billy Burt's, the county clerk."

"Wish it was Garrett's. It'd tickle me to ride away on old Pat's horse. But go catch him and bring him here."

Goss with a bridle in his hand went out into the pasture to catch the horse. The pony was young and mettlesome and moreover was enjoying his banquet of grass along the asequia. Goss was old and somewhat doddering, and catching a spirited horse that did not wish to be caught in a two-acre pasture was no easy task. Dodging about on his ancient legs, Goss hemmed the pony in one corner and then hemmed him in another and always the horse, snorting, head and tail in air, broke away and went galloping to another part of the field. Meantime, the Kid lounged in the courtyard with unperturbed patience, rolling cigarettes and whiffing them in leisurely fashion, the body of the man he had killed within a few feet of him.

Goss's chase of the black pony wasted more than an hour. Finally the horse grew tired of the pastime and submitted to the bridle. Goss led him in and cinched a saddle on him. The old man was fearfully apologetic.

"You seen how the darn critter acted," he explained. "I done my best, but I couldn't ketch him no quicker."

"Oh, that's all right," returned the Kid easily.

Through the pasture gate at the northwest corner of the

building, the Kid led the horse out into the street. The group of a half-dozen men was still standing curiously on the porch of the Wortley Hotel waiting for the show to continue. They perked up interest now; here was the next act. The Kid gathered up his bridle reins, gripped the pommel, and swung into the saddle. Burdened with his two six-shooters, rifle, and heavy cartridge belts, he was immediately bucked off. He struck the ground on his hands and knees, still holding to the bridle. He leaped to his feet; for a moment he stood there in the middle of the sun-drenched road, legs braced, rifle cocked and ready for instant use, a tense, thrilling figure of a fighting man at bay. The watchers on the porch made no move but on their minds this quick picture of Billy the Kid remained indelibly engraved for all their lives.

Again the Kid swung into the saddle. This time he settled himself comfortably and, waving his hand in farewell to the group of men, rode out of town at an easy gallop. At the edge of the village he passed a Mexican urchin and, at that time, according to the boy, he was whistling a merry little tune.

CHAPTER XVIII

THE LURE OF BLACK EYES

DUE west from Lincoln the Kid rode. A mile and a half out he turned north-by-west into Baca road. Here Bonito Cañon widens into a beautiful valley. Down across the bottom-lands and vegas he passed, his horse at a swift gallop. The hay meadows, full of new grass, spread about him enamelled with wild flowers. Now and then a jackrabbit stood on its haunches and eyed him curiously. An occasional field lark piped an accompaniment to his pony's drumming hoofs.

The drowsy murmur of the Bonito River began to fill his ears, its winding course for miles up and down the valley marked by groves of walnut, box-elder, cottonwood, and willow. Here and there in the distance he had a glimpse of a white slant of rapids or a long reach of shining water. Never drawing rein, he splashed across the stream where, under shade of trees, it poured over golden gravel at the Baca ford.

On the benches of land beyond, he kept on through the ploughed fields, at the edges of which stood the adobe houses of Mexican farmers. Through a deep gap in the bulwark of colossal yellow piñon-splotched hills ahead loomed Capitan Mountain, deep in purple sleep. On a height over which the trail climbed he turned in his saddle for a farewell look at Lincoln. Far across the sunlit valley, the little town, half-buried in blooming orchards, seemed a picture of peace. He wondered what was hap-

pening there, what furore of excitement his escape had
aroused, what hurried plans of pursuit were taking shape.
His distant view from the hilltop was the last he ever had
in life of the mountain village that had been the scene of
his most thrilling exploits and desperate adventures.   A
moment more and the valley was left behind and he was
swallowed up between the towering walls of Baca Cañon.

A few miles up the cañon where the trail turned west
along the foot of the mountain range stood the little adobe
jacal of Jesus José Padilla.   Directly above it Capitan
peak went up to the blue sky in heavily wooded, tumultuous slopes.   The clatter of hoofs brought old man
Padilla to the door.

"*Tengo mucho hambre, amigo,*" said the Kid, dismounting
with a clank of leg chains.   "*Tiene Usted alguna cosa
para comer ?*"

The Mexican bustled about the house and set out
bread, goat's cheese, and cold coffee, upon which Billy
fell with gusto.

"*Ahora dame un pedaso de papel,*" said the Kid when
he had finished eating.   Padilla brought him a piece of
writing paper upon which in pencil the Kid wrote a note
to Billy Burt, county clerk at Lincoln, on whose black
horse he had escaped.   The missive read, according to
Martin Chavez, who saw it later:

BILLY BURT—You would cry if you lost your horse.   I won't need
him any more.   I am sending him back to you.   Much obliged.   Give
my regards to Pat Garrett.   Tell him to look out or he will be next.

BILLY THE KID.

Folding the note in his bandanna handkerchief, the
Kid tied it to one of the cantle strings on the saddle and,
taking the bridle off the horse's head, fastened it securely

to the pommel. Then turning the pony's head toward Lincoln, he gave it a resounding slap on its hind quarters and off it went briskly down the cañon road homeward bound. At dusk Old Man Goss was surprised to see the animal standing at the bars of the jail pasture in Lincoln. Billy Burt, thankful enough to get back the horse, which he never expected to see again, preserved the note for years and spoke with a certain touch of kindliness of the Kid ever afterward.

On foot, the Kid struck westward from Padilla's, avoiding the road and keeping well back in the timbered hills where progress was slower but safer. All the while he expected every minute to see a posse clatter by in pursuit, but none appeared. The red sun sank behind the mountains, and in the stillness of dusk he came back to the lonely trail, where he made better speed. It was far in the night and the moon was up when he turned northward and began the long climb through Capitan Gap. Walking was not his habit. All his life he had been half-centaur, Encumbered by his leg irons and weighted down by his rifle, two six-shooters, and two heavy, full-charged cartridge belts, travelling over the mountain roads was slow and wearying.

While crossing the pass, he turned off the trail a little north of the crest of the divide and lightened his load by hiding one of his six-shooters in the forks of a juniper tree. He told Sepia Salazar in Las Tablas of this cache and suggested, if he wanted a good gun, that he go and find it. His directions were explicit. The juniper tree stood in the pass, he said, one hundred and twenty steps off the road to the east on the far side of a rocky gully and at the foot of a cliff overgrown with moss and vines. Salazar hunted for the gun and failed to find it. He told some of his friends later who also searched for it without success. As years went by Billy the Kid's six-shooter hidden in the forks of the juniper tree in Capitan Gap became a tradition like Captain Kidd's buried treasure. It is still talked about in that country, and many people have hunted for it; but if it was ever found, the finder kept the secret—and the gun—to himself.

The Kid arrived early in the morning at the goat ranch of José Cordoba. Greatly astonished was Cordoba to see him here at his door.

"I thought," he said, "they were getting ready to hang you in Lincoln."

"Maybe they are," replied Billy, "but I won't be there."

"What is that rattling sound I hear when you walk?"

"My leg irons. Can you take them off?"

"*Facilmente, amigo.* Come with me."

Cordoba maintained a wayside smithy where he did odd jobs of tinkering and horseshoeing for the neighbourhood. He conducted the Kid into the blacksmith shop where, with file and pincers, Benito Rodriguez, Cordoba's helper, soon freed the Kid's ankles of their steel gyves.

"Now," said the Kid, standing up and stamping his unencumbered feet, "I am myself again. I will never wear any such things on my legs again unless they put them on me dead."

Cordoba invited him to get some sleep on his bed but the Kid declined.

"Pat Garrett and his men may come riding along any minute," he said. "If they do," he added, "I'll get Garrett the first one. I won't care much what happens to me then. I'll get a little sleep in the woods somewhere on the road to Las Tablas."

"Ighenio Salazar lives in Las Tablas now, and if you look him up, he will take care of you," Cordoba told him, and gave him directions how to find the house.

"You bet I'll look up my old compadre," said Billy, and he started off again along the mountain trail.

Las Tablas is a little Mexican village near the edge of the foothills on the north side of the Capitan range. It was night, and a half-moon was shining when the Kid drew near. Following Cordoba's directions it was easy to pick out the home of Ighenio Salazar, close friend of other days who had fought by his side in the three-days' battle at the McSween house in Lincoln. Hidden on a dark hillside by the road, the Kid gave a shrill whistle.

"I was getting ready for bed," so Salazar tells the story, "when I heard the whistle. I cocked my ears. It was repeated several times. I said to my wife, 'What do you suppose that is?' She was a little alarmed. 'I don't know,' she answered, 'but you better stay in the house.' Those were bad times and I had made enemies in the Lincoln County war. I hesitated to investigate. But the whistle kept up so persistently that at last I opened the door and stepped outside. The hills were dark. The village was silent; most everyone had gone to bed. I could see nobody. Again I heard the whistle. It came from close by. I walked up the road toward it. Finally I made out a man standing at the edge of some piñon brush, and he was waving at me.

"I could hardly believe my eyes when I saw Billy the Kid standing before me. The news of his escape had not yet travelled across the mountains.

"'*Nombre de Dios*, Billy,' I said, 'can this be you?'

"'It's me, all right, Ighenio,' he answered.

"'Why, I dropped in to see you only—— When was it?'

"'A week ago.'

"'And you were a prisoner then, bound hand and foot and sentenced to die on the gallows in only a few days more.'

"'Yes, Ighenio, but the idea of dying on the gallows somehow didn't have any special attraction for me. So I pulled my freight. I was sorry to disappoint a lot of people who expected to see a good show but I had other plans. But, say, *amigo*, I'm hungry. Can't you rustle me something to eat?'

"I took him to my home and my wife cooked him a nice, hot meal. He was nervous inside four walls, and as soon as he had eaten, he and I went off into the brush where we sat down on the ground and Billy told me the details of his escape. He said he had been watching and waiting for just such an opportunity ever since he had been a prisoner. He felt sure, if he could get a weapon, he could shoot his way out. All his plans centred on getting a weapon. He did not think there ever would be a possibility of getting Ollinger's six-shooter; Ollinger watched him too closely all the time. Bell was not so vigilant. He played cards with Bell every day, and at every game he figured how he could grab Bell's revolver. He seemed to feel a real regret at Bell's death.

"'Bell had been good to me,' he said. 'I never intended to kill him and I wouldn't have done so if he had permitted me to lock him in the armoury. It was foolish of him to run down the stairs. Then there was nothing left but to kill him. He ought to have known that; and I couldn't have missed him if I had tried.'

"But when the Kid told of Ollinger's death, he spoke with bitterness and, even in the darkness, I could see his eyes flash.

"'Ollinger was the meanest man that ever lived,' he said, 'and I hated him worse than any man on earth. When I shot Bell, I thought Ollinger would do exactly what he did—come running over to see what was the matter. As I stood by the window with the shotgun ready for him and saw him start across the road, I knew I had him. He played right into my hand. But I didn't want him to die without knowing I was the man who killed him. So I called, 'Hello, Bob,' to make him look up. You ought to have seen his face when he saw me sighting at him over the barrel of his own gun with which, just a little while before, he had threatened to kill me. He knew he was gone, and the coward's eyes popped out of his head with terror. It was the happiest moment of my life when I pulled the trigger and filled him full of buckshot. My only regret was that I could kill him only once. No matter what chances I had to take, I never would have left Lincoln until I had killed him.'

"I asked the Kid what he proposed to do now," Salazar continued. "He said he was going to Fort Sumner to see his sweetheart.

"'It will be very dangerous to go there,' I told him. 'Garrett's posses will soon be scouring the country for you, and Fort Sumner will be one of the first places they will search. You ought to start for the border at once and get into Mexico where you will be safe.'

"'I'm going to see my girl,' he said, 'if it costs me my life.'

"We talked until midnight. He wouldn't come to my house to sleep. He was expecting pursuit and thought it wiser to sleep out. I brought him some blankets and he made his bed down in the brush.

"'I will never be taken alive again, Ighenio,' he said

as we parted for the night. 'I got too close to a rope for comfort. If they get me again, it will have to be with a bullet.'

"He meant every word of that," Salazar added. "I knew they would have to kill him ever to take him again. He was plainly desperate."

The Kid hung about Las Tablas two days. Salazar saw him several times more, and the Kid met several other Mexicans, including Sepia Salazar and Martin Chavez, now a merchant in Santa Fé. To Chavez, an old friend, he also confided that he was bound for Fort Sumner to see his sweetheart. As he was about to leave the mountains now and strike off across the plains, he needed a horse again. José Jorado borrowed a pony for him from Andy Richardson, manager of the Block ranch. So from peaceful little Las Tablas the Kid rode out of the hills northward for Fort Sumner, his sweetheart's black eyes his lure and guiding stars and the winding trail Destiny's road leading toward the final, inevitable tragedy.

Back in Lincoln, no sooner had the Kid galloped out of town than the street, empty a moment before, suddenly swarmed with excited men, women, and children. Everybody had something to say as to what could have been done or should have been done. Wise plans were advanced for locking the stable door after the horse had been stolen. But there was no pursuit. The prudent villagers did not feel called upon to follow such a dangerous fugitive, who had left behind two corpses as proof of his prowess, and decided to leave the chase to officers paid to risk their lives in such work. They viewed the two dead bodies with curious interest but, strangely enough, left them lying where they had fallen until Sheriff Garrett's return next day. They thronged into the courthouse to read the story of the tragedy as best they might in what tell-tale evidence remained. The monte layout was still spread on the table, the matches and scattered deck of cards near it and the jack of hearts on the floor. Bell's six-shooter with one chamber empty was found in the armoury where the Kid had laid it when he rearmed himself. At the turn of the back stairs, the bullet that had killed Bell was embedded in the wall. The hole is there to this day. It must have been a centre shot. Between the top of the stairs and the hole in the wall is a straight line about on a level with a man's heart.

Though at least two hours elapsed, by the most reliable estimates, between the time Bell and Ollinger were killed and the moment the Kid rode away, no plans of any kind were made by Lincoln citizens to prevent his escape. Tom Larue, the storekeeper, had a thought of interfering and Lincoln still talks about his thought as rather heroic. When he heard the shot that killed Bell, Larue stepped out on the front porch of his store in time to see Ollinger fall. Then, hurrying back into the house, he got his shotgun and was on the point of rushing out when his wife threw her arms around his neck and dissuaded him. So, instead of rushing out, he locked up his store and remained discreetly inside until the Kid was well on his way to the mountains.

"I was a little boy," says Miguel Luna, "and was spinning tops with Savero Gallegos in the road in front of Larue's store. When I heard the shot that killed Bell, I stood looking toward the courthouse wondering what it meant. I saw Ollinger run across the street and the Kid lean out the window with a queer smile on his face and shoot him down. Savero Gallegos and I hid among the ruins of the old McSween home and watched developments. We saw old Goss chasing Billy Burt's pony in the jail pasture. Then we saw the Kid bucked off the first time he mounted. That surprised us because we had seen him ride many a time and he was a cracker-jack rider. As he rode out of town, he met Manuel Baldano, who now lives in Carrizozo. Manuel had a new rope and Billy asked him for it to use in picketing his pony Manuel said it was his brother's, and wouldn't give it to him. But Billy was in a hurry just then and didn't have time for arguments. So he threw a gun down on the boy and got the rope. He tossed Manuel a dollar as he galloped away."

CHAPTER XIX

THE peace of morning lay on White Oaks. The little bowl of a valley was a chalice brimming over with the crystal wine of the sunlight. The green grass on the slopes was like the velvet nap of a rug on which piñon copses formed dark arabesques. Against the turquoise of the April sky the mountains stood with etching-like distinctness.

"I've been busy for the past two months gathering evidence against Pat Coughlin," John W. Poe was saying to Sheriff Garrett, as the two men stood at the edge of the sidewalk in front of the Long Branch saloon. "Billy the Kid with his stolen cattle has made the King of Tularosa rich. I just got back from Tombstone. I found that steers from the last herd the Kid stole on the Canadian River had been sold by Coughlin as far to the southwest as that. I've found a lot of hides with Canadian River brands on them hanging out to dry around Fort Stanton. These also were cattle the Kid had stolen and Coughlin had sold. I'll be ready to lay my evidence before the grand jury as soon as——"

There was a sudden whirr of excitement among the loungers along the street. A Mexican horseman was seen riding toward town out of a tumult of dust on the Carrizozo road. He dipped out of sight in the deep arroyo of the creek, came racing into view again, and, rounding into the main street, halted abruptly beside the two officers, his pony marbled with sweat and foam.

"*El Chivato*," he announced excitedly, "*asesinó a sus dos guardias en Lincoln y se escapó a las sierras. Cogió la pistola de Bell mientras jugaban a monte y tiró una bala dejándole muerto. Luego mató a Ollinger con su propria escopeta cuando éste corrió a través de la calle. Después montó a caballo y huyó del pueblo hacia el poniente. Nadie sabe donde se encuentra ahora.*"

Which conveyed succinctly the news of the tragedy in Lincoln and the escape of Billy the Kid.

Garrett stared at Poe and Poe stared at Garrett. For an interval neither uttered a word. The news struck them like a blow between the eyes.

"Ain't that hell?" said Garrett at length. "I told those fellows to watch the Kid. They must have got careless. Now they're dead and the Kid's gone. That means I've got to do it all over again. Now I've got to kill the Kid or get killed trying. He won't be taken alive again. Well, no use crying over spilt milk. I'll saddle up and strike back for Lincoln."

A few minutes later, Sheriff Garrett went galloping out of town. Out of the mountains about White Oaks, across the Carrizozo plains, up the steep hairpin curves of Nogal Hill, along the edges of dizzy precipices with a thousand-feet drop beneath him, and then on the long down-grade beyond, he travelled under whip and spur, driving his pony to the last limit of its speed. He startled the Mexican farmers in their little jacals along the road as he went dashing past with thunder of hoofs and swirls of dust. Into the pleasant valley of the Bonito he came at last and without drawing rein burst into Lincoln, his sweat-lathered horse staggering with exhaustion.

There was much to be done and no time to lose. With quick decision, Garrett organized his plans to hunt down the escaped outlaw. He gathered a posse of a dozen picked men in Lincoln. He rushed off orders for other posses to take the field from Roswell, Tularosa, and Seven Rivers. He had only a vague idea of the direction the Kid had taken. He could only guess at what place of refuge the fugitive would aim. Every avenue of escape out of the country must be guarded. The dragnet was to be far-flung. The sheriff proposed in his search to comb New Mexico.

The hour for the start was set. The posse assembled in the sheriff's office in Lincoln courthouse for a final council of war.

"I figure," said Garrett, "the Kid's headin' for old Mexico. Once across the border, he'll be safe. Our only chance is to head him off before he gets there. With good luck, we can do it."

"I got an idea the Kid might hole up at Fort Sumner," interposed Former Sheriff "Dad" Peppin.

"No chance," retorted Garrett. "Fort Sumner's only ninety miles. The Kid's no fool. He won't hang around so close, with posses rakin' the whole country for him and knowin' he's got to swing if he's caught."

"That's just it," Peppin answered. "He might calculate you'd think just that way."

"The Kid's too smart to take a chance like that."

"If you don't aim to look for him in Fort Sumner, I'd call it mighty smart in him to go there. He'd be among his friends."

"That's true enough. He's got plenty of friends there. But I don't know as he'd trust 'em. There's that big

reward out for him dead or alive.   Money has been known
to turn friends."

"What's more," persisted Peppin, "he's got a sweetheart in Fort Sumner."

"What does the Kid care about sweethearts?" Garrett
replied with scorn.   "He's thinkin' of no sweethearts.
He's figurin' right now on savin' his neck from the noose.
I tell you he's ridin' hard for the Rio Grande.   His only
hope is Mexico."

"Well, you're bossin' the job," said Peppin, "and that
settles the argument."

"One last word before we hit the trail, boys," added the
sheriff.   "The Kid's desperate.   He ain't goin' to be
taken alive.   You can gamble on that.   If we jump him,
we've got to kill him.   Don't take any chances.   As soon
as you sight him, start shootin'."

So westward out of Lincoln rode Sheriff Garrett and his
posse, gaunt, hawk-eyed men, bronzed with weather
six-shooters jostling in scabbards, sun flashing on rifles
their hunting field New Mexico, their quarry a slendeɪ
youth, five feet eight in his boots, hidden somewhere out
in the vastness of deserts and mountains.

They followed the Kid's trail without knowing it to the
point where he had turned off into Baca road toward
Fort Sumner.   As Garrett had thrown Fort Sumner out
of his calculations they kept on west.   Spreading out, they
ransacked the mountain coverts around Fort Stanton
where the Kid once had had a rendezvous.   They passed
out of the hills and scoured the Carrizozo plains and the
desolate Mal Pais beyond.   They beat across the ghastly,
gleaming chaos of the White Sands.   Far and wide over
the sombre lava desert which an ancient crater spread

along the eastern slopes of the Oscuros—a black wilderness
of jagged iron rocks sentinelled by weird cactus shapes—
they circled and quartered like foxhounds questing on a
cold trail.   They whipped the wild ravines of Chupadero
Mesa.   They searched among the ruins of the Gran
Quivera.   Turning south, they passed through the Three
Rivers country, traversed the Jornado del Muerto, ex-
plored the cañons and valleys of the Organ Mountains,
and came at the end of a bootless hunt into Mesilla.
Not a clue had they found, not a word had they heard of
the Kid's whereabouts.   So, weary, discouraged, and
bedraggled, they trooped back to Lincoln.

The other posses reported equally unsuccessful results.
But Garrett was not yet ready to give up.   He had one
more card to play.   From the Mescalero reservation he
summoned two Apache trailers, lithe, half-naked, moc-
casined fellows, famous among their people for skill in
tracking game and men through trackless wastes.   Given
the direction of the Kid's flight, these human sleuth-
hounds set out from Lincoln on foot.   Along the sides of
the road they worked slowly, patiently, their keen eyes
scrutinizing every inch of ground, until they came to the
trail that branched off to Baca Cañon.   Here where the
Kid had turned they turned also.   Some sign that no
white man could have detected—a stone streaked by the
swift impact of a horseshoe, a weed broken at a certain
height from the ground and at a certain angle, a hoofprint
of more than usual depth—guided these savage trackers
in the right direction.   They broke into a dog-trot, crossed
the Bonito, plunged into Baca Cañon.   To Padilla's
ranch they came at length, led by what microscopic trail
marks no man might know except themselves.   Padilla,
good friend of the Kid that he was, kept a silent tongue

in his head.   Beyond his jacal, the Indians lost the scent.
Turning back to Lincoln, they reported the trail was too
old and too cold to follow.

So the man-hunt ended and Garrett settled down to
watch and wait.   Sooner or later news would reach him.
A rumour would come on the wind out of the dark.   Something somewhere somehow would happen.   In some lonely
bar over the whisky glasses a tongue would wag.   Out
in the vagueness of the Southwest, a leaf would rustle, a
twig would crack.   Abruptly the empty silence would
find a voice.   The Kid's hiding place would be betrayed.
Sooner or later.   But for the time being, the outlaw had
disappeared as if the mountains had opened and engulfed
him.

Poe, who had been appointed one of Garrett's deputies,
remained in White Oaks during May and June busy on
the Coughlin case.   A remarkable man was Poe with a
record behind him and a future ahead.   Standing more
than six feet in height, broad shouldered, and as straight
as a mountain pine, he was a determined, resourceful
man with courage and honesty clearly legible in his frank
face and clear blue eyes.   A native of Kentucky, he had
lived in Texas since early manhood.   As marshal of
Tascosa, hard-boiled cowboy capital of the Panhandle, he
had established a reputation for fearless performance of
duty.   Stories of his exploits still linger along the Canadian.   When Jim Oglesby, bad man from the Indian
Nations, was painting the town, Poe, without drawing a
weapon, disarmed him in mid-rampage and led him off
tamely to the calaboose.   When infuriated citizens
surrounded him and threatened to lynch a prisoner in
his custody, Poe, standing alone, drew his six-shooter and
told them they would have to kill him first and some of

them would die before he did; his quiet heroism bringing the mob to its senses and saving the day. He moved later to Moobeetie, lively little town of the Texas cattle ranges, and was appointed by the Canadian River Cattlemen's Association to ferret out and bring to justice the rich patrons of Billy the Kid, who supported that young outlaw in his rustling operations by buying his stolen cattle. His campaign against Pat Coughlin, King of Tularosa, was his first successful work as a cattle detective in New Mexico.

There dwelt in White Oaks a certain George Graham, who was living out the age-old tragedy of a drunkard. He had once been a man of substance in Texas. But drink and dissipation had played havoc with his means; he had slipped gradually into the depths and was now a down-at-heels derelict making shift to exist as a hanger-on around White Oaks saloons and gambling halls. In more prosperous days, he had known Sam and Dan Dedrick, who kept a livery barn in the mining camp. Since what few coins he managed to scrape together went for whisky and he had no money to pay for a bed, they permitted him, out of charity, to sleep in the haymow of their establishment.

One night in July, two months after Billy the Kid had escaped, Graham crawled into the hay and composed himself for slumber. He was just dozing off when he heard voices in the livery office. He pricked up his ears. The Dedrick brothers were talking together. They exchanged confidences. Evidently in the silence and seclusion of their livery barn at midnight they felt no fear of eavesdroppers. For the moment they had forgotten the derelict stretched in the hay.

What Graham heard startled him into intense wakefulness. He became suddenly aware that he was the possessor of a dangerous secret. The thought troubled him. For hours he tossed in nervous restlessness. It was not until the small hours of morning that he was able to fall asleep.

Standing on the street next day, Poe was speculating idly on the enigma of the Kid's disappearance. Garrett, it seemed, was right. The Kid by this time was doubtless safe across the border in Mexico. Well, at least he would not come back to harry Canadian River herds, and Poe's employers were as well off as though the Kid had been hanged. A trampish man slouched by. Poe rested a casual eye upon him. He had no idea who the fellow was. From the looks of him, he didn't care to know. But to Poe's surprise, the seedy stranger flashed him a look of recognition and, with an almost imperceptible motion of the head, tipped him a signal to follow. Here was a mystery which at first glance did not seem intriguing. But Poe followed—first to the edge of the town and then on a little way into the country. At a point in the road screened from observation by piñon trees, the vagabond turned and faced him.

"Do you remember me?" he asked.

Poe, after a moment's scrutiny, shook his head.

"George Graham."

"Oh, yes," answered Poe. "Back in Tascosa. Of course. How are you, George?"

"Down and out. That's how I am. Which it's no use to tell you. You can see it."

"What's the matter?"

"This is what drink has done to a man who was once a fairly prosperous citizen. But I didn't bring you out here to tell you my troubles. You were my friend in

Tascosa. I have news for you. I know what you're here for."

This mysterious fellow was talking in riddles. Poe wondered if his misfortunes might not have unhinged his mind.

"But I'd be killed if it was ever found out I told you," Graham added. "You must give me your word you'll never mention my name."

Poe promised secrecy.

Graham looked in all directions to make sure no one was in sight.

"All right," he said. "Here it is. Billy the Kid is in Fort Sumner!"

The words gave Poe a thrill.

"What makes you think that?" he asked.

"Listen. You know the Dedrick boys? They have been friends of the Kid for years. The Kid used to hang out at their ranch over in the Bosque Grande country. Whenever he came to White Oaks he made their livery stable his headquarters. Last night, when I had gone to bed in the haymow, I overheard Sam and Dan Dedrick speaking about the Kid. They know where he is. They said he has been in White Oaks since his escape at Lincoln."

Poe smiled incredulously.

"I'm telling you what they said," insisted Graham. "Believe it or not. The Kid, they said, has been right here in White Oaks. They kept him hid in their livery barn several days. What do you think of that? And you walking past the barn a dozen times a day and within a few feet of him. Ever since he killed his guards and got away, the Kid, the Dedricks said, has been hanging around Fort Sumner. Expects to skip to Mexico some time soon. But he hasn't gone yet. He's in Fort Sumner now."

Poe hardly knew what to think. The information was, at least, impressive.

"What you tell me may be true," he said at length. "But it's hard to believe. However, it may be worth investigating. Here's a dollar for you. Go buy yourself a few drinks."

So Billy the Kid was betrayed for a silver dollar by a rum-soaked bum of the boozing-kens. Four drinks of whisky, according to current quotations in White Oaks bars, was the price paid for the secret upon which his life hung as by a hair.

Poe walked in on Garrett in Lincoln next day.

"I don't believe it," said Garrett.

"Neither do I," replied Poe.   "But let's take a chance."

"Humph!" Garrett rubbed his nose reflectively. "Well, we'll go.   But I warn you it'll be just another wild-goose chase."

Sheriff Garrett and Poe rode into Roswell next day and laid the clue before Tip McKinney, one of Garrett's deputies, a veteran man-hunter hailing from Uvalde in Texas.

"I don't take any more stock in it than you fellows," said McKinney. "There's about as much chance of the Kid being in Fort Sumner as of me flying to the moon."

But that evening at sundown the expedition of the three sceptics started from Roswell. They headed toward Lincoln to avert suspicion as to their destination. Ten miles out, they turned sharply to the north. That way Fort Sumner lay.

They rode till midnight, when they picketed their horses and slept on their saddle-blankets. Next day they travelled fifty-five miles and camped for the night in the sandhills six miles from Fort Sumner.

"One of us ought to ride into Fort Sumner now and reconnoitre," said Garrett. "Nose around. Take a drink or two at old Beaver Smith's bar and talk with the fellows. Might learn something if there's anything to learn. But I can't go. Everybody knows me. I lived there two years."

"I can't either," spoke up McKinney. "I've been here half-a-dozen times, and quite a few know me."

"Nobody knows me," said Poe. "I'll go."

"If you don't pick up any information in Fort Sumner," said Garrett, "ride on to Charlie Rudolph's ranch seven miles out on the Las Vegas road. Charlie's an old-timer and a friend of mine and you can lay your cards on the table with him. If the Kid's in the country, he'll tell you. I'll give you a note to him."

Garrett tore a page out of his pocket notebook, scratched off a few lines to Rudolph and gave the paper to Poe.

"McKinney and I will wait here in the sandhills for you until dark," he added. "If you don't come back, we'll ride to the end of the double row of cottonwoods four miles north of Fort Sumner near the little Mexican village of Punta de la Glorietta and meet you there at nine o'clock."

It was ten o'clock in the morning of July 14th when Poe rode into Fort Sumner and hitched his horse in front of Beaver Smith's saloon. The grizzled old proprietor stood in the door.

"Warm day," observed Poe ingratiatingly.

"Where you from?" asked old Beaver, waiving formalities.

"White Oaks."

"Live there?"

"Been doing a little mining. Not much luck. On the way back to my home in Moopeetie."

The little street had been empty when Poe arrived. Now he noted men strolling toward him with a casual air from all directions.   He was soon surrounded by a dozen citizens, all wearing six-shooters, all viewing him with cold-eyed suspicion.

"Stranger in these parts?"

"Where you from?"

"Where you bound?"

They were violating the frontier's code of courtesy in which questions to a stranger had no part.   Being a frontiersman, Poe knew it.   Also he knew why.   But he answered their queries with easy politeness as he had answered Beaver Smith's.

"Come on in and let's have a drink," he suggested.

After the whisky the situation eased a trifle.   Poe discussed crops.   He had a word to say about cattle.   He dropped a few wise reflections on politics.

"Pat Garrett," he remarked at last, slipping in the parenthesis rather adroitly, "was in White Oaks the day I left, looking for the Kid.   They say the Kid's been seen there since his escape."

Sudden profound silence greeted his observation.   His auditors looked at him sullenly and shot furtive glances at one another.   Poe went back to crops, cattle, and politics for an hour or so.   Then he tried again.

"Billy the Kid must be a fine fellow," he said, taking a new tack.   "I don't know anything about him, being a stranger in New Mexico.   But I've been interested in the stories I've heard.   They say he has a sweetheart in Fort Sumner and paid her a flying visit after he broke jail.   Eh?"

Another profound silence shot through with suspicion. It was plain Poe could learn nothing.   These were all friends of the Kid.   Whatever they knew they were keeping to themselves.   To save his visit from being a total loss, Poe went to a restaurant and ate a good meal.   He had had no food except a pocket sandwich since leaving Roswell.

Poe left Fort Sumner in the middle of the afternoon, starting eastward.   A few miles out, he cut across country westward to the Las Vegas road on which Rudolph's ranch was located.   He arrived at Rudolph's at sundown, presented Garrett's note, and was cordially received.

After supper the two men sat on the porch in casual conversation.   Poe's first mention of Billy the Kid had a marked effect upon his host.   Rudolph fidgeted in his chair and tried to change the subject.

"I've heard," remarked Poe relentlessly, "the Kid's been in hiding in Fort Sumner ever since his escape."

"No truth to that," snapped Rudolph with notable perturbation.   "Such a report is silly.   The Kid's too shrewd to be caught lingering around here with a price on his head and posses hunting him everywhere."

Poe played cautiously a little longer and then, following Garrett's advice, laid his cards on the table.

"Sheriff Garrett," he said, "is waiting for me now near Fort Sumner.   We have reason to believe the Kid is there.   Garrett has sent me to you for definite information as to the Kid's hiding place.   I'd like the straight truth from you."

"I know nothing about the Kid," Rudolph protested, his excitement changing to downright alarm.   "I can't tell you a thing.   If the Kid was around here and I told you where he could be found, my life wouldn't be worth a penny.   But I don't believe he's around Fort Sumner.   You can set that report down as a lie."

Poe joined Garrett and McKinney at nine o'clock that night at the appointed meeting place at the north end of the double row of cottonwoods and recounted his day's experiences. The suspicion he encountered in Fort Sumner and Rudolph's agitation convinced him, he said, that the Kid was somewhere in the Fort Sumner vicinage. Garrett was not so sanguine.

"But as long as we are here," Garrett said, "we might as well try watching Charlie Bowdre's old home in Fort Sumner. Manuela Bowdre, Charlie Bowdre's widow, still lives there with her mother, and if the Kid's in these parts, he's probably hiding there."

They set off from Fort Sumner through the four-mile avenue of cottonwoods. A quarter of a mile from town, they hid their horses in a grove of trees on the Pecos and took a position in the old peach orchard at the north edge of the village. Just across the road from their place of concealment stood the old military hospital in which Manuela Bowdre had her home. A full moon was in the sky, making the landscape as bright as day, but the peach trees were in full leaf, and in the deep shadows they were safe from chance discovery. For two hours they remained there silently watching the Bowdre door like three cats at a mouse hole. But no sign of the Kid rewarded their patience. It was hard on midnight when they decided to abandon their vigil.

"I had no faith in this trip in the first place," growled Garrett. "I'm willing to bet the Kid ain't in Fort Sumner and never has been here since his escape. We'll go back to our horses now and start for Roswell. Best to put a little distance between us and Fort Sumner before day-break."

"Let's go see Pete Maxwell before we give it up,"

insisted Poe doggedly. "If the Kid's in Fort Sumner or has been here, he'll know beyond a doubt. Maybe he'll tell us."

"Maybe," replied Garrett dubiously, "and maybe he won't. If the Kid happened to hear Maxwell had betrayed him, Pete would be due to start on a long journey. But just to satisfy you, Poe, we'll see him."

They crossed the road, white with moonl ght, slipped into the sleeping town, stole noiselessly through the streets in the shadows of the houses, and came out into the broad open space that had once been the parade ground of the army post. Before them stood the Maxwell home.

Once used as officers' quarters, it was a large two-story building containing twenty rooms, its lower walls of adobe bricks sustaining a frame superstructure with a row of dormer windows along its gable roof opening from the upper rooms. A wide sheltered veranda ran across its front and along the north and south sides. It faced east on the old parade ground, from which it was separated by a low picket fence that extended fifty feet to the south to a row of adobe houses along the side yard. A cannon, relic of old soldier days, stood outside the fence near the northeast corner. At the southeast corner beside the front gate grew a tall cottonwood tree.

"Pete Maxwell's sleeping room is right there in the southeast corner of the house," said Garrett when they reached the gate. "You fellows wait here outside and I'll go in and have a talk with him."

Garrett stepped across the porch and enteredt he door of Maxwell's room which, on this warm summer night, had been left open. Poe sat down on the edge of the porch at the gateway. McKinney squatted down on his heels, cowboy fashion, just outside the picket fence and rolled himself a cigarette. The moon was riding westward from the zenith and the two men, sitting in silence, merged into the dark, heavy shadows falling eastward from the building.

Maxwell's room was in deep darkness. Garrett paused just inside the door for a moment until his eyes grew accustomed to the obscurity. Then, groping his way to a chair at the head of the bed, he sat down and gently roused Maxwell.

The room was twenty feet square. There were three windows, two in the front and one in the south wall near the door, but the roof of the porch prevented even a faint reflection of moonlight from entering. Maxwell's bed stood against the south wall, its foot near the door, its head against the front wall. There was a bureau in the northwest corner, a fireplace in the west wall, and a washstand between the fireplace and the door. The floor was carpeted.

Maxwell was surprised when he awoke from a deep sleep and saw Garrett sitting at his bedside. He rubbed his eyes.

"Oh, hello, Pat," he mumbled. *"Qué hace Usted aquí?"*

"About the Kid, Pete," said Garrett in Spanish. "I've had word——"

A voice sounded outside—a voice that Garrett knew. He cut short his words. He sat in tense, sudden silence, listening. . . .

When Garrett and his deputies stole into Fort Sumner from the peach orchard, Billy the Kid was in the house of Saval Gutierrez, Pat Garrett's brother-in-law, which stood at the south edge of the Maxwell side yard not more than fifty feet from the Maxwell home. He had come in only a few minutes before from a sheep ranch several miles south on the Pecos. He was tired. He took off his coat, boots, and hat and threw himself on a bed. He smiled to himself as he thought how neatly he had thrown Garrett off the scent. While the posses were sweeping New Mexico, he had been safe in Fort Sumner among friends. But it was time for him to get out of the country. These bloodhounds on his trail would nose him out sooner or later. He would start for Mexico to-morrow night. And while the Kid dreamed his dream, death was waiting in ambush for him fifty feet away.

"Celsa," he called.

Celsa Gutierrez, Saval's wife, who had been waiting up for the Kid to come in from the sheep camp, stepped into the room from the kitchen.

"I'm hungry, Celsa," said the Kid. "Can't you get me a bite to eat?"

Celsa rummaged through her pantry.

"There is nothing here but some cold tortillas and coffee, Chiquito," she said, "but Pete Maxwell killed a beef to-day. It is hanging in the north porch of the Maxwell house. I'll go cut you off a steak and cook you a good supper."

She went back into the kitchen and got her butcher knife. She was reaching for her *rebozo* hanging on a nail on the wall to throw over her head against the night damp.

"I'll go for the meat," said the Kid, getting up from the bed.

"No, *muchacho*," protested Celsa. "You must stay here. There is no telling what might happen to you. Danger is always near you. You must not venture out to-night."

On this night of nights, Fate, it might seem, was setting the stage. There was no need for the Kid to come in from the sheep camp.   But he had come.   There was now no need for him to go for the meat.   But he went.

"There is no danger, Celsa," he said.   "Give me the butcher knife."

So the Kid started out for the meat just as he was, bareheaded, coatless, with only socks on his feet, the butcher knife in his right hand and, naturally enough, as he was left-handed, his forty-one calibre double-action revolver in its scabbard at his left side.   He stepped from the door of Saval Gutierrez's home not more than a minute after Garrett had entered Pete Maxwell's room.

The familiar scene outdoors was more than usually serene in the pale moonlight.   The deep hush of midnight lay upon the slumbering town.   The great, dark, silent mass of the Maxwell home loomed fifty feet ahead of him.   There was no movement, no sound to indicate danger, nothing to warn him to be on guard.   He was hungry. The carcass of beef hung in the north porch.   He would cut off a good steak for himself.   There was no better cook in Fort Sumner than Celsa.   He would have a regular feast.   .   .   .   He did not see the two deputies sitting in the heavy shadows of the porch.   With quick, easy stride, still thinking of his supper, he walked straight toward them, his soul off watch.

Poe saw him coming.   McKinney, squatting behind the palings rolling a cigarette, neither saw nor heard him. The Kid's figure stood out clearly in the moonlight as he moved noiselessly on bootless feet over the matted grass. Not a flash of suspicion disturbed Poe's mind that this was the desperado he was hunting, whom he knew he had to kill on sight, who otherwise would kill him instantly and without mercy.   Strangely enough at this tense, critical moment of the long chase, the deputy's wits seem

to have been wool-gathering. He looked at the approaching figure with only casual interest, wondered in a mildly
curious way who this half-dressed youth might be wandering about at midnight, and contented himself with the
half-formed, passing thought that probably it was one of
Pete Maxwell's sheep herders.

Coming on rapidly, the Kid stepped up on the porch
and almost stumbled over Poe before he saw him. If his
soul had been off watch before, that instant it sprang to
hair-trigger alertness. There was a lightning-quick movement of his left hand and Poe was staring in astonishment
into the muzzle of the Kid's revolver.

"*Quién es?*"

The Kid's voice was vibrant with a suddenly awakened
sense of danger. Who were these two armed strangers
at Pete Maxwell's house at midnight? He began to back
away across the porch.

Poe was nonplussed, his mind somehow still out of focus.
He thought with a certain touch of pity that, without
intention, he had frightened this poor sheep herder. It
seemed to him vaguely that he owed the simple rustic
some sort of apology. He got to his feet and took a step
toward the Kid.

"Don't be scared," he said reassuringly. "I'm not going to hurt you."

The Kid kept backing away.

"*Quién es?*" he snapped out again.

Poe said nothing more. He did not know what to say.
He had never seen a sheep herder act like this. The
fellow must be crazy. It did not occur to him to draw
his six-shooter. He stood there feeling rather foolish,
the Kid's gun all the while pointed at his breast.
McKinney had stepped up on the porch and was standing

now a pace behind Poe. He, too, fancied the Kid a sheep
herder and was equally at a loss to understand the situation.

The Kid backed into the doorway of Maxwell's room.
There he paused for an instant, half-hidden by the thick
adobe wall, his gun still at aim.

"*Quién es?*" he called a third time.

Then he turned and stepped into the black darkness
of the chamber; into security, as he fancied; into a death
trap, in reality. In the darkness, Death crouched,
waiting, ready.

Coming in out of the bright moonlight, the Kid could
hardly see his hand before him. But he did not need to
see. He knew the room of old, the arrangement of the
furniture—every detail. He groped to the foot of the
bed, stepped around to the side, leaned slightly over
Maxwell.

"*Quiénes son esos hombres afuera*, Pete?" he asked.
(Who are those fellows outside?)

Garrett, sitting silent in the darkness at the head of the
bed, could have stretched out a hand and touched the
Kid. He knew at once this was the Kid. He had recognized his voice when the Kid had flashed his first Spanish
question at Poe outside on the porch. He had recognized
the familiar figure silhouetted against a patch of moonlight as the Kid came in the door. If no doubt was in his
mind of the Kid's identity, neither was there doubt as to
what he himself must do and do quickly if he was to live
to see the light of another day. His mind was instantly
made up.

As the Kid entered, Garrett, still sitting in his chair,
reached for his six-shooter. But so quickly did the little
drama in the darkness rush to its climax, he was still in

the act of drawing his weapon from its scabbard when the Kid, two feet away, was bending over Maxwell with the query that was never answered. The Kid felt, rather than saw, the noiseless movement of Garrett's arm. He caught a sudden, vague glimpse of Garrett's form bulking dimly in the darkness. He sprang back to the middle of the room and threw his revolver to a level.

"*Quién es?*" he demanded sharply.

Dropping over sideways from the chair toward the floor in a tricky, dodging movement, Garrett answered the question with a shot. A flare of lurid flame lighted up the darkness for an instant, the room shook with a sudden crashing explosion, and Billy the Kid fell dead with a bullet through his heart.

Garrett fired a second shot as quickly as his finger could pull the trigger and, bolting for the door, was out of the room in three strides. Pete Maxwell, in wild panic, scrambled over the foot of his bed and, hard on Garrett's heels, dashed outside, a fat, ludicrous figure clad only in his nightshirt. He blundered on the porch into Poe, who shoved his six-shooter into his stomach and would have killed him, had not Garrett, with a hurried explanation, knocked the weapon aside.

"It was the Kid who came in there on to me," Garrett told Poe, "and I think I got him."

"Pat," replied Poe, still under the sheep-herder hallucination, "I believe you have killed the wrong man."

"I'm sure it was the Kid," responded Garrett, "for I knew his voice and could not have been mistaken."

They heard several gurgling gasps inside. Then there was silence. But no one dared enter that room of death. A spectre of fear stood in the darkness like the menacing ghost of the dead. ......

.   .   .   Paulita Maxwell, aroused from sleep, came out on the porch and joined the four men huddled along the wall. They broke the news to her. She received it in silence without show of emotion. Pete Maxwell hurried into the house and returned with a tallow candle. Also with trousers on. He reached out a cautious hand and set the lighted taper on the window sill. Peeping furtively into the room now faintly illuminated by the flickering flame, he saw the Kid stretched out face downward in the centre of the floor.

They went in then. Upon examining the body they found that Garrett's first bullet had struck the Kid directly over the heart, a centre shot, passing through him and burying itself in the west wall. What had become of his second bullet they were at that time unable to discover. The Kid had not fired a shot. He lay with his gun still clutched in his left hand and, in his right, Celsa Gutierrez's kitchen butcher knife. Every cartridge chamber of his revolver was loaded.

They carried the body across the Maxwell yard into a deserted carpenter shop, full of dust and cobwebs, its floor littered with shavings, and laid it on an old work bench. The town was aroused by now. Excited Mexican men and women gathered at the scene and crowded into the shop. When the women saw the Kid lying dead, the moon shining on his white face through a weather-stained window, they broke into a hysteria of tears and grief, filling the place with their cries. Celsa Gutierrez screamed as one demented. Nasaria Yerbe lifted up her voice in wild lamentations. Abrana Garcia, a figure of tragedy, pale with fury, shook her clenched fists aloft, called down curses on Pat Garrett, shouted threats to kill him. Deluvina Maxwell, the Navajo servant of the

Maxwell household, whose idol the Kid had been, burst into a passion of sobs.   Throwing her arms about the Kid, she covered his face with her tears.   "*Mim uchacho!*" she wailed, "*Mi pobre muchacho!*"

Bringing candles, the women lighted them about the body.   In the shine of the candles, the Kid lay all night in rude state, the dusty work bench for his bier.   And all night the women in their black dresses, with their black *rebozos* about their heads, crouched along the walls in the dim, dingy room, weeping.

It was a wild night in Fort Sumner.   Men stood in groups in the street and about the Maxwell home.   All had six-shooters.   Some had rifles.   They discussed the Kid's death in muttered undertones.   "Shot down in the dark." "Never had a chance."   "Nothing but straight murder." They worked themselves up to a fever pitch of excitement.   They threatened vengeance.   Garrett, Poe, and McKinney sat until daybreak in a room in the Maxwell home, their guns in their hands ready for instant action. They expected an attack from the Kid's friends.   But no openly hostile demonstration developed.   After the inquest next morning, held by a justice of the peace, they mounted their horses and set off for Roswell, their departure watched by grim, sullen groups that hurled savage imprecations after them.

What became of Garrett's second bullet remained an unsolved enigma for years.   No trace of it and no mark it had left could be found.   Finally it was discovered embedded in the underside of the top of the washstand which had stood across the room from Garrett.   From the angle at which it had struck, it must have been fired almost from the level of the floor when Garrett dropped over sideways from his chair. The twisted lump of lead bore silent and unmistakable witness to a panic. It must have missed the Kid by six feet.

Calm analysis of the tragedy reveals unaccountable blunders. The Kid made two egregious mistakes and, though the explanation of each is obvious, both were out of keeping with his usual methods and his desperate character. He could have killed Poe and McKinney when he had them covered on the porch. He could have killed Garrett when he threw down his gun on his shadowy form in the darkness. These were two chances to save his life; he took advantage of neither. It is evident that the dubious thought that the three men might be friends of Maxwell's bent upon some peaceful mission stayed the Kid's deadly trigger finger. It would have been more like his true self to shoot first and ask questions afterward. Yet he did nothing but ask questions. He hesitated, perhaps for the first time in his life, and death was the result of his hesitation. According to Poe, not more than thirty seconds elapsed from the moment the Kid entered Maxwell's room until he was killed. Blundering strangely from the beginning of the episode to its fatal termination, the Kid, in his last flash of consciousness, it is safe to say, did not know who killed him.

The mistake credited to Poe and McKinney savours of a momentary aberration in view of the time, place, and circumstances. Their failure to suspect the Kid's identity is incomprehensible and their persistence in the belief that he was a harmless sheep herder, even after he had jerked out his gun, seems sheer stupidity. Both were men of fine minds, and their dullness in such a desperate crisis is hard to explain. Either could have killed the

Kid as he came toward them in the moonlight except for this singular apathy. Only the Kid's own blunder kept their mistake from costing their lives.

Though the cards were stacked against the Kid that night and it was written in the stars that he must die, Garrett was the only one of the four principals in the tragedy who acted as he might logically have been expected to act and as the occasion demanded he should act. Everything he did and everything he did not do proved the shrewdness and craft of an alert, quick-thinking brain. If he had spoken, the Kid would have recognized him by his voice. If he had risen from his chair, the Kid would have recognized him by his height. In either case, he would have died instantly. But Garrett did not speak, did not rise, did not hesitate. He fired. He alone made no mistake.

Fort Sumner had been home to the Kid, if under Heaven he had had a home, and the last rites were a labour of love in which all Fort Sumner joined. Domingo Lubacher, man of all work, knocked together a coffin of rough pine boards. Francisco Medina, who still lives on the ranch of Don Manuel Abreu, dug the grave. The hearse was a rickety old wagon drawn by a pair of scrawny Mexican ponies. Not six people were left in Fort Sumner during the funeral. The entire population, men, women, and children, turned out to do the Kid last honours and followed his corpse to the little military cemetery a short distance east of town. A stranger might have thought the funeral that of Fort Sumner's most distinguished citizen.

They laid the Kid to rest beside Charlie Bowdre and Tom O'Folliard, his old-time comrades in many a foray and desperate adventure. His grave was at one end of the row, O'Folliard's at the other, and Bowdre's in the middle. Pat Garrett had killed them all. At the head of the little mound they set a wooden cross on which was painted in crude zigzag letters, "Billy the Kid."

The row of three graves in the little cemetery on the windswept, desolate river flats marked the end of the long campaign to establish law and order west of the Pecos. The Kid was dead; his outlaw band was wiped out. Sheriff Garrett's work was done.

CHAPTER XX

HO! FOR old Fort Sumner. You set out gaily. Your fancy conjures up quaint pictures of the romantic old place. How does it look now? Is it the same as in old frontier days? You propose to ramble through the old home of Pete Maxwell and his sister, Paulita. You will see the room in which Billy the Kid was killed. You will stroll through the shady aisles of the old peach orchard. You will visit old Beaver Smith's former drink-parlour. You revel in pleasant anticipations.

From new Fort Sumner, the commonplace town by the railroad, your road leads south along the famous avenue of cottonwoods through irrigated farmlands. The avenue is still an avenue but there are woeful gaps in the twin rows of giant trees. Pecos Valley farmers care more for wheat, beans, potatoes, than for beauty. Where the old trees shut off the sunlight from their precious acres, they have chopped them down. Which in this treeless land seems a sort of crime.

"Under ditch, this land's worth two and three hundred dollars an acre," says Old Man Charlie Foor, your guide. "But where you can't get water on it, it ain't worth settin' a Mexican to plough it."

You come at length to the southern edges of cultivation. The double row of cottonwoods ends abruptly. Before you, to the south, as far as the eye can see, stretches a grassy level plain between the Pecos River and the table-top hills along the east. Range cattle are pasturing here and there. Coming from the northwest, the river bends to the south and loses itself in the far distance. You have a view of a broad reach of bronze water which, in the sun, looks like a highway paved with gold. Old Man Foor halts. You look at him curiously, expecting an explanation.

"There it is," he says.

"There what is?"

"Old Fort Sumner."

He sweeps the empty landscape with a casual wave of his hand.

You gulp down your astonishment. You had expected to find much. You find nothing.

"There ain't no such place as old Fort Sumner," Foor tells you. "Not now. It's gone."

Gone absolutely. Engulfed in the past. A town that was. As if it had never been. Not a house standing. Nothing to suggest its old life, business, bustle, gaiety. Its site a waste expanse of grass and weeds. Gone back to wilderness. Wild flowers waving above it like banners of victory. The old four-mile avenue of cottonwoods, once the trail to romance, now a road to desolation.

Surely, you think, Old Man Foor has made a mistake. But no. Old Man Foor has lived in and around old Fort Sumner for forty-odd years. He kept a saloon in the town. He was postmaster for twenty years. He knows the old place like a book. He is knocking around seventy now, as he tells you; a white-haired, white-moustached, kindly old philosopher; a good, steady-going, old-time Western man, who has seen hard knocks in his day and emerged out of rough pioneer experiences into a mellow old age.

He conducts you to a great, irregular, grass-grown mound.

"This," he says, "was the old military hospital. Where that steer's grazin', the old Texas road come in from the east. Charlie Bowdre used to live here with his wife, Manuela. Pat Garrett killed Tom O'Folliard right over there. Over yonder was the old peach orchard where Garrett, Poe, and McKinney hid on the night Billy the Kid was killed. It used to spread over a powerful lot of ground. You never seen anything prettier than when it was in full bloom in the spring o' the year. See them two lone trees? They're all that's left of thousands. They're the old peach orchard now."

A little to the south across an irrigating ditch emptying into the Pecos River is a long, low, tumbled mound buried under bunchgrass and sunflowers. This, Foor tells you, is the remains of the barracks of the soldiers. Fifty yards farther south is another mound of the same kind, marking the second row of barracks. Along this mound, Foor points out where stood the home of Saval Gutierrez, out of which Billy the Kid walked to his death.

Main Street was once along the river bank. Now it is an indistinguishable part of the cattle range. The Pecos has eaten away most of the land on which stood the stores and bars that formerly fronted on the ancient thorough-fare. The site of Beaver Smith's famous old saloon is probably by now at the bottom of the Gulf of Mexico. Off to the east, still plainly marked, is the old parade ground, a gravelly tract on which weeds and grass grow thinly. As you skirt its edges, a jackrabbit jumps up almost from under your feet and scuttles off in a lop-sided run.

Between the river and the old parade ground is the site of the old Maxwell home. Its adobe foundation walls, now rounded, grass-green mounds, mark off a great rectangle, divided into what were once the ground-floor rooms. Foor helped to tear down the old house when Lonny Horn, a cattleman of Trinidad, bought it and took out its timbers and beams to be used in the house he built on his cattle ranch thirty miles to the east.

"This is the room," says Foor, standing in the sunlight knee-deep in grass in a square depression, "where Billy the Kid was killed. There in that corner stood Pete Maxwell's bed. Against that east wall sat Pat Garrett. Right out there was the corner of the porch where Poe and McKinney was waitin' for him. Here where this bunch of sacatone is growin' was the door the Kid come in at, and here in the centre of the room where I'm standing now, he fell dead."

The scene is undramatic. You see some grass, an old man mopping his perspiring brow with a red bandanna, over there a cow grazing; the river in the background. Sunlight is picking out all the secret places of the midnight tragedy of long ago. This is the bare stage of the drama, all the properties vanished, all the actors gone. Yet somehow the spot is grippingly impressive. It pulls at the imagination. For one tense, thrilling moment you see the old tragedy enacted over again almost within arm's reach. There is Billy the Kid coming silently toward you across the yard in the moonlight. You hear his sharp, "*Quién es?*" as he stumbles upon Poe and McKinney on the porch. You hear his tense question to Pete Maxwell as he steps swiftly to the side of the bed.   In the sudden illuminating glare of Pat Garrett's six-shooter, you have a quick vision of him standing there in the centre of the room only a few feet from you, taut, alert, suddenly at bay, his revolver pointing.   He crashes down at full length at your very feet.   You hear his last choking gasps for breath. . . .

"Right here," Old Man Foor is saying as he pokes a finger into the atmosphere at a level with his breast, "was where Pat Garrett's bullet buried itself in the west wall after passing through the Kid's heart.   When Pete Maxwell hired me to fix up the old house, I covered the bullet hole under a new coat of wall paper."

Billy the Kid lies buried in what it is easy to fancy is the dreariest little cemetery in all the world.   A quarter of a mile from the spot at which he met death is a half-acre of half-desert land enclosed by a barbed-wire fence. It might pass at a glance for an abandoned cattle corral. The flat ground is sparsely covered with salt grass, bunch-grass, prickly pear, sagebrush, greasewood, and Spanish gourd.   Here and there are half-wrecked paling enclosures about neglected graves; here and there, broken, mouldering crosses half fallen or leaning at crazy angles.   In the summer sunshine, the place looks God-forsaken; a mocking bird singing happily on a fence post fails to relieve its grimness.   On a leaden day of cold rain, it is the concentrated essence of loneliness and desolation.   When winds are asweep through the Pecos Valley, they whimper and moan in the barbed-wire fence like troubled ghosts.

"The cemetery," says Old Man Foor, "used to have an adobe wall around it with an arched gateway with a cross on top.   It was the burying ground of the army post at first.   Sixty soldiers was buried here, quite a few of 'em killed in Indian wars. When the Government decided to abandon Fort Sumner as a military post, the bodies was moved to the national cemetery at Santa Fé. The graveyard was then laid out with gravelled paths. The headstones and wooden crosses had names and dates on 'em. You'd see flowers on the graves now and then. The place, you might say, was a decent spot for dead men to sleep in. It looked like holy ground—a *campo santo*, as the Mexicans called it. But that was long ago. Now the name it goes by is 'Hell's Half-Acre.' It looks blighted; like it had a curse on it. It's a graveyard of murdered men. Twelve men who died with their boots on are buried in it. They say it's haunted. Some folks'll drive a mile out of their way at night to keep from passin' it."

Old Man Foor knocks the dottle of tobacco out of his pipe against the heel of his boot.

"Of the twelve men who was killed," he goes on, "two was Mexicans, one a Negro soldier who had deserted from the army, and the other nine white men. Maybe I can remember 'em—le'me see. There was Billy the Kid, Charlie Bowdre, and Tom O'Folliard; they're buried together in a row. There was George Peacock, killed by a fellow named White. Then Felipe Beaubien. They said he was killed while tryin' to hold up Felipe Holtman's store, but I never believed that; I think it was plain murder. Francisco Gallego, killed by Tom Moran, a cowpuncher, was another. And John Legg, a saloon keeper. John Farris, killed by Barney Mason, is buried here, too. Joe Grant, killed by Billy the Kid in José Valdez's saloon, lies just a few feet from the man who killed him. That's nine. The Negro deserter makes ten. I forget who the other two were. They were all killed in old Fort Sumner.

It was a right lively little town in its day and a powerful easy place to get killed in.   None of the graves are marked and mighty few people now know where any of them are."

Old Man Foor looks at the gate to get his bearings, walks a little distance, as by a compass, and halts.   With a knotted forefinger he points down to a strip of flat, yellow, sun-cracked earth that is strangely bare.

"This is the spot," says the old man.   "Under this strip of baked clay lies Billy the Kid."

The bare space is perhaps the length of a man's body. Salt grass grows in a mat all around it, but queerly enough stops short at the edges and not a blade sprouts upon it. A Spanish gourd vine with ghostly gray pointed leaves stretches its trailing length toward the blighted spot but, within a few inches of its margin, veers sharply off to one side as if with conscious purpose to avoid contagion. Perfectly bare the space is except for a shoot of prickly pear that crawls across it like a green snake; a gnarled, bristly, heat-cursed desert cactus crawling like a snake across the heart of Billy the Kid.

"It's always bare like this," says Old Man Foor, standing back from the spot as if half-afraid of some inexplicable contamination.   "I don't know why.   Grass or nothin' else won't grow on it—that's all.   You might almost think there's poison in the ground."

Narrow cracks made by the blistering sun have outlined on the hard yellow surface the crude suggestion of a picture.

"If you stand at a certain angle," says Foor, "them cracks look a little like a skeleton hand.   Stand over here. See?   Can you make it out?   Them four lines there look like a dead man's long, crooked fingers reachin' out for something; and this short line here mightily resembles a bony thumb. Funny, ain't it?"

You look closely, curiously, at the sun-drawn skiagraph. The resemblance is unmistakable. The weird shape startles you. Can it be the thing has some cryptic, fathomless meaning? What are those long, bony fingers reaching for? Who knows? But there it is clearly sketched in the hard yellow clay—a skeleton hand, reaching . . . reaching ......

"I reckon if you dug down under there, you wouldn't find much of the Kid left," says Old Man Foor. "It's more than forty years since they put him away. You might, maybe, find his skull. They say the skull goes last. The Kid used to have buck teeth that made him look like he was laughin' when he wasn't. And like as not, his buck teeth make his skull look like it's laughin' yet. It kind o' gives you the creeps to think of him down there under the earth still laughin'."

Foor takes a few steps toward the north.

"Bowdre's grave is here," he says, "and O'Folliard's here at the other end of the row. Them three fellers was pals in life and they're pals in death. There wouldn't be no finding the graves they sleep in unless you knew where to look. There's mighty few people left alive who know exactly where Billy the Kid's grave is. There's Mrs. Paulita Jaramillo, who was Paulita Maxwell when she was a girl—she knows; and Francisco Medina, who dug the grave; and Deluvina Maxwell, the old Navajo woman who lives with the family of Don Manuel Abreu; and myself. I reckon that's about all. There was once a path running through the centre of the cemetery from north to south, and the Kid's grave was three feet west of this path and thirty-one steps from the gate. I knew the grave when it was new-made and had a cross with the Kid's name on it at the head of it, and fresh flowers on it every day that the Mexican women of old Fort Sumner used to put there. The cross was shot away in 1883. Some soldiers passing through in charge of a bunch of Ute Indians sat on the adobe wall around the cemetery and popped away at the cross with their rifles in drunken devilment. Shot it plumb to kindling wood. And it never was replaced. I came out here with Pat Garrett years after the cross had been shot away. He knew about where the Kid's grave was but I had to show him the exact spot.

"'God rest his soul,' said Pat. 'If it wasn't him sleeping here it might be me. He would have killed me if I hadn't killed him.'"

Old Man Foor tamps some plug-cut into his pipe and, lighting a match on the seat of his trousers, gets a smoke under way with a few resounding puffs.

"There was once some talk about erectin' a monument over the Kid's grave," he resumes. "Somebody tried to start a public subscription. But people in New Mexico seemed scandalized. 'Why, he killed twenty-one men,' they said. 'Contribute to a monument for such a terrible desperado? Not on your life.' So the scheme fell through. Then I heard talk of Frank Coe settin' up a tombstone. He was a great friend of the Kid, and he's pretty well off now and could afford to do it if he wanted to. But he ain't made no special move in that direction yet that I know of. Anyway, the Kid's grave is still unmarked."

Old Man Foor pulls reflectively at his white moustache.

"Seems to me the grave ought to have some sort of marker," he says. "Sightseers and tourists come out here every year to see it. You might think it was some kind of a shrine, to hear them talk. There was one lady I brought out here once who got all riled up when she didn't find no tombstone. 'It's a shame,' says she. 'It ain't decent. The State of New Mexico or the State Historical Society or somebody owes it to posterity,' she says, 'to set up some kind of a tablet or a monument or a tombstone. Why,' says she, 'Billy the Kid's grave is one of the shrines of romance of the Southwest.' I never heard nobody carry on so. She seemed real disturbed about it.

"Well," concludes Old Man Foor, shooting a stream of tobacco smoke out into the sunshine, "the Kid was a bad feller; I ain't disputin' that. But he made considerable history in New Mexico as long as his trigger finger held out. I wouldn't say the kind of history he made entitled him to no monument, but it does seem to me that a fellow that raised as much hell as he did in early days deserves some kind of a marker over his last resting place. It don't have to be a equestrian statue nor nothing big and fine. Just a plain little slab of gray granite would do. If they don't hurry up and put up some kind of stone the site of his grave will be lost. The old-timers who know where it is are dying off mighty fast these days."

Romance weaves no magic glamour in this Hell's Half-Acre where the Kid sleeps his last sleep. From this coign of disillusion one sees his tragic life in stark perspective, crowded with outlawry, vendetta, hatreds, murders; twenty-one dead men like ghostly mile posts marking his brief journey of twenty-one years, a journey that through all the twists and turns of its crimson trail marched inevitably toward this lozenge of cactus-shadowed desolation.

As you stand in a mood of reverie above the lonely spot,

a vagrant wind whisks across the plain a tiny dust-devil that spins for a moment madly, futilely, and is swallowed up in nothingness. This, in quick apocalypse, is the life of Billy the Kid—a little cyclone of deadliness whirling furiously, purposelessly, vainly, between two eternities. A little space of bare desert earth lost in the sagebrush is the guerdon of all his glory. For this, he lived and died. Here in his nameless grave on the dreary, wind-swept Pecos flats under sun and rain and drifting snows, the boy of the tiger heart rests at last in peace.

CHAPTER XXI

HISTORY, that records the long fight of sheriffs and marshals and peacemakers of all kinds to tame the West and establish law and order, furnishes few finer examples of the frontier sheriff than Pat Garrett. He was brave, resourceful, tireless, and in the conscientious performance of his duty, as cold and impersonal as the law itself. His psychology was that of a sheriff. The law was explicit; it pointed out his path of duty clearly; and he carried out the law to the last letter without sentiment or malice or resentment. No personal feeling of any kind ever clouded his ideas of the law or his duty under the law. He was in a way a legal machine. He moved along his path of duty as crushingly and inexorably as a steam-roller. If he set out to arrest a man, he arrested him or killed him. When he took a trail, he followed it to the end.

Cold and relentless as he undoubtedly was, he was not instinctively a killer. He killed only three men in his life—Tom O'Folliard, Charlie Bowdre, and Billy the Kd —and in each instance the killing was justified by the circumstances. He was free of any taint of blood-thirstiness. In that time and country, it was "Hands up!" with every man he arrested, and if he had been dominated by a murderous spirit, he could have killed many men with impunity and within the law. But beneath his hard surface was a certain kindly humanity, and in many crises he refrained from bloodshed when a less merciful man in his position would have killed without hesitation.

Garrett was virtually unknown when he killed Billy the Kid, and the Kid's death made him famous overnight. The report of the six-shooter that ended the outlaw's career was heard throughout the nation. Newspaper readers everywhere knew of New Mexico's desperado who had killed twenty-one men when he was twenty-one years old, and to whatever far corner the Kid's name had been borne, there also travelled the name of the man who had killed him. It was as if Garrett had become heir to the Kid's fame.

Fame, in fact, came to Garrett in a sort of deluge. He became suddenly a heroic and outstanding figure. Distinguished people sought his acquaintance. Everybody was eager to know him. His advent in any town caused a stir of excited interest and people pointed him out and whispered, "There goes Pat Garrett, the man who killed Billy the Kid." Visitors to New Mexico who had never heard of Glorietta Pass or Truches Peak or Taos or the Zuni villages had heard of Pat Garrett and wanted to see him, to meet him, to shake his hand. He was honoured everywhere. He walked in an aura of glory.

But Garrett had a level head on his shoulders that was not to be turned by flattery and applause. He took glory as coolly as he took danger. He remained the same calm, poised, homespun personality, the same Pat Garrett who had been a professional buffalo hunter in the Panhandle and a saloon keeper in old Fort Sumner. Though he had moods of taciturnity, he was, on the whole, an easy-going, good-natured man, who loved the society of boon companions, a drink, a joke, a good story. He had a drawling speech and a dry, sly humour, and though his gray eyes looked rather tragic and the expression of his asymmetrical face was saturnine, there was usually a smile or a laugh just beneath the surface.

It is interesting to know that Garrett, who was Billy the Kid's friend for two years, who played monte with him, drank with him, and danced with the same Mexican girls at Fort Sumner, and who at last stalked him and killed him, placed a high estimate on the Kid as a man and a fighter.

"The Kid was a likable fellow," said Garrett. "He was quiet. There wasn't any fuss or bluster in him. He was not quarrelsome; he never hunted trouble. If you'd never met him before or heard of him, you'd have thought him a mild, inoffensive sort of boy. You certainly never would have taken him for a fighter or a killer. But there was something about him even when he was friendliest that made you feel that he was mighty dangerous to take any liberties with. I don't know what it was, but it was something and you could feel it. I never saw him mad in my life; I hardly remember him when he wasn't smiling; but he was the most murderous youth that ever stood in shoe-leather, and he was game all the way through. He had everything that goes into the make-up of a desperado—cold nerve, the killer's instinct, and marvellous quickness and sureness with a six-shooter.

"When I was elected sheriff, he and I broke friendship. When I started in to hunt him down, I hoped to capture him; I didn't want to kill him. I was happy when I took him alive at Stinking Spring. I expected he'd be put away in prison for a long term. Just when I thought my troubles were over, he made his escape at Lincoln. If there was ever any such marvellous escape as that before,

I never heard of it. I don't know yet how, with his hands and feet manacled, he managed to kill Ollinger and Bell. I don't believe many men ever lived who could have done the same thing under the same circumstances. After that I knew that if ever I cornered him again, I'd have to kill him or he'd kill me.

"When he finally came in on me in Pete Maxwell's bedroom, I played in luck. I knew him and he didn't know me. My eyes had grown used to the darkness and I could see him from the time he came in the door. He couldn't see me at first. When at last he caught a vague glimpse of me and threw his gun on me, I was nearer death than I ever was in my life. But still he didn't recognize me; that's all that saved me. He must have thought I was some friend of Maxwell's. I killed him before he changed his mind. I had to kill him; if he had remained alive a second longer, they'd have carried me out of that room feet first. I had a shade the best of the situation. That's the only reason he's dead and I'm alive. But just as I say, he was a good, game boy— rest his soul! I wish him luck in the other world."

Garrett knew, from much personal experience, "the virtue of the drop." He never underestimated it but he viewed it philosophically, much as he did a gambler's "system" at faro—sometimes it worked and sometimes it didn't.

"There's no doubt about the importance of the drop in professional matters," said Garrett. "In the old days, an officer who didn't get it when he could was a fool. With the drop on your man, you were absolute master of the situation. The crook of your trigger finger could settle all argument. But the drop didn't always have the effect you might think it would. Say a man was

wanted for murder and knew he would be hanged if taken.
That man might have made up his mind that he preferred
to die by a bullet rather than be dropped through the
trapdoor of a gallows. If you got the drop on that kind
of fellow, he was pretty sure to make a break to get away
or put up a fight. Other men when covered wouldn't
give in because there was a doubt in their minds that the
sheriff had the nerve to pull the trigger. Others were
just naturally reckless and not afraid of a gun. There
was always this gambling uncertainty about a sheriff's
work, but as a rule the drop was good medicine and the
man who had a six-shooter shoved in his belly usually
threw up his hands.

"I remember over in Alamogordo once I saw a man I
wanted. His offense was not serious and I didn't look
for any trouble in taking him. I stepped up to him and,
tapping him on the arm, told him he was under arrest.
But that fellow, thinking I was unarmed, my gun being
out of sight in my hip pocket, turned on me like a wildcat
and ranted and swore and abused me something scandal-
ous. I took it for a minute. It had been a long time
since I had been in a row. I hardly knew what to do; I
didn't want to kill him. Says I to myself, 'Pat, you must
be getting old; you're losing your nerve.' Then, all of a
sudden, the feeling of old times came over me. Maybe
I got a little mad; I don't know. But I jerked out my gun
and stuck it against his stomach so hard it made him bend
double. His hands went up like I'd touched a spring.
'It's all right, old man,' he said as meek as a lamb, 'but
I'd give just a hundred dollars to know where you got
that gun.' I guess I was a little quick for him.

"I once got word from a Texas sheriff," Garrett went
on, "that a man wanted for murder was supposed to be

in my part of the country. He was red-headed, freckled, and had a red spot in the pupil of his left eye, so the description said, and there was a reward of twelve hundred dollars for him. I heard that a red-headed man had opened a little cantina on the Pecos a few miles below Fort Sumner and, taking a deputy, I went out there. I told my deputy not to go for his gun till I gave him the sign; I didn't want to make a foolish mistake and arrest the wrong man. A red head and freckles weren't enough; I had to see that red spot in the left eye.

"The red-headed man was behind the bar when we walked in and called for a drink. He hardly looked at us. While he was setting out the bottle and glasses, he kept his eyes lowered. I pretended not to pay any attention to him. I poured out my liquor and as I raised my glass to my mouth, I looked at him. He stood with his two hands spread out on the bar and was looking at me. There, as plain as day, was the red spot in his left eye. I let the liquor gurgle down my throat and set down my glass. Then I reached below the bar as if for a handkerchief to wipe my lips, and came up with my six-shooter.

"'Throw up your hands!' I said.

"But he didn't throw them up. He just stood there looking at me with his hands spread out on the bar. I kept telling him to throw 'em up or I'd kill him. But he didn't make a move. I knew that just below the bar he had a six-shooter and I could read his mind. He was figuring whether it was better to go back to Texas and be hanged or get killed right there. He finally decided it was wiser to take a chance on death several months off than to die on the spot. His hands went up slowly; he came out from behind the bar holding them in the air and my six-shooter on him all the time. I put the irons on him. On the way to Las Vegas he confessed and, later on, he was hanged in Texas. But that fellow had guts. The drop didn't scare him at all, but it saved my life.

"While I was sheriff of Doña Ana County," Garrett said, dropping into another reminiscence, "a sheriff from over in the Indian Nations rode into Las Cruces one day. He was trailing a convict who had broken out of the penitentiary back there after killing a guard and had sworn he'd never be taken alive. I located the fugitive on a ranch a few miles from town where he was cooking for a cattle outfit. Leaving the officer behind because the convict knew him, I rode out to the ranch with a Mexican deputy. I posted my deputy on guard outside and I stepped into the house.

"I sneaked along the hall with my six-shooter in my hand and ran on to my man in the kitchen. He was a strapping, powerful fellow and was wiping his hands on a towel, having just finished washing the dinner dishes. As I cracked down on him with my gun, he leaped at me and smashed me in the face with his fist. It was a punch like the kick of a mule. I staggered against the wall; he jumped out of the window. I clawed at him with my hands and tore the shirt off his back but he wriggled out of my grip. I rushed out the door and we met again head-on on the porch. I smashed him over the head with my revolver and knocked him flat. But he leaped up and tore into me. I don't know why I didn't kill him; I could have done it any time. We fought all over the porch. Finally he broke away and darted into a door. He was running through a hall to his room to get his gun. But my Mexican stepped inside just then and put a bullet in his back between the shoulder blades, dropping him dead. I was glad, because if the Mexican hadn't killed him, I'd have had to do it myself.

"The reward was a sizable sum of money and the Indian Nations sheriff offered to give it all to me; but I wouldn't take it nor any part of it. I didn't want any pay for doing a fellow officer a little courtesy like that. I had done only what I'd have expected him to do if I had happened to drop over into his country on a little matter of business. That sheriff, after that, always thought pretty well of me. A little politeness goes a long ways."

Billy Wilson was one man who held Garrett in an esteem little short of worship. Wilson had ridden with Billy the Kid and was captured in the fight at Stinking Spring. He was a handsome, dashing young outlaw, but of his many adventures none was more dramatic than the episode that occurred long after his days of adventure were supposed to be over and through which he learned for the first time the kindly generous human side of the sheriff who had once pursued him with deadly purpose.

After Wilson had been released from the Santa Fé jail, he settled down under a new name to peaceful pursuits near Uvalde in Texas. He was at first a cowboy, then a ranch foreman, and eventually acquired a ranch and cattle of his own. When Garrett, then sheriff of Doña Ana County in New Mexico, visited Uvalde, Wilson was married and prosperous, his outlaw past a dim memory to himself and known only to one or two intimate friends in that part of the country who guarded his secret closely.

One old Federal warrant charging mail robbery still stood against Wilson. It was like a past reaching out clutching fingers for him. As long as that old warrant remained valid, all his years of honest effort and good citizenship might be swallowed up at any time in the shadows of prison tragedy.

When Wilson heard of Garrett's presence in Uvalde, he supposed the sword that had hung above his life by a thread was about to fall and sent a friend to plead his cause. This friend, a former merchant of White Oaks, laid the facts before Garrett and asked that Wilson be left unmolested to pursue his career as a good citizen.

"Go back," said Garrett, "and tell Wilson to rest his mind in peace. I wouldn't for money put a stumbling block in his way. I believe I know a way to make his future safe. I'll see what I can do."

Months afterward, Wilson received a letter from Garrett. It read: "Would like to see you at my office in Mesilla." That was all. What the message meant Wilson did not know, but he had faith in Garrett and answered the summons.

"Hello, Billy," said Garrett as Wilson walked into the sheriff's office in Mesilla. "I've got a little something for you."

Garrett stepped over to his safe, drew out a paper, and laid it in Wilson's hand. It was a pardon signed by President Grover Cleveland. Wilson read it through a haze of tears. For a moment, he stood white-faced and silent.

"Pat," he said at length brokenly, "I don't know how to thank you. You can have anything I've got any time —my last dollar, the shirt off my back. You've made no mistake. I'll live up to this piece of paper the rest of my life. You can gamble on that."

He reached out a hand that trembled as if he had the ague, and Garrett gripped it.

"I believe you, Billy," said the sheriff. "I've done my part. Now you do yours. Live straight. Make good. That'll be all the thanks I want."

So, with his slate wiped clean, Wilson went back to his home in Texas and, still under his assumed name, lived cleanly and honestly and prosperously ever after. He may be living yet.

Tom Pickett, another of the Kid's followers who was in the Stinking Spring affair and who rode into Fort Sumner with Tom O'Folliard the night the latter was killed by Garrett, also turned straight after the Kid's death. In the little town in New Mexico where he settled down, it tickled his vanity to be pointed out as one of the Kid's old buccaneers, and he swaggered about the streets with two heavy six-shooters buckled around him. He handled his weapons neatly and was a crack shot, and his fellow townsmen treated him with the cautious consideration usually accorded a bad man. Sheriff Garrett unexpectedly dropped into Pickett's home town one day. Whereupon, to everyone's surprise, Pickett mounted his pony in a hurry and rode off into the hills, where he remained in hiding until Garrett departed. His neighbours made unmerciful fun of Pickett for running away. "We thought you were a bad man and a fighter," they laughed, "and the first chance you get to show us how brave you are, you take to the tall timber." Pickett accepted the ridicule with good-humoured frankness. "I know that long-legged fellow," he said, "and don't want his game." The panic into which Garrett threw him unintentionally had a salutary effect. He was laughed out of his reputation as a bad man, laid aside his guns, and went seriously to work. When, years afterward, he was gathered to his fathers, he was a well-to-do and respected citizen.

Garrett had an invincible sense of humour, oblique at
times perhaps, but always keen. There was not more
fun in his life than might be, but what there was he enjoyed with huge gusto. There were ridiculous murders
and absurd tragedies that appealed to him as jokes.
He was not to be denied his laugh when Death played the
clown.

"Tom Hill's death," said Garrett, "was as funny as a
farce-comedy on the stage. After the Lincoln County
war, he doubled up with Jesse Evans and they started out
as regular highwaymen. Hill was the man who killed
Tunstall and had besides two or three other notches on
his gun. Evans was a jolly kind of daredevil but he
was as tough as Hill. These two famous fighters and bad
men picked out an old German living down Alamogordo
way as an easy fellow to rob. The old German used to
drive about the country selling goods and usually carried
quite a large sum of money in a box under his wagon seat.
He never went armed, and to these two bold desperadoes
he seemed such a harmless, helpless old chap that they
would have been ashamed to rob him if they hadn't
needed the money. But they did need it and they figured
it would be about the easiest money they ever stole.

"They ran on to his camp while the old German was
off a ways in the hills gathering some wood for his fire.
When the old fellow came back and saw Hill and Evans
rummaging through his wagon, he hardly knew what to
make of it at first. He had never had any personal
experience with robbers before. 'Hey, vat you do dere?'
he called, more in curiosity than anger. Hill and Evans
didn't pay any attention to him. Both being crack shots,
they could have killed him, but they didn't think this
'harmless old Dutchman' was worth shooting. The old

fellow stood staring at them for quite a while before he could bring himself to believe that he was being robbed.

"'Py golly,' he cried out, 'you iss robbers, ain'd it? Yah. Raus mit you.'

"Hill and Evans went on quietly looking for the money box. The old man spied Hill's rifle leaning against one of the wagon wheels. He had a sudden idea that the rifle spoke a language that maybe the robbers could understand better than his broken English. Just as the old German grabbed the rifle, Hill rose up from beneath the wagon seat with the money box in his hands. There was a look of pained surprise on Hill's face as a bullet caught him just over the left eye and he pitched dead out of the wagon on his head, scattering money all over the ground.

"Evans was not too surprised to jerk out his six-shooter, but the gun fell out of his hand when one of the old German's bullets broke his right arm and another crashed through his lungs. Evans toppled out of the wagon almost on top of Hill, but, badly wounded as he was, he bolted for his pony and, managing somehow to scramble into the saddle, never stopped going until he had put sixty miles between himself and this 'harmless old Dutchman.' He found refuge at a ranch in the San Augustine Mountains, where Deputy Sheriff Dave Wood arrested him a few days later. He was taken to the hospital at Fort Stanton, where he was kept until he got well. Then he strolled away and disappeared.

"Hill was generally hated. The only tears shed over his death were tears of laughter. The frontier split its sides at the way this bad man cashed out. The old German was greeted everywhere with laughter and applause. People seemed to think him a sort of humorist.

"Jesse Evans and his brother, George Davis—Davis being the family name—got mixed up in a robbery down around Pecos City," Garrett went on, "and in a fight with Texas Rangers, George was killed and Jesse sent to the Texas penitentiary for twenty years. While he was serving his term, a queer little incident occurred that always puzzled me. I was sitting in my office in Lincoln one day in 1882 when a Mexican came in and told me Jesse Evans was in town and he and several other Mexicans had talked with him. I hurried out and searched everywhere, but not a trace of Evans could I find. There is no doubt that Jesse was then in the Texas penitentiary, but the Mexicans, who knew him well, swore they had met him face to face in Lincoln and could not have been mistaken. Mexicans are a superstitious lot and believe in ghosts, witches, wraiths, and such things, and there is an old myth among them that by some kind of magic certain persons have appeared at the same time in places a thousand miles apart. When I told my Mexican friends that Evans was in the Texas penitentiary at the moment they thought they were talking with him in Lincoln, they were sure they had seen a wraith. If it wasn't a wraith, I don't know what it was. Certainly it was not Jesse Evans."

What became of this former crony of Billy the Kid is not definitely known. Some say he died in the penitentiary; others that he served out his twenty-year sentence. When he was released, according to one story, he went to his native town of Texarkana, where he found that his wife, who had supposed him dead, had taken a new husband. He did not reveal himself to her, it is said, but leaving her happy with the other man, took himself off quietly to Arizona, where all trace of him was lost.

A little before his election as sheriff of Lincoln County, Garrett had settled on a ranch a mile east of Roswell. Land was worth almost nothing, and he eventually acquired twelve hundred and fifty acres along the Hondo River not far from its junction with the Pecos. After his term as sheriff had expired, he came back to his ranch, but the lure of a more exciting life led him, in 1884, to accept the captaincy of a company of Texas Rangers with headquarters at Atacosa. A year and a half passed in this capacity and he became manager of a cattle detective agency in the Panhandle and did effective work in breaking up a band of cattle rustlers and trail cutters that preyed on herds bound north from Texas ranges to the Kansas railroads. He later managed a cattle ranch in the White Mountains, and in 1887 returned to his Roswell ranch.

He was credited with the discovery of the great reservoir of artesian water underlying the country about Roswell, and was one of the organizers of the Pecos Valley Irrigation Company, an enterprise which twenty years later would have made his fortune but which, in that day of meagre settlement, did not realize the bonanza hopes of its promoters. Embittered by defeat when he ran for sheriff of the newly formed county of Chavez, which had been cut out of Lincoln County, he sold his land and moved to Uvalde, Texas. His new trail led him away from the wealth that inevitably would have come to him if he had waited patiently on his ranch. Artesian water eventually transformed the region around Roswell into a rich agricultural oasis. The land he owned is valued today at one hundred and fifty dollars an acre.

For five years he was a rancher near Uvalde. Then Governor W. T. Thornton of New Mexico appointed him sheriff of Doña Ana County to fill the unexpired term of Numa Raymond. For two subsequent terms Garrett was elected to the office. When President Roosevelt visited new Mexico in 1901, he met the famous frontier sheriff, conceived for him one of his impulsive but warm and lasting friendships, and soon afterward appointed Garrett Collector of Customs at El Paso. Garrett held this position four years.

At the close of his El Paso collectorship, Garrett settled in Las Cruces. He had saved a little money; he acquired several ranches and mining properties. For a few years his affairs were prosperous. He lived in a comfortable home with his wife and five children. Miss Elizabeth Garrett, a blind daughter, was a talented musician; after her father's death, she won some celebrity on the concert stage, singing songs of her own composition. But toward the close of his life, Garrett lost most of his money—he was a soldier of fortune rather than a business man—and in cramped circumstances, worries and anxieties preyed upon him.

He rented one of his ranches in 1907 to Wayne Brazel, a young stockman, who ran sheep and goats on it. Six months later, Brazel sublet the property to J. P. Turner of Fort Worth and Carl Adamson of Roswell, who agreed to buy his sheep and goats. This subletting of his land angered Garrett. He maintained that Brazel by this action had forfeited his lease. He had several stormy interviews with Brazel. He demanded that Brazel surrender his lease. Brazel refused. Garrett quibbled over Brazel's goats. Running goats on the land, Garrett insisted, was contrary to the terms of the lease. He threatened court action. It is said, also, on what seems good authority, that he made threats against Brazel's life.

Still Brazel stood firm, convinced that legally he had the better side of the argument.

Garrett was in his fifty-ninth year. Old age was upon him. He had slowed down in mind and body. His eye was growing dim; his trigger finger had lost its quickness. As a gunman, he had little left but his indomitable courage and his reputation. His life had been hard; the years had not mellowed him. He was no longer the calmly poised soul that in old days had taken "the thunder and the sunshine" with equal temper. His old geniality and spirit of comradeship were gone. He had become a sombre man, sour of outlook, embittered, irascible, easily stirred to dangerous moods.

Brazel, on the other hand, was thirty. Born and brought up in the range country of New Mexico, he had dealt with hard conditions and hard men all his life. He was reserved, cool, resolute, mindful of his own affairs, neither courting trouble nor inclined to avoid it—a quietly dangerous man. On his side were the quick resources of youth. He was not afraid either of Garrett's reputation or of Garrett himself. The cause of quarrel between the two men seems, in retrospect, to have been rather trivial, but out of its stupidity and triviality flamed the ultimate tragedy of Garrett's life.

Accompanied by Carl Adamson, Garrett, driving a pair of horses to a buckboard, set out for Las Cruces from his Bear Cañon ranch in the Organ Mountains on the morning of February 28, 1908. Before starting, he slipped two cartridges loaded with buckshot into his shotgun, which he stowed in the bottom of the buggy. "I might need this gun before I get to Las Cruces," he remarked to Adamson. As the team trotted along a lonely stretch of road between the little village of Organ and Las Cruces,

Garrett spied a solitary horseman jogging ahead in the same direction.

"I wonder who that is," he said.

He soon recognized the bay horse as Brazel's and the stalwart young figure sitting in the saddle with the nonchalant grace of a veteran range rider as Brazel himself. As his team, moving at a smart clip, cut down the intervening distance, Garrett was soon able to note the details of the horseman's attire—gray sombrero set squarely on the head, tan overalls, gray coat beneath which projected the yellow leather holster of a six-shooter, a red-and-black knitted scarf around the throat against a tang of cold in the February morning. Hard lines appeared about Garrett's eyes, and his lips tightened as he clucked up his horses. He seemed grimly pleased at the prospect of this accidental meeting.

"I'll give that young fellow a piece of my mind," he said.

Brazel looked surprised but in no wise disconcerted as Garrett drew alongside and pulled his team to a walk.

"I am goin' to give you mighty little more time to get off my land," said Garrett.

"I'll take all the time I want," Brazel replied with crisp deliberation. "You ain't goin' to get that land back till my lease is up. I've told you that before."

"I'll show you. If the law don't put you off, I will."

"You can't bluff me and no use trying."

"Moreover, you've got no right running goats on my land."

"I'll run any kind of stock on it I please."

"And you can't sublet it under the lease."

"I've already sublet it."

So they snarled and snapped at each other. Their angry argument was two miles long with the horses at a

walk. The backing-strap of one of Garrett's horses became unbuckled. He stopped his team, climbed out, and
rebuckled it. Brazel reined his horse to a standstill at
the side of the road and waited for the journey and the
argument to begin again. He sat in his saddle, silent,
watchful, defiant. Garrett stepped back to the space
between the wheels. He stood for a moment facing his
enemy, his tall, lank form rigid, his face twisted with rage,
murder blazing in his eyes. His words had been wasted;
it was time for buckshot.

"God damn you," he said, "if I can't get you off my
land one way, I will another."

He reached into the buckboard and snatched up his
gun. He wheeled with the gun almost to his shoulder.
But quick as he was, the old fighter was not quick enough
for his young antagonist. At Garrett's first hostile move,
Brazel jerked out his six-shooter and, at a distance of
ten feet, fired twice. The first bullet drove through
Garrett's heart, the second struck him between the eyes.
Either would have been fatal. Garrett crashed to the
ground at full length on his face, almost against the fore
feet of Brazel's horse, both hands still gripping his shotgun
firmly, a finger of his right hand against the trigger.

Levelling the six-shooter at Adamson, who still sat in the
buckboard, Brazel said, "You'll come on with me to Las
Cruces and tell this thing exactly as it happened." So,
leaving the dead man lying in the road, Brazel and Adamson journeyed on to Las Cruces, where Brazel surrendered
to Sheriff Lucero, who locked him in jail. Garrett's body
lay in the lonely mountain road for five hours; a party
of his friends drove out from Las Cruces in a wagon and
brought it into town toward sunset. The killing plunged
Las Cruces into a fever of excitement. There was some

talk of lynching Brazel, but it soon died out; Brazel himself had many friends among the town people.

At the coroner's inquest next day, Brazel told the story of the tragedy as it has been set down here, and Adamson, the only other eyewitness, corroborated it in every detail. Brazel was released on ten-thousand-dollar bonds on March 4th, after a preliminary hearing before Justice Manuel Lopez, Attorney-General Harvey representing the territory. Adamson repeated the story he had told at the inquest and made out a clear case of self-defense. Brazel's bondsmen were cattlemen and merchants of Las Cruces.

Garrett's death stirred the Southwest. From Yuma to Brownsville and from the Rio Grande to the Ratons, no man was better known. He was sincerely mourned by thousands. Many of his old friends came from all over New Mexico, from Texas and Arizona, to pay their last respects at his grave. His funeral was one of the largest that part of the country ever knew. Governor George Curry of New Mexico was one of the pallbearers. Followed by a long cortège of buggies, wagons, and men and women on foot, his body was borne to the little cemetery on the outskirts of Las Cruces. It was a barren enclosure; you see such little *campo santos* all over the Southwest— many wooden crosses, a few gravestones, little grass or shrubbery, no flowers except those left upon the graves by those who mourn for the dead.

Tom Powers of El Paso acted as master of ceremonies. Everybody in the crowd knew Powers; there were few in all that land who did not know him. For years he kept a saloon in El Paso; he was a kindly, hospitable man; over his bar he dispensed good fellowship as well as good liquor. His saloon was famous; it was the meeting place for old-timers—Texas Rangers, cowboys, cattlemen, mining men, men of the deserts and mountains of all the country along the Mexican border, who wore the white steeple hat with a rolling brim that marked them as the breed of the Southwest, native and to the manner born.   Powers is dead now —rest his soul—but every one in the Southwest will tell you that a friendlier, whiter, squarer man never lived.

So, at the open grave, Powers read Robert Ingersoll's oration on the burial of his brother—a beautiful, eloquent address filled with human charity and kindliness and love and the sadness of farewell.   It seemed fitting; Garrett, it is said—though certain of his friends deny it—had been an atheist.   The solemn service over, the grave was filled, the rounded mound of earth above it was heaped with flowers, and the crowd filed back to town, leaving the dead man to his long sleep.   *In pace requiescat.*

Brazel was placed on trial in Las Cruces on a charge of murder on May 4, 1909.   A. B. Fall, one of the political powers of New Mexico, later United States Senator and Secretary of the Interior under President Harding, appeared as counsel for the defense and District Attorney Mark B. Thompson for the territory.   Brazel took the stand and testified that Garrett had made threats on several occasions to kill him and said that he shot only when it became necessary to save his own life.   The only other witnesses were Sheriff Lucero, W. C. Field, Hugh Clarey, S. S. Pedregon, and Fay Sperry, the last four, members of the coroner's jury.   Carl Adamson, the only eyewitness except Brazel himself, did not appear.   Garrett's friends made much of this fact and started the report that Adamson had been influenced to remain absent.   As he already had told his story twice under oath, however, it is not probable that his testimony would have changed the verdict. The trial lasted only one day. The jury deliberated only fifteen minutes and returned a verdict of acquittal.

Shortly after Garrett's death, a rumour became rife that he was murdered as the result of a conspiracy. It was said that Garrett was hunted to his death by men who had been arrested and prosecuted by Garrett while he was sheriff of Doña Ana County. It became known that when he was killed, he was on his way to Las Cruces to have a conference with J. B. Miller, who was said to have killed several men and was known as "Killing Miller." According to the conspiracy theory, Miller had hired Brazel to kill Garrett, and then, as part of the plot, had summoned Garrett to Las Cruces to afford Brazel an opportunity to commit the murder on the lonely road. This story was again bruited when, a short time before Brazel's trial, Miller, with three other men, charged with the murder of A. A. Babbitt, a cattleman, was taken from jail at Ada, Oklahoma, and lynched by a mob. The unexpected and unexplained absence of eyewitness Adamson from Brazel's trial seemed to many to lend colour to the suspicion that Garrett's death had been planned. No case of conspiracy, however, was ever definitely made out, and from all the evidence there is every reason to believe that Brazel shot in self-defense and was justly acquitted. Brazel continued to live near Las Cruces and is to-day a prosperous ranchman of the region.

New Mexico owes much to Garrett. He brought law and order west of the Pecos. He stabilized the land, made it safe to live in and build homes in, cleared the way for statehood. He was the last great sheriff of the old frontier, constructive through destruction, establishing peace on a foundation of graves, the leaping flame from the muzzle of his six-shooter the beacon of prosperity. He had a job to do and he did it; a mission to fulfil and he fulfilled it.   His death was a period to completed labours, tragically in keeping with his tragic life, "last scene of all that ends this strange, eventful history."

THE END